THE LOGIPHRO DILEMMA

THE LOGIPHRO DILEMMA

An Examination of the Relationship between God and Logic

James C. McGlothlin

☙PICKWICK *Publications* · Eugene, Oregon

THE LOGIPHRO DILEMMA
An Examination of the Relationship between God and Logic

Copyright © 2017 James C. McGlothlin. All rights reserved. Except for brief quotations in critical publications or reviews, no part of this book may be reproduced in any manner without prior written permission from the publisher. Write: Permissions, Wipf and Stock Publishers, 199 W. 8th Ave., Suite 3, Eugene, OR 97401.

Pickwick Publications
An Imprint of Wipf and Stock Publishers
199 W. 8th Ave., Suite 3
Eugene, OR 97401

www.wipfandstock.com

PAPERBACK ISBN: 978-1-4982-8223-9
HARDCOVER ISBN: 978-1-4982-8225-3
EBOOK ISBN: 978-1-4982-8224-6

Cataloguing-in-Publication data:

Names: McGlothlin, James C.

Title: The logiphro dilemma : an examination of the relationship between God and logic / James C. McGlothlin.

Description: Eugene, OR: Pickwick Publications, 2017 | Includes bibliographical references and index.

Identifiers: ISBN 978-1-4982-8223-9 (paperback) | ISBN 978-1-4982-8225-3 (hardcover) | ISBN 978-1-4982-8224-6 (ebook)

Subjects: LCSH: God (Christianity) | Logic | Philosophy and religion | Metaphysics

Classification: BT103 M23 2017 (paperback) | BT103 (ebook)

Manufactured in the U.S.A.   01/03/17

To W. Wiley Richards

My first philosophy professor

CONTENTS

ACKNOWLEDGMENTS | ix
INTRODUCTION | xi

1 PROLEGOMENA | 1
2 THE *LOGICAL* EUTHYPHRO DILEMMA | 27
3 LOGICAL VOLUNTARISM | 43
4 LOGICAL NON-VOLUNTARISM | 85
5 A VIABLE THIRD ALTERNATIVE | 128

BIBLIOGRAPHY | 169
SUBJECT INDEX | 175
NAME INDEX | 181

ACKNOWLEDGMENTS

This book, in an earlier form, was my doctoral dissertation. Thus, thanks of course go to my dissertation committee: Stewart Shapiro, Tamar Rudavsky, and Chris Pincock for all of their advisement, criticisms, and help throughout the dissertation process. I would like to especially thank Stewart Shapiro who patiently guided me throughout my graduate career, particularly when I wanted to quit. Thanks also to all of the professors in the philosophy department of The Ohio State University (both current and now elsewhere) who have helped me at every step. Much thanks to my wife Cynthia—the one person who *really* knows how difficult the whole process of doctoral studies has been for me. I also want to give thanks to my editor Robin Parry at Pickwick. His corrections and suggestions were incredibly helpful, though all remaining problems here are still clearly mine. Finally, all thanks to him who undoubtedly has kept me and blessed me (Numbers 6:24–26).

INTRODUCTION

In this book I set out to answer the following main question: What is the relationship between God and logic? I argue for an answer to this question by first examining two possible options and then give my own philosophical explanation that I believe overcomes the problems associated with these two options.

In chapter 1 I first define and clarify the desiderata of my main question. I understand God to be the divine being of classical theism shared by Jews, Christians, and Muslims. I understand logic as primarily about the logical consequence relation. I characterize this relation in terms of necessity and universal applicability (or form), which captures various popular intuitions concerning logic. Therefore, my main question is refined to: What is the relationship between the God of classical theism and logical consequence?

In chapter 2 I investigate an ancient question and dilemma presented by Plato in his *Euthyphro* dialogue, known popularly as the Euthyphro dilemma. I suggest that the structure of this question naturally lends itself to the investigation of my question—what I call the logical Euthyphro dilemma, or the Logiphro dilemma for short. As the name suggests, this dilemma gives us at least two options for thinking about the relationship between God and logic: (1) logical voluntarism: the view that claims the logical consequence relation is the result of God's commands or will or (2) logical non-voluntarism: the view that the logical consequence relation is completely independent of God's commands or will, including being independent of his creating or sustaining power. I then set out to investigate both of these positions each in turn.

In chapter 3 I investigate logical voluntarism. I clarify what the position amounts to and then investigate a few possible historical proponents to see what might motivate this view, including some non-theistic motivations. I

INTRODUCTION

then investigate various objections to logical voluntarism, especially focusing on one of these objections and the negative results for accepting the consequences of this objection. I conclude that logical voluntarism cannot provide an answer to my main question.

In chapter 4 I investigate logical non-voluntarism. I clarify what the position of logical non-voluntarism amounts to and note its advantages over logical voluntarism. I clarify that it can be construed either as a Platonist theory (i.e., explicitly appealing to abstract objects) or as a nominalist theory (i.e. explicitly *not* appealing to abstract objects). I investigate the Platonist version first noting several objections to it from classical theism. I then investigate the nominalist version showing that it is a poor account of logic. I conclude that logical non-voluntarism (both versions) cannot provide an answer to my main question.

In chapter 5 I give my positive account to explain the relationship between God and logic. I first re-investigate the original Euthyphro dilemma and find that the literature discussing this dilemma suggests a third alternative. I suggest that an analogous third alternative is available to the Logiphro dilemma as well. Borrowing from Greg Welty's account of modality and God, which in turn is based upon Aquinas, I argue for a model of logical consequence constituted by mental objects within the mind of God, which I call *theistic conceptual logical realism*. I conclude that this model explains the relationship between God and logic while overcoming the problems associated with both logical voluntarism and logical non-voluntarism.

1

PROLEGOMENA

My primary question in this book: What is the relationship between logic and God? In the whole of the following I will investigate and attempt to explain the nature of this relationship. It should go without saying that a good explanation of this relationship, or any relationship, will be restricted by our understanding of the desiderata involved. Thus, in this first chapter, I will attempt to clarify what I mean be the terms "logic" and "God." Once a clearer understanding of these notions is in place, we will then be in a better position to proceed towards seeing what the nature of the relationship between logic and God might be.

This chapter is divided into two main sections. In section 1.1 I will attempt to clarify the desideratum of "logic," primarily by restricting it to what I take the primary focus of logic to be. Though I believe I won't be saying much that is controversial in this section, I'll argue for a certain way to understand logic's primary focus. In the second section, 1.2, I will attempt to clarify the desideratum of "God." Since the divine is usually seen by most philosophers as an epistemologically challenging subject for exploration, I will investigate the two broad theological methodologies that are usually appealed to in making claims about God. I'll address some challenges with the methodology I will be mainly siding with and then explain the particular way I take myself to be epistemically justified in making philosophical claims concerning the being referenced as "God." Even though this is strictly a philosophical investigation, I will also clarify the notion of the

Western or Abrahamic religious tradition I'll be assuming throughout this work.

I believe this chapter will sufficiently define our desiderata of "logic" and "God" in order that we may go forward with our investigation as to what sort of relationship exists between the two.

1.1 DEFINING LOGIC

1.1.1 Logic's Primary Focus

What do I mean by "logic" when I say I'm interested in the relationship between God and logic? Generally, logic is taken to be the study of correct reasoning.[1] More particularly, it is often characterized as the study of assessing good arguments from bad arguments in a particular (i.e., logical) way. In this context, the word "argument" typically does not mean a shouting match between two or more people but a stretch of indicative discourse where at least one claim is intended to be supported by one or more other claims. The claim that is intended to be supported is often called a "conclusion" while the claim, or claims, intended to do the supporting are often called "premises." So, the technical term "argument," in logic, refers to a collection of claims that includes one or more premises and a single conclusion with this sort of supporting relationship between them.[2] It is usually claimed that logic's particular means of assessment—what I'll call its primary focus—is the supporting logical relation between the premises and conclusion. This sort of relationship goes by various names such as *deductive (or logical): validity, entailment,* or *consequence.* Thus, logic seems to be primarily about the business of distinguishing "good" arguments as *deductively valid* from "bad" arguments as *deductively invalid*. In this work I'll simply call this relationship between a conclusion and its premises *the logical consequence relation*.

In our day, most logicians and philosophers of logic will agree that logic's primary focus is the logical consequence relation. However, at one

---

1. As with most things in philosophy, the "general" view has its respectable detractors. Philosopher of note Gil Harman challenges the straightforward connection between reasoning and logic in his books *Change in View* and *Thought*.

2. A couple of caveats to this description I should add: (1) On most accounts of logic some conclusions need no support from other claims ($[\emptyset] \vdash \Phi$), i.e., the set of premises may be empty; and (2) at least on most accounts of logic it is trivially true that a claim can support (imply) itself ($\Phi \vdash \Phi$).

PROLEGOMENA

time *logical truth* was seen as the primary focus of logic.[3] As philosopher Stephen Read briefly comments:

> In the early twentieth century a number of authors (perhaps under the influence of the axiomatic method) seem to have concentrated on logical truth as the primary logical notion and logical consequence became an afterthought. This is a grave mistake, completely reversing the real situation.[4]

Why was this a "grave mistake"? Read goes on to give us two arguments to show why. First, Read claims that holding logical truth as the primary notion and logical consequence as "an afterthought" completely reverses the real situation. How so? Note that a logical truth is usually defined as the conclusion of a valid argument with no premises (i.e., $[\emptyset] \vdash \Phi$). Observe here that logical truth is being defined *in terms of* logical consequence. Read points out, the converse is not possible: logical consequence cannot be defined in terms of logical truth. This being the case, consequence seems like a more foundational notion than truth in logic and so consequence should indeed be recognized as the primary focus of logic.

Second, Read points out that logical truths, when counted among the premises of an argument, are unnecessary; or, put another way, premises that are logical truths may be suppressed. To see this point, take some argument where the conclusion Φ follows validly from a collection of premises Γ. Now suppose one of those premises in Γ is a logical truth. Logical validity is usually taken to mean that the conclusion follows from its premises *alone*. For if an argument is valid, then any interpretation that makes the conclusion false must make at least one of the other premises false too. But of course, the premise of an argument that is a logical truth cannot be made false. So the validity of this argument will not be affected by omitting the logical truth. Thus, the logical truth is redundant and so can be suppressed.

---

3. Some notable examples of this traditional view include Gottlob Frege who focused primarily upon logical truth. For example he says: "Just as 'beautiful' points the way for aesthetics and 'good' for ethics, so do words like 'true' for logic. . . . To discover truths is the task of all sciences; it falls to logic to discern the laws of truth," from his "Thought," in *Frege Reader*, 325. W. V. Quine also focused on logical truth as well: "Logic is, in the jargon of mechanics, the resultant of two components: grammar and truth" from his *Philosophy of Logic*, 60. A more contemporary example is Penelope Maddy's *Second Philosophy*, which centers on logical truths as the central notion in logic. However, I find her discussion somewhat ambiguous. She claims to focus upon logical truth but it seems she spends a majority of her discussion on logic dealing with logical consequence instead.

4. Stephen Read, *Thinking About Logic*, 38.

The conclusion that Read draws, along with the majority of logicians and philosophers of logic today, is that the notion of logical consequence is more central to logic than logical truth. Thus, in this book, I will also take the notion of logical consequence as the primary focus of logic as well.

1.1.2 Defining Logical Consequence

But how exactly should we understand this notion of logical consequence? If it is the primary focus of logic, it would also seem that logical consequence would probably be the primary focus of most any formal logical system.[5] Indeed, this is usually the case. In such systems, which are typically about formal languages, consequence is often characterized in one or two closely related ways. Let L stand for any formal system of language, let Γ stand for a set of premise claims and let Φ be a single concluding claim. With this terminology in place, one formal notion of consequence that can be recognized is *syntactic* logical consequence and is usually defined in the following way:

> $(\Gamma \vdash \Phi)$ is syntactically valid in L just in case Φ is derivable from Γ, and the axioms of L, if any, by the rules of inference of L.

A second formal notion of consequence that can be recognized is *semantic* logical consequence and is usually defined this way:

> $(\Gamma \vdash \Phi)$ is semantically valid in L just in case Φ is true in all interpretations in which every member of Γ is true.[6]

Given that these are sharply defined notions on a formal language L, relations between them are a purely formal matter and so various formal results could be deduced from them. For instance, systems like L are considered *sound* if every syntactically valid argument in L is also a semantically valid argument in L; and L is considered *complete* if every semantically valid argument in L is also a syntactically valid argument in L. And since logical consequence is usually understood in these formal ways, like the above, distinguishing valid from invalid arguments is usually done

---

5. Formal logical systems can have other goals, such as relevance or rhetorical power. For a discussion of such goals in various formal logical systems see Susan Haack, *Philosophy of Logics*, 11–13.

6. A logical truth is usually taken to be a valid instance of $(\Gamma \vdash \Phi)$ where $\Gamma = [\emptyset]$.

by applying such a sharply defined formal interpretation of consequence within some strictly formal system L.

It thus makes sense then why logicians and philosophers of logic usually talk and think about logic, and logical consequence in particular, in terms of some specific formal system L. However, in pursuing the philosophical question about the relationship between God and logic, I need to be clear that I'm not interested in the relationship between God and some formal system L. (Though I'm sure there are interesting questions there.) Rather, I'm interested with the relationship between God and that which I believe such formal logical systems are usually attempting to model or capture—again, what I'm calling the primary focus of logic—the notion of logical consequence. It seems to me that just as formal grammatical rules for a natural language are attempts to capture the implicit rules of that natural language, in a similar way, I take it that formal logical notions for a formal language are attempts to capture the implicit notions of natural argumentation. If this is right, logical consequence is not primarily in the domain of formal logical systems, even if it is easier to talk about it in such systems.

But what exactly constitutes logical consequence then? If not formal notions, then what sorts of things make up logical consequence? I take this to be primarily a metaphysical question and historically there have been various suggested answers to it. Some candidates for what constitute logical consequence include mental entities (like thoughts, beliefs, etc.), or concrete objects in the world (such as sentence tokens), or abstract objects (propositions, possible worlds, sets, etc.).[7] Since throughout this work I will be attempting to understand what relationship exists between God and logic, this will include attempting an answer to what sorts of entities constitute the logical consequence relationship. But, in order to not beg any questions at this point, I'll remain neutral as to the exact sort of metaphysical nature that constitutes logical consequence. However, I will be returning to this question throughout this work, especially in chapters 4 and 5.

In order to attempt an answer to this metaphysical question later though, we still need to understand more clearly what sort of notion the logical consequence relation we are working with. I clearly see the

---

7. There is a large body of literature that treats the issues of ontology in logic, as well as the related field of mathematics. A few works that serve as excellent introductions include Stephen Read, *Thinking About Logic*, Stewart Shapiro's *Thinking About Mathematics*, and Shapiro's edited volume *The Oxford Handbook of Philosophy of Mathematics and Logic*.

attraction for logicians and philosophers to primarily think of logic in terms of a formal system. Since, as argued above, logic is primarily focused upon the notion of logical consequence, then having a formal conception of logic enables us to characterize a fairly crisp view of consequence thus giving us a nicely demarcated referential target for the term "logic." However, I'm proposing that we conceive of logic extra-systematically, i.e., non-formally, and I'm also wanting to remain (non-question-beggingly) neutral as to logic's exact metaphysical nature at this point in the book. Yet, it is incumbent upon me to try to give a clear (as far as possible), non-formal characterization of logical consequence that I believe most formal systems are attempting to represent. In doing so I need to give a characterization of the logical consequence relation that endeavors to capture at least some of the most commonly accepted and intuitive notions that are often associated with logic. There are actually several such characterizations one could adopt here.[8] I will mention four basic non-formal characterizations of logical consequence that will end up helping to inform my own suggested notion and my rationale for adopting it.

The first non-formal characterization of logical consequence intuitively suggests that the modal concepts of necessity and possibility are at the heart of logic. This characterization has a long and distinguished history tracing back to at least Aristotle. On this modal characterization logical consequence can be rendered the following way (remember that Φ is a conclusion claim and Γ a set of premise claims):

> (M) Φ is a logical consequence of Γ if it is not possible for the members of Γ to be true and Φ false.

Nowadays it is common to talk of modal notions in terms of possible worlds. So our first characterization (M) could be restated in this way:

> (PW) Φ is a logical consequence of Γ if Φ is true in every possible world in which every member of Γ is true.

However, with the semantic turn in analytic philosophy it has sometimes been claimed that logical consequence should eschew metaphysically rich notions like modality and possible worlds and be rooted in something more readily accessible, like the meaning or use of language. This suggests

---

8. This section is primarily informed by Stewart Shapiro's essay "Necessity, Meaning, and Rationality," 227–40. As Shapiro argues there, some of the different notions of logical consequence do not cohere with others. I hope my discussion here clarifies that claim.

a second non-formal characterization of logical consequence, call it the semantic notion:

> (S) Φ is a logical consequence of Γ if the truth of the members of Γ guarantees the truth of Φ in virtue of the meanings of the terms in those sentences.

However, this characterization of logical consequence has taken its share of criticisms as well, which I won't discuss here.[9] But given these criticisms, a third characterization of logical consequence attempts to follow (S) but leave out the seemingly vague notion of meaning. This might be called a formal characterization (though not to be confused with the earlier notion of "formal" that I'm leaving aside):

> (F) Φ is a logical consequence of Γ if there is no uniform substitution of the non-logical terminology that renders every member of Γ true and Φ false.

Fourth and lastly, another fairly intuitive characterization of logical consequence claims to have something to do with the idea of rationality. It can be defined in this way:

> (R) Φ is a logical consequence of Γ if it is irrational to maintain that every member of Γ is true and that Φ is false. The premises of Γ alone *justify* the conclusion Φ.

I take all of these four characterizations of logical consequence to be *prima facie* intuitive. I think one could give a plausible case for each characterization that it is the best description of the primary focus of logic. Nevertheless, as I mentioned for a few, I think each has its shortcomings. In light of this I suggest adopting the following extra-systematic characterization of logical consequence instead:

> (LC) Φ is a logical consequence of Γ, if at every possible world in which the uniform substitution of the non-logical content in Γ and Φ renders every member of Γ true, then it also renders Φ true.[10]

---

9. See chapter one of W. V. Quine, *Philosophy of Logic* for a brief but clear discussion of some criticisms of the traditional notion of meaning.

10 I stress here that the possible worlds talk in (LC) can be interpreted in variously excluded ways. Thus, I'm not presupposing any sort of metaphysical position about logical consequence here. It should also be noted that (LC) can also be stated in the following equivalent way:

(LC1) Φ is a logical consequence of Γ, if there is no possible world at which the uniform substitution of the non-logical content renders every member of Γ true, it also

By submitting this extra-systematic characterization as the way to think of logical consequence I'm claiming that (LC) best represents the sort of relationship of support between ($\Gamma \vdash \Phi$) (i.e., logical consequence) that many formal logical systems are attempting to represent, even if some of these systems might give contrary evaluations of validity than what (LC) would deliver for the exact same sequence of claims. In other words, it could very well be (and most likely is) that not every formal system L will capture (LC) perfectly. But this should come as no surprise given that the same can be said for competing formal systems of each other.

But what is my rationale for submitting (LC) as *the* basic non-formal concept of logical validity? First, like (M) and (PW), (LC) contains the commonly held intuitive notion of necessity. (LC) claims that if Φ is a logical consequence of Γ, then this shows that the relationship between conclusion and premise(s) (if any) is a *necessary* one. As mentioned above this has been a long and well-recognized core component of logic. But I believe the notion of necessity is strongly tied to another notion that (LC) also represents and that also supports the intuition of necessity. The following quote from philosophers J. C. Beall and Greg Restall explains:

> The fact that logical consequence is necessary means that logical consequence applies under any conditions whatsoever. If we consider what might happen *if* A were the case, and we reason from the premise that A, validly to a conclusion B, we ought, by rights, be able to conclude that if A were the case then B would be the case too. The applicability of logic is not a contingent matter; it works come what may, whatever hypotheses we care to entertain.[11]

To say that a valid argument is *necessarily* valid seems to imply that the validity of an argument is something that cannot be mucked around with—that nothing could possibly change it. This is why Beall and Restall above closely tie the notion of necessity in logical consequence to the notion of *universal applicability*. For, it seems clearly true, that if a logical argument is necessarily valid, then it seems its validity must hold "come what may." This intuitive idea usually involves logical consequence with the notion of *logical form*, i.e., the substitution of non-logical content does *not* affect deductive validity. My characterization (LC) captures this notion as well. For if ($\Gamma \vdash \Phi$) is truly a valid argument, it seems it should be valid no matter what non-logical content may be represented in Γ and Φ.

renders Φ false.

11. J. C. Beall and Greg Restall, *Logical Pluralism*, 15–16.

PROLEGOMENA

I think the notions of universal applicability and logical form can be well illustrated and motivated with what is sometimes called the "locked room metaphor."[12] This metaphor claims that we should be able to correctly recognize inferences that are instances of valid logical arguments even if we were locked in a dark windowless room knowing nothing of the outside world. As the metaphor highlights, if we were in such a situation we would then have to evaluate sequences of claims exclusively on the basis of our linguistic competence of logical terms alone. In other words, one need not know anything about the content of the non-logical terms involved (i.e., "nothing about the outside world") in order to determine the validity of an argument. Again, this seems intuitive, for if p then q, and p together validly implies q, surely this argument is valid *regardless* of what is being represented by p and q.

However, appealing to the notion of logical form pushes us to ask how we know what terms within claims counts as *logical content* and what terms do not. For if the notion of logical form, as represented by (LC), is to truly characterize the extra-systematic notion of logical consequence, then we must be able to successfully distinguish logical content from non-logical content within claims. Historically there have been many and varied attempts to make the demarcation between the logical and non-logical crisp and clear. Nevertheless, as far as I can tell, there is still very little philosophical consensus about how to make a definitive distinction here.[13] Interestingly though, a clear distinction is still very popular and almost uniformly held to in logical practice among philosophers, logicians, and more importantly, logic textbooks. This is usually done by adopting the practice of simply listing commonly accepted logical terms. The typically stipulated list includes truth-functional connectives ("not," "and," "or," "if ... then"), quantifiers ("some," "all"), variables (p, q, etc.) and identity ("=").

---

12. See E. Bencivenga's essay "What is Logic About?" 6–7.

13. For a good discussion of the problems that have plagued trying to distinguish logical content from non-logical content, see John MacFarlane, "Logical Constants," in *Stanford Encyclopedia of Philosophy*, accessed June 6, 2016, http://plato.stanford.edu/entries/logical-constants/. MacFarlane puts forward the notion of permutation invariance as the most hopeful way to eventually make this distinction clear. But it seems to me that his discussion does much to highlight various worries he has concerning permutation invariance. Thus, in the end, the distinction between logical and non-logical content still seems difficult to clearly and successfully demarcate.

THE LOGIPHRO DILEMMA

Though I agree with this list as well, I find this approach a little unsatisfying. Therefore, I believe I need to say a little more here to motivate this common move.

How can one be epistemically justified in holding that the terms in some set S (like the logical terms listed above) are truly *logical* terms? It seems to me that this is closely akin to asking how am I epistemically justified in holding that a particular argument A is valid? For if we *know* that A is a logically valid argument, and validity is a matter of form (in accordance with my characterization (LC)), then it seems that we must *know* what content in the argument is the logical content. I find Stewart Shapiro's explanation of epistemic justification of logic to be helpful here.[14]

Shapiro argues that the adoption of a formal system of logic can become an objective justification for logic if two questions are settled. (Those familiar with soundness and completeness proofs should recognize some similarities here.) First, does every deducible argument in the formal system correspond to a correct inference in the natural language under study? In other words, do the valid arguments in our formal logic match the acceptable inferences that we make in our non-formal, everyday talk? Second, is the formal system exhaustive in the sense that every correct inference of natural language corresponds to a deducible argument in the formal system? Put conversely, do the acceptable inferences in our non-formal, everyday talk match to valid argument forms in our formal logic? Shapiro notes the rather common sense observation that "we somehow recognize the correctness of at least some inferences in natural language, and that we do in fact recognize the correctness of inferences modeled by deducible arguments."[15] In context, Shapiro is explaining how valid logical arguments are usually thought to be *a priori* justified by way of a formal system; yet, as his suggested questions show, he initially appeals to the idea that we must first start with such psychological phenomena as subjective introspection and community beliefs about inferences. Shapiro gives a story of how he thinks this process most likely goes:

> At the outset of theory, when considering the "data" with which one is to begin, "there is no logic and epistemology independent

---

14. The argument expounded here is from the second chapter of Stewart Shapiro, *Foundations Without Foundationalism*.

15. Ibid., 33. Shapiro points out though that neither stance could assure us that the system is exhaustive, i.e., that *every* correct inference of the natural language is modeled in the deductive system.

of psychology." It is, in effect, a working hypothesis that the inferences and propositions that seem correct are correct. What else is there to go on? The stronger our intersubjective certainty about a given inference, the less likely it is that it will be challenged or revised in the light of theory. In some cases, we simply cannot imagine revision, at least not now. This applies to logic . . . once theory has begun and shows signs of success (whatever that may be), then our intuitions can be modified by its light. That is, theory can guide our dispositions to judge, just as dispositions guide theory. Indeed, at any given time, these "intuitions" are the product of one's background training, and that is, at least in part, the product of previous intellectual endeavors.[16]

In that our introspective and commonly held beliefs are providing some initial justification for the validity of logical arguments, Shapiro recognizes that this is a concession, of sorts, to psychologism—an almost universally discredited way of thinking about logic. But Shapiro thinks that psychologism is later expelled in that once we have a logic that "shows signs of success" in place we can then make a distinction between intersubjective certainty and epistemic justification. That is, we no longer have to rely solely upon our intuitions to epistemically justify our logical inferences once we have a commonly accepted formal system in place that comes in and takes over that epistemic load. Thus, the formal system, i.e., the logic that "shows signs of success," eventually acquires a normative status within the community of users who have adopted it. Shapiro notes that though this approach may sound objectionably circular, "we now have the benefit of historical hindsight. The [formal] systems have proved fruitful and they do conform to our *current* dispositions concerning correct inference."[17]

In a like fashion, it seems to me that we can similarly provide an epistemological justification for accepting the typical list of logical terms that we usually do. The usual list, being part of most formal logical systems, is part of that proven track record of being fruitful in our logical practice and it also conforms to our current dispositions concerning what counts as logical terminology. Even though (LC) is strictly an extra-systematic account of logical consequence, the notion of form that is included in this

16. Ibid., 34. See also Michael Resnik, "Logic, Normative or Descriptive?" 221–38 for a similar and fuller discussion of this sort of approach.

17. Shapiro, *Foundations Without Foundationalism*, 34. I think this is a bit overstated given that we have a plethora of voices today espousing various competing logics. But I agree with the general notion: there seems to be an overwhelming consensus on many logical notions, including what terms count as logical.

characterization is partially informed by logical practice and familiarity with current formal logical systems. It seems to me that the position I'm advocating here is similar to what philosopher John MacFarlane calls the Deflater position:

> Like the Relativist, the *Deflater* seeks a moderate middle ground between the Demarcater [one who believes there is a principled distinction between logical and non-logical] and the Debunker [one who denies the Demarcater's thesis]. The Deflater agrees with the Demarcater that there is a real distinction between logical and nonlogical constants, and between formally and materially valid arguments. She rejects the Relativist's position that logical consequence is a relative notion. But she also rejects the Demarcater's project of finding precise and illuminating necessary and sufficient conditions for logical constancy. "Logical constant," she holds, is a "family resemblance" term, so we should not expect to uncover a hidden essence that all logical constants share.... That does not mean that there is no distinction between logical and nonlogical constants, any more than our inability to give a precise definition of "game" means that there is no difference between games and other activities. Nor does it mean that the distinction does not matter. What it means is that we should not expect a principled criterion for logical constancy that explains why logic has a privileged epistemological or semantic status.[18]

I part ways a bit with the Deflater in that I don't overtly reject the Demarcater's project; I'm just not very hopeful that it will ever succeed. But, given that we have a commonly accepted list of logical "constants" (i.e., logical terms) already, then, along with the Deflater, I don't see the question of finding a principled distinction as terribly pressing. With this sort of epistemological or Deflater picture in mind, I also think we have a fairly intuitive grasp of what terms count as logical and thus we can recognize logical content within claims. In sum then, I think we have epistemological justification for the notion of logical form represented in (LC).

Some further rationale for submitting (LC) as *the* basic non-formal concept of logical validity, I need to say a little more about (LC)'s relation to the four characterizations of logical consequence given earlier. First, I should say that though (LC) appeals to "possible worlds" language, at this point in the book this language should be read neutrally. I am making no

---

18. John MacFarlane, "Logical Constants." For a detailed defense of the Deflater position, see Mario Gomez-Torrente, "The Problem of Logical Constants," 1–37.

PROLEGOMENA

explicit metaphysical claims at this point. Second, note that (LC) is a synthesis of the earlier characterizations of necessity (PW) and formality (F), which implies that I've ruled out the notions of meaning (S) and rationality (R). Why rule these latter two notions out?

I excluded any sort of semantic notion of consequence (i.e., (S)) from (LC) because it includes an idea of linguistic competence that seems contrary to universal applicability that the locked room metaphor suggests. As I argued above, some form of minimal linguistic competency is obviously needed for identifying the distinction between logical and non-logical content and thus in order to identify the notion of logical form included in (LC). But this sort of linguistic competency is a much shallower notion of "meaning" than the richer semantic content that (S) suggests.

My exclusion of (R), which includes the notion of rationality, is more nuanced though. I've already affirmed that logic should be universally applicable. Similarly, following Shapiro and MacFarlane, I've also already affirmed that logic has its place in normatively governing how we should reason and think about things. As Frege famously said, from logic "there follow prescriptions about asserting, thinking, judging, inferring. And we may very well speak of laws of thought . . . ."[19] As Joan Weiner explains, Frege thought logic was "meant to offer us tools for evaluating inferences when our aim is to make true judgments. . . . What distinguishes these guiding principles from other laws of this sort is that they apply to *every* domain."[20] But to say that logical consequence *informs* our norms of rationality, is not the same as saying that rationality, and its normative force, just *is* logical consequence. In other words, I believe we should not confuse one of the primary uses of logic with what logic actually is. As Frege also famously said, "an explanation of a mental process that ends in taking something to be true, can never take the place of providing what is taken to be true."[21] Frege's latter reference is to logic—the former reference is to how logic is used.

Let me summarize what I take myself to have done in this section. I set out to clearly define the term "logic." I have argued that logic is primarily focused upon the notion of logical consequence. Though many formal logical systems are attempts to capture or model the non-formal notion of logical consequence, I'm not interested in the relationship between God

---

19. Frege, "Thought," 325.
20. Joan Weiner, *Frege Explained*, 148.
21. Frege, "Thought," 326.

and some formal system but between God and the extra-systematic notion of logical consequence. I take no stand, at this point, upon the metaphysical nature of whatever constitutes this notion. However, I've argued that (LC) best characterizes it. That is, I believe the best and most intuitive way to understand logical consequence, apart from a formal system, is by (LC).

Therefore, by pursuing the question, "What is the relationship between logic and God?" I am more precisely asking, "What is the relationship between what constitutes logical consequence, as characterized by (LC), and God?" I'll now proceed to get clearer on what I mean by the term "God."

1.2 DEFINING GOD

What do I mean by "God" when I say I'm interested in the relationship between logic and God? In this section I will attempt to get clear on what sort of divine being I'm referring to when I use the word "God," as well as defining the tradition that I see this term as part of. But before doing so, we must first ask: How does one know that one's conception of "God," whatever that conception may be, accurately describes the divine being that he is referring to? This question highlights the need to explain how claims about God are epistemically justified, what is sometimes called a *theological method*. In the following I will investigate two broad methodologies that have historically been appealed to as well as challenges to the method I will largely side with. I will then explain my own epistemological approach for making claims about God in this work. By the end of this section we should have a much clearer account of how I understand the term "God."

1.2.1 Revealed and Natural Theology

Theology, the study of God, has historically been divided into two broad approaches, or two methods of inquiry, which may be generally referenced as *revealed theology* and *natural theology*, respectively. One traditional slogan that is thought to aptly distinguish these two approaches from each other claims, "It is the difference between God's movement toward man [revealed theology] and man's movement toward God [natural theology]."[22] As with most distinctions though the one between revealed and natural

---

22. Ed. L. Miller, *God and Reason*, 12.

theology is not always a sharp one. However, I will try to make the distinction as clear as I can.

Revealed theology, as a rule, constitutes claims about God acquired (at least primarily) through revealed means. The two word phrase "revealed means" focuses upon one of the distinctive features of the Western religious tradition (sometimes called the Abrahamic tradition): the belief that God can and has manifested himself to human beings in various ways, sometimes called *special* revelation. One of the primary ways it is believed that God has manifested himself is by literally speaking to particular members of humanity throughout history, usually revealing claims about himself or his purposes. Since only a certain limited number of people have received this divine information first-hand, it is usually testified to others orally or by means of some written text where the grounds for belief in the items of knowledge available to the first recipients are obviously different than those grounds available to others. Therefore, given the uniqueness of special revelation, revealed theology usually focuses upon the written testimonial accounts of those who have claimed to be first-hand recipients of this special revelation. I will reference such written testimonial accounts in this work as "Scripture."[23] It should be clear that if Scripture is truly a record of revelation from God, then such data is obviously a central and primary means by which theists would make claims about God. For if one wants to find out information about some person P, apart from investigating or interviewing P first-hand, then he or she would certainly take written testimony from first-hand witnesses of P to be a most important resource of coming to know and understand P. Of course, even within the main branches of the Western tradition of religion (i.e., Judaism, Christianity, and Islam), what counts as authentic Scripture as long been debated. And even when this is agreed upon within a subset of similarly minded theists, there are also disagreements about what Scripture actually claims or does not claim.[24]

---

23. "Scripture" often refers to a type of special or divine revelation. That is, for example, the Bible just *is* special revelation from God. For my purposes, "Scripture" need only be understood as a human *record* of divine revelation. I don't deny that Scripture is divine revelation, but I only need the latter, less robust notion, for this project. In this work I'm not mainly concerned with the nature of Scripture but that it is a reliable testimonial source of special revelation. For a helpful discussion of this subject, see the relevant section in Richard Swinburne, *Revelation*, 239–88.

24. I take "Scripture" to be a synonym for "*the* Bible." But, as I'll explain in the last part of this chapter, when I appeal to the notion of Scripture, I only plan on appealing to the so-called Old Testament, which Jews and Christians take to be common property and seems to at least be respected among Muslims. I'm following Brian Leftow here (*God*

Nevertheless, such disagreements do not negate the idea that Scripture, whatever counts as such, can operate as a primary testimonial source of information about God. No one automatically disregards testimony just because there is counter-testimony to it. Such difficulties just require more research and evidence; they don't disqualify the notion of testimony.

In contradistinction to revealed theology, natural theology is constituted by knowledge claims about God acquired through the publicly available means of common philosophical analysis.[25] Sometimes natural theology is distinguished from revealed theology by making a conscious effort to *not* appeal to special revelation.[26] In any case, this approach to theology primarily relies upon the traditional tools of philosophical investigation, such as the active employment of observation, reflection, and inference, among others. This is why natural theology is sometimes simply called *philosophical theology*. Examples of natural theology are usually thought to include things such as the traditional arguments for God's existence, the Anselmian tradition of "perfect-being" theology, et al. Thus, claims and philosophical arguments about God, many times apart from special revelation, exemplify the method of natural theology.

Since the present work takes itself to be a work of philosophy, I plan on mainly relying upon a certain methodology of natural theology (to be explained in §1.2.3 below). However, since natural theology has been challenged in various ways, from both non-theistic and theistic opponents, I think it's incumbent upon me to address at least some of these challenges, particularly from theistic opponents.

1.2.2 Challenges to Natural Theology

Especially from within the Western or Abrahamic tradition of religion, there have been staunch criticisms against natural or philosophical theology as a means of making and establishing truth-claims about God. Thus, these critics claim, we should only appeal to revealed theology in making

and Necessity, 3 n.9), who says: "An outsider, noting the Koran's habit of citing, commenting on, and revising OT stories, can find it hard to resist calling the OT a source of the Koran."

25. A typical definition, this one taken from Richard Swinburne, *Faith and Reason*, 107.

26. For instance, philosopher Anthony Kenny claims to want to "discuss the concept of God and his attributes in the light of reason without accepting as authoritative any claim to revelation, such as the Christian revelation." *The God of the Philosophers*, 3.

PROLEGOMENA

our claims about God. Since the present work is primarily a philosophical one, I want to investigate this allegation that philosophical theology is inadequate or problematic compared to revealed theology. As far as I can tell, there are two main criticisms from the Western theistic tradition that seek to dismiss natural theology in favor of revealed theology.

First, there is the seemingly extreme position that claims that human reason (in general, and the study of philosophy in particular) is not equipped to deal with issues of theology either by the utter uniqueness of divine matters[27] or because humans have damaged rational or moral capacities that disallow them from being able to do so.[28] For instance, it has been thought that the apostle Paul held such a view when he warned the Christians in first-century Colossae with the following: "See to it that no one takes you captive by philosophy and empty deceit, according to human tradition . . . and not according to Christ" (Col 2:8).[29] This viewpoint that reason, and philosophy in particular, should be held in suspicion in relation to theological claims is sometimes called *fideism*. Specifically, fideism is the view that theological claims cannot be the result of rational investigation, or, sometimes added, that theological claims are not even subject to rational evaluation. Thus, for example, a fideist would most likely claim that his belief that God exists does *not* depend on any reasoning and would most likely see trying to prove God's existence by argument as a waste of time and effort.

But how does a fideist, for example, *know* that God exists? Such a theist might appeal to various things such as his own personal experience,

---

27. For example, Gregory of Nazianzus (AD 320–390) seems to represent something like this sort of view when he says the following: "To tell of God is not possible . . . but to know him is even less possible. For language may show the known if not adequately, at least faintly, to a person not totally deaf and dumb of mind. But mentally to grasp so great a matter is utterly beyond real possibility." Quoted from Stephen D. Boyer and Christopher A. Hall, *The Mystery of God*, 39. Gregory seems to think that God is so utterly different from humans that we cannot think, talk, or reason intelligibly about the divine.

28. For example, the Protestant Christian tradition of religion often maintains that humans have a general ability to think well, but due to their personal sins against God they (at least sometimes) lack the moral ability to do so. The idea is that our sinful inclinations tend to push us away from thinking the way we should about the divine. For, so the reasoning goes, if we thought rightly about God we would all turn to him in repentance; but many obviously do not. For more details on this position see Michael Horton, *The Christian Faith*, 431–32.

29. I personally do not think that is what the apostle is claiming here, but I won't take the time to defend that claim. For a friendlier perspective, like my own, on the meaning of this verse, see J. P. Moreland and William Lane Craig, *Philosophical Foundations*, 18.

intuition, or perhaps Scripture; but any explanation given by a consistent fideist would be done with the caveat that such knowledge was *not* the result of philosophical reasoning or argument. If fideism were adopted as the only legitimate way to make theological claims, then natural theology would obviously be a futile and irrelevant path to knowledge of God. As a popular and seemingly fideist slogan goes: religion is a matter of the heart, not the head!

I suspect fideistic attitudes against natural theology are also sometimes fueled by an overreaction to certain epistemological views, such as those espoused by W. K. Clifford's classic essay "Ethics of Belief."[30] Clifford set forth the historic and definitive, modern version of evidentialistic epistemology arguing that it is *never* morally acceptable to believe *anything* without sufficient evidence. Unable to provide the amount or sort of evidence for claims about God that epistemologies like Clifford's demands, perhaps some theists have retreated to a fideistic safety to shelter their religious beliefs from such attacks. However, in recent decades this sort of highly demanding epistemology has fallen out of favor due to various inextricable problems associated with it.[31]

Whatever the motivations, I believe that fideism, or a fideistic attitude, should be rejected as a reason against eschewing natural theology because fideism is simply self-refuting. To show this, take the following, which I believe is a fair representation of the fideistic position towards natural theology:

(1) Any view that aspires to make theological claims by using rational (or philosophical) reasoning should be rejected.

(2) Natural theology aspires to make theological claims using rational (or philosophical) reasoning.

(3) So, natural theology must be rejected as a means of making theological claims.

This is a valid argument. But, as I think should be obviously clear, any fideist who relies upon it is actually using or relying upon rational (or philosophical) reasoning—even if only implicitly or vaguely—in order to reject rational (or philosophical) reasoning concerning God. I think there are

---

30. One place where this famous essay can be found is in Louis P. Pojman, ed., *The Theory of Knowledge*, 515–18.

31. A good summary of these problems is provided by Peter van Inwagen "Quam Dilecta," in Robert V. Morris, ed., *God and the Philosophers*, 31–60.

other ways to characterize this view. But regardless, I think it's clear that this problem generalizes to any accurate characterization of fideism. Therefore, since fideistic reasoning against rationality in general, and philosophy in particular, is using the very means it claims to be rejecting, fideism is thus self-refuting. And so, it cannot be appealed to as a ground for dismissing natural theology.[32]

A more informed criticism that adherents of the Western or Abrahamic tradition might use to dismiss natural theology as a means of making theological claims is the worry that natural theology could possibly be a corrupting influence on their respective religion. More particularly, I think the worry could be that the terms and concepts usually associated with natural theology—and so the picture of theism implicitly or explicitly delivered by natural theology—may not cohere well with the picture of theism implicitly or explicitly delivered by revealed theology. Something like this criticism can be seen as early as the Christian thinker Tertullian (AD 160–220) who famously asked: "What has Athens to do with Jerusalem?" I think this worry is often why many religious thinkers throughout Western thought have derogatorily referenced the God presented by natural theology, and by extension classical theism (see below), as the "God of the philosophers." A sample of how this worry has been fairly constant throughout, for example, the history of Christianity, is recounted by theologian Michael Horton:

> The seventeenth-century Genevan theologian Francis Turretin pointed out that the Socians reproached the traditional doctrine of God on the basis that "the whole doctrine is metaphysical" (i.e., philosophical) rather than biblical. Specifically, they charged that God's simplicity, aseity, immutability, and exhaustive foreknowledge originated in Stoic philosophy—a claim that has been repeated consistently down to our own day. In the same vein, Albrecht Ritschl attempted to eliminate all "metaphysical" ideas from Christian theology. The late nineteenth-century historical theologian Adolf von Harnack advanced his thesis that nearly everything we regard as Christian "orthodoxy"—"the Catholic element"—is in fact the result of "the acute Hellenization of the church."[33]

As we can see, and as with Tertullian's comment before, this concern is sometimes worded in terms of "Greek" or "Hellenistic" philosophy. Again, I

---

32. Perhaps fideism might qualify natural theology in some way, but it is clearly a hypocritical position if it's taken to be a refutation of natural theology.
33. Horton, *The Christian Faith*, 226.

think the fear is that by importing certain terms or concepts—those that do not seem to exist within the resources of special revelation—theology can become corrupted in the sense that theological claims informed by natural theology may not accurately represent the God presented by special revelation. And I think this is a perfectly legitimate concern. It makes more sense to give primacy to first hand accounts of P rather than resting upon philosophical claims and formulations concerning P not primarily informed by first hand accounts of P. Second hand data is obviously epistemologically weaker, i.e., further conditions must be met to qualify that we know it. Therefore, why rely upon such second hand data (i.e., natural theology), if first hand data (i.e., revealed theology) is available?

However, this criticism, or worry, does not necessarily imply that the more secondary approach to making claims about P is incoherent with the data of first hand accounts of P. Moreover, it seems to me that philosophical claims concerning P can and should be made *in accordance with* the first hand accounts of P. In reference to the Hebrew Bible, Horton points out that the story of Scripture gives rise to particular doctrines in that "Not only are the people of Israel able to infer certain attributes or characteristics of their God from his mighty acts; God himself interprets these for them. Israel's lexicon of divine attributes does not come in the form of a systematic theology, . . . but in narrative, instruction, liturgy, and law."[34] As Horton suggests, surely one of the primary motivations for attributing philosophical terms and concepts of natural theology to God are predominantly based on special revelation (and records of it), even if the vocabulary in which the matter gets discussed is philosophical, i.e., not originally in Scripture. Therefore, since there is no automatic incoherence between natural and revealed theology, I think this criticism is, at best, overblown. And, as I'm hinting at in my comments here, I think some sort of synthesis could be made between natural and revealed theology.

1.2.3 Synthesis of Natural and Revealed Theology

Various thinkers throughout the history of the Western tradition of religion have sought to show a compatibility between the picture of theism delivered by natural theology and with their religious tradition, which is usually considered rooted in revealed theology. Attempts to show compatibility between natural and revealed theology seem to imply attempting a

34. Ibid., 225.

synthesis between the methodologies of natural and revealed theology. But what might such a synthesis look like?

Philosophers of religion J. P. Moreland and William Lane Craig give a very informative suggestion with the following. They claim that "[s]ince the concept of God is underdetermined by the [i.e., scriptural] data... philosophers working within the [western religious] tradition enjoy considerable latitude in formulating a philosophically coherent and [i.e., scripturally] faithful doctrine of God."[35] By claiming that the concept of God is "underdetermined by the [i.e., scriptural] data," I take Moreland and Craig to mean that Scripture sometimes does not address many philosophical issues and questions that may concern us about God, e.g., like the relationship between God and logic. On this point they are surely correct. For example, given the Christian belief in special revelation, Christians in antiquity wondered how it could be that Jesus of Nazareth was God when the Father in Heaven was obviously God. The Christian concepts of the Trinity (i.e., that God is three in person, but one in essence), and Chalcedonian Christology (i.e., that Christ has a fully divine as well as a fully human nature) are examples of philosophical formulation and extrapolation that the original writers of Scripture seemed to simply assume or cared little about explaining. To say that the concept of God is underdetermined by Scripture is not so much a criticism of Scripture as a resource for making theological assertions as it is a claim that in imparting revelation to the original recorders of these documents God had little interest in answering or clarifying many such philosophical questions and concerns. Nevertheless, scriptural paucity pushes those who are interested in such questions to look outside of Scripture (in addition to Scripture) in their thinking about God. Such efforts would be, I take it, examples of natural theology.

And so, I am suggesting the following sort of synthesis between revealed and natural theology: I take the testimonial documents of revealed theology (i.e., Scripture) to be reliable and primary data, while natural theology comes along as a means of clarifying such data and extrapolating to coherent and philosophical formulations that are consistent with this data. I think philosopher Ed. Miller explains this sort of dual approach to understanding God quite well:

---

35. Moreland and Craig, *Philosophical Foundations*, 501. I've replaced "western religious" for their word "Christian" and "scriptural" for their word "biblical" since my focus here is a bit broader.

> [The philosopher of religion] ought, as much as possible, to pursue philosophical knowledge concerning the divine since he, being a man, possesses a natural desire and proper inclination to understand what he already accepts on faith. Reason, moreover, is necessary for clarification and explanation of revealed doctrines, the refutation of opposing and erroneous teachings, and for the apologetic purpose of reasoning with those who do not accept the authority of the Scriptures.[36]

I think this suggested synthesis between natural and revealed theology seems like a very reasonable epistemological or theological method, while still acknowledging special revelation as having primacy. Therefore, throughout this work, in making claims about God I will be appealing to the philosophical methodology of natural theology. Yet, as the above synthesis has set out, this natural theology approach will seek to respect (i.e., remain coherent with) the claims of revealed theology, i.e., Scripture.

1.2.4 Classical Theism and the Western Religious Tradition

Now that I have a theological methodology clarified and in place, I can now attempt to get clearer on the meaning of the word "God," and thus my conception of God, that I will adopt and be working with throughout this book. The divine being I have in mind is part of a picture that is often called *classical theism*.[37] Classical theism is a conception of God generally shared by most adherents of the Western religious tradition, which includes the *main* branches of the religions of Judaism, Christianity, and Islam. There are various compatible ways to describe the God of classical theism. Not exhaustive, but here is just one brief synopsis:

> God is a *person*: that is, a being with intellect and will. A person has (or can have) knowledge and belief, but also affections, loves, and hates; a person, furthermore, also has or can have intentions, and can act so as to fulfill them. God has all of these qualities and has some (knowledge, power, and love, for example) to the maximal degree. God is thus all-knowing and all-powerful; he is also

---

36. Miller, *God and Reason*, 123.

37. Rather than a singular conception, some have claimed that classical theism should be seen as a family of conceptions. However, I think there is enough of an overriding conception to identify a single notion of God that can be recognizably acknowledged by most adherents of the classical picture. See Michael Peterson, William Hasker, Bruce Reichenbach, and David Basinger, *Reason and Religious Belief*, 81, note 3.

perfectly good and wholly loving. Still further, he has created the universe and constantly upholds and providentially guides it.[38]

Another familiar but more technical way to describe the God of classical theism is to broadly distinguish God's *incommunicable* attributes from his *communicable* attributes. The former attributes are so called in order to delineate those attributes that belong to God uniquely. God's incommunicable attributes are often identified by negation by stating those respects in which God is *not* like us. Thus, some of God's incommunicable attributes include immortality (since we are mortal), invisibility (since we are visible), and immutability (since we are changeable and changing), among others. But the communicable attributes of God are those characteristics that humans seemingly share (if only by analogy) with God, though obviously humans have these in a qualitatively much inferior way to God. For example, to say "God is wise" and to say that "Plato is wise" is to identify something similar between God and Plato. Yet, classical theism maintains that God's wisdom far surpasses that of Plato's or anyone else's wisdom. Some of God's communicable attributes include omniscience (since humans have some knowledge), omnipotence (since humans have some causal power), and omnipresence (since humans are spatio-temporally located), among others.

This classical theistic picture is a fairly common understanding of God in Western philosophical and theological thought. For example, many theological works that are explicitly based upon revealed theology often use the categories of classical theism (e.g., omniscience, omnipotence, etc.) even though these categories and terms do not appear in Scripture. Likewise, many atheists and agnostics also share this conception of classical theism in their understanding of God. For instance, the so-called problem of evil, an argument usually taken to be evidence against believing in God, has as its target the divine being as described by classical theism. Indeed, the familiar problem of evil argument only makes sense as a discussion between theists and atheists with this view of God held in common.[39]

---

38. Alvin Plantinga, *Warranted Christian Belief*, vii.

39. The problem of evil references the argument that the following three propositions cannot be jointly and simultaneously true:
(1) God is all-powerful (i.e., omnipotent);
(2) God is all-good (i.e., omnibenevolent);
(3) Evil exists.
Both opponents and proponents of this argument agree that to deny (1) or (2) is equivalent to the claim that "God does not exist." For if God does exist, as classical theism claims, then (1) and (2) must both be true of him.

So this is my understanding of the term "God" as I'll use it in this book. And since this is a generally accepted conception of God in the Western religious tradition, and given the purposes of the present project, I don't see the need to attempt an exhaustive description here of the word "God" as it is understood in classical theism. In the following chapters I will often cite various traditional doctrines (teachings that claim what the God of classical theism is like or not like) to see whether a particular explanation of the relationship between God and logic can be counted as acceptable. In other words, I take it that at least some of the characteristics and aspects of the God of classical theism must be respected in order for an explanation of the relationship between God and logic to count as a good explanation. But the doctrines I will refer to in this book are not controversial, in the sense that it is not in question whether they are a generally recognized part of classical theism.

There is one more matter I need to briefly address before summarizing this section. Throughout my discussion here I've been using phrases like "the Western religious tradition," or "the Abrahamic tradition," which I take to be synonymous with each other. I should be clear on what I mean by these phrases, particularly as they relate to the notion of Scripture. Normally, and as I've already designated, the "Abrahamic tradition" is a rubric that includes the main branches of the monotheistic religions of Judaism, Christianity, and Islam.[40] Though there is much disagreement among these branches, there is also quite a bit of overlap—mainly overlap concerning the picture of God that is called classical theism. Since the classical theism I am adopting is a fairly detailed and complex picture of God that has been worked out over the centuries in the Western religious tradition by Jewish, Christian and Islamic theologians and philosophers, then everything I will be arguing for in this work—as far as I can tell—should be consistent with Judaism, Christianity, and Islam. In line with this thought, whenever I reference Scripture as data I will be usually focusing upon the so-called Old Testament books since they are the common property of Jews and Christians and respected among Muslims (since they are often quoted in

---

40. Another purpose in calling these "western" is that I'm primarily trying to distinguish the eastern tradition of Christianity as shaped by Basil and Gregory of Nyssa, and Gregory of Nazianzus from the Western tradition of Christianity as shaped by Augustine, Anselm, and Aquinas. This distinction does not deny that there is much overlap between the eastern and Western traditions of Christianity; but given certain differences, to be identified later, I want to segregate off the eastern tradition from this rubric of "Abrahamic" or "western" religion.

PROLEGOMENA

the *Koran*). Thus, whenever I appeal to the notion of revelation (mainly in chapter 3) it should be understood as a case that applies to all three Western monotheistic religions.[41]

As a further note, I take the phrase "traditional Western theist" to refer to a believer and practitioner of mainline Jewish, Christian, or Muslim tradition, such that, if any of the claims or practices of a respective branch of this tradition were clearly characterized, then any well-educated person who identifies with that respective branch of this religious tradition would more than likely agree that the claim or practice in question is true or part of that tradition.

Let me reiterate that this present work is strictly a work of *philosophical* theology. As such, in line with the natural theological method laid out in this chapter, I do not intend to use Scripture as evidence (such as quoting sacred texts for proof of some point). Rather, given the importance of Scripture within the Western religious tradition, I will treat Scripture as data that I will seek to be consistent with. In other words, if my project presented a picture of the relationship between God and logic that could not be made to cohere well with the generally accepted account of classical theism as proffered by the Scripture of that tradition, then I would take this project to be a failure in finding an adequate explanation of the relationship between God and logic.

In summary of §1.2, I conclude that the term "God" references the being presented by the picture of classical theism. I understand this picture as being primarily informed by the Scripture of revealed theology in the Western religious tradition and extrapolated and built upon by the resources of natural theology. Since the present work is a philosophical one, I will primarily be relying upon the methodology of natural theology though seeking to be consistent with Scripture, and the Western tradition, of revealed theology. In trying to answer the question, "What is the relationship between God and logic?" I will thus more precisely be asking, "What is the relationship between the God of classical theism and logic?"

---

41. I clearly and proudly count myself within the Christian (Protestant) tradition. I'm not denying or hiding this fact. But I don't think I argue for anything within this work that is unique to a Christian perspective.

1.3 SUMMARY

In summary of this chapter, I understand logic to be primarily about logical consequence, which I think is best represented by my characterization (LC). Again, I assume that whatever sort of entities constitute logical consequence is what most formal logical systems are attempting to capture or model. But I remain neutral on the metaphysics of logical consequence at this point. I understand God to be the divine being presented by classical theism. The special revelation of revealed theology, presented in Scripture, functions as the "raw data" of theology, while natural or philosophical theology seeks to theorize and extrapolate from this data coherent views concerning God, especially as it relates to concerns not addressed, or not addressed sufficiently, within Scripture. This current work is primarily a work of natural theology, but will seek to be consistent with the claims of special revelation (i.e., the so-called Old Testament) in the Western tradition, or at minimum, those claims from the Old Testament that Muslims can theologically agree with Christians and Jews about. In addition, I'm arguing for a position that I believe coheres with the whole of classical theism, namely, all three main branches of the Western Abrahamic tradition. Therefore, I will attempt to argue for my thesis with this broad notion of Western religion in mind.

I think this prolegomena is sufficient for understanding the desiderata that I want to respect when asking the question: "What is the relationship between logic and God?" Throughout this work I will often word the question stated in this more simple way; but it should be understood more precisely as asking, "What is the relationship between what constitutes the logical consequence relation, as characterized by (LC), and the God of classical theism?" Now that I have my terms clarified, what is the best way to proceed in conducting our investigation of our question concerning God and logic? This is the subject of the next chapter.

2

THE *LOGICAL* EUTHYPHRO DILEMMA

Now that I've clarified how I understand the terms "God" and "logic," we can now focus on the primary question: What relationship exists between God and logic? But how exactly shall we go about investigating and answering this question? In this chapter I will suggest a track of investigation by way of a classic query and problem that is found in philosophical antiquity. I believe this ancient question, and its ensuing dilemma, present a good starting point for approaching how God and morality relate to each other. In addition, I believe an investigation of the structure of this classic question and dilemma will suggest an interesting, analogous way to begin thinking about the relationship between God and logic. In §2.1 I will explore this ancient question briefly laying out the problems it presents to any kind of theory that attempts to explain morality in virtue of God's will or commands. In §2.2 I will then attempt to motivate an analogous dilemma structure for our investigation concerning God and logic. As we'll see, this approach lays out quite nicely at least two options for thinking about what relationship might exist between God and logic. In §2.3 I'll try to deflect the objection, or at least the worry, that this sort of approach is a bad way to investigate the relationship between God and logic.

THE LOGIPHRO DILEMMA

2.1 THE EUTHYPHRO DILEMMA

Historically, religiously minded ethicists have often sought to ground morality in God, in some way, where God plays some central role in explaining the very nature of morality. There are various sorts of ethical theories that offer such an account, including theological versions of virtue ethics and natural law approaches.[1] However, another way to explain morality in virtue of God, and one that has also been popular among many theists, is that ethics is grounded in the explicit commands, or will, of God. Such an ethical theory claims that morally evaluable entities, of whatever kind, have at least some of their moral statuses in virtue of acts of divine command or will. For example, according to such a theory an act of kindness would be morally good if and only if God had in fact commanded or willed humans to act kind. Such an ethical view is standardly known as some sort of *divine command theory*. However, divine command theories have suffered a long history of criticisms. Many of these criticisms usually trace back to what is often called *the Euthyphro dilemma*. In the following section I want to investigate the original, as well as an updated, Euthyphro dilemma and the problems that it poses for divine command theorists.

2.1.1 The Original (and Updated) Euthyphro Dilemma

The Euthyphro dilemma finds its origin in an early Socratic dialogue entitled, appropriately enough, *Euthyphro*.[2] Written by his student Plato, it features Socrates questioning the young religious zealot and presumed prophet Euthyphro. The dialogue begins with Socrates and Euthyphro meeting each other on the way to court: Socrates to answer for an indictment of corrupting young men, Euthyphro bringing murder charges against his very own father. In light of his supposed prophetic knowledge, Euthyphro makes several confident assertions to Socrates concerning piety. Socrates, seeking to be enlightened in order that he may effectively answer his prosecutors, begins to question Euthyphro on the nature of piety. In response, Euthyphro initially proclaims that "what is dear to the gods is

---

1. For a helpful and sympathetic introduction to various such approaches see Wadell, *Happiness and the Christian Moral Life*.
2. For analysis and commentary on Plato's *Euthyphro* see Geach, "Plato's *Euthyphro*," 369–82, Sharvy, "*Euthyphro* 9b–11b: Analysis," 119–37, and Hare, *Plato's Euthyphro*. In the following I give a fairly common interpretation of the Euthyphro dilemma that largely agrees with these commentators.

THE *LOGICAL* EUTHYPHRO DILEMMA

pious, what is not is impious" (7a).³ But Socrates points out that the gods are not always unified on what is dear to them for one god may favor one thing, another god another thing. But Euthyphro insists, to the contrary, that the gods *are* together on such matters. He clarifies that "the pious is what all the gods love, and the opposite, what all the gods hate, is the impious" (9e). So, in sum, Euthyphro proclaims that if all the gods support some practice because they love it, then it's an act of piety; if they all denounce some practice because they hate it, then it's an act of impiety.

But then Socrates asks the following question, one that has ever since haunted ethicists who desire to make a strong connection between divine will and morality: "Is the pious being loved by the gods because it is pious, or is it pious because it is being loved by the gods?" (10a). This seemingly innocent question presents two options to Euthyphro and divine command theorists. Both options are usually taken to be fraught with undefeatable difficulties.

However, before going on to these difficulties, we should note that in our day most philosophers who might be sympathetic to some sort of divine command theory will be monotheists, unlike the polytheistic Greeks of antiquity that this Socratic question challenges. This being so, we should update the wording of Socrates' original question a bit. It is widely agreed that doing so will not blunt any of the force of Scorates' original challenge. Philosopher Louise Antony helpfully provides an updated translation: "Are morally good actions morally good simply in virtue of God's favoring them? Or does God favor them because they are—independently of his favoring them—morally good?"⁴ I think Antony's revision is a fair rendering of Socrates' original question. The plural "gods" is replaced with the monotheists' "God," "piety" is taken to mean "goodness" (i.e., moral goodness), and Antony replaces the "loves" of the gods with God's "favor," where favor is thought of in terms of God's commands. However, one objection one might bring against this translation is that piety is not especially connected to morality and so "goodness" is not an acceptable gloss here. This objection claims that someone could be religiously pious (i.e., strictly following religious duties and practices) without being moral.⁵ Nevertheless, I think it's clear that piety is usually thought as being tightly connected to

---

3. Quotations and parenthetical references come from Plato's *Euthyphro* found in *Plato: Complete Works*.
4. Louise Antony, "Atheism as Perfect Piety," 71.
5. See *Euthyphro* (11e) ff. Thanks to Stewart Shapiro for pressing this point.

morality. To be moral seems synonymous with being pious and being pious seems synonymous with being moral. Moreover, the context of Plato's dialogue seems to assume this connection as well. Also, the rationale for the translation of "loves" to "favor" is built on the idea that if, for example, God commands us to be merciful to one another, then it is reasonably thought that this shows his favor of such actions.

2.1.2 Problems for Divine Moral Command Theories

Now that we've updated Socrates' original question to fit our contemporary context, let's now look at the two horns, or two problematic options, that this question seems to imply for the monotheistic divine command theorist.

The first horn of the Euthyphro dilemma: Morally good actions are morally good simply in virtue of God's favoring them. This first option suggests that God's commands or will determine what is morally good, and God's prohibitions, or negative will, determine what is morally bad.[6] If God commands or wills some action, then it's morally good in virtue of his commanding or willing it. If God prohibits some action, then it's morally bad in virtue of his prohibiting it or willing against it. Thus, this view claims that what is morally good is the case *solely* because God has commanded or willed it. Moreover, there is nothing more to say concerning a particular action being morally good other than that God commanded or willed it. To affirm this position is to embrace a *voluntarist* theory of moral goodness—a straightforward divine command theory.

The second horn of the Euthyphro dilemma: God favors morally good actions because they are, independently of his favoring them, morally good. This second option suggests that God's commands or will concerning morality are what they are in virtue of God recognizing what is already morally good. On this view, the moral goodness of an action is a feature independent of, and antecedent to, God's commanding or willing it. Thus, when God makes moral commands or morally wills something, it is because such commands are (or his will is) rooted in that which is already and independently morally good. This view also usually claims that God, being good himself, only commands or wills what is antecedently good. So God's

---

6. By explicitly designating goodness as *moral* goodness, we are implicitly claiming that this option is silent as to the determination of other kinds of goodness, e.g., aesthetic goodness.

moral commands or will are thought to consistently track what is indeed morally good. Call this view a *non-voluntarist* theory of moral goodness.

Unfortunately, for divine command ethicists, neither the voluntarist nor the non-voluntarist option is considered unproblematic. I'll not offer an exhaustive list here of all the problems for either of these positions; but let's briefly look at some of the usual objections that are given to each.

Concerning the first option, the voluntarist option, critics have often pointed out that if God's commands or will are the sole determinants for why particular actions are morally wrong (e.g., rape or genocide), then it seems that the moral status of such actions are entirely a reflection of God's capricious whim. For if there are no prior or further reasons for why such actions are morally wrong, then they are wrong simply because God said or willed so. Call this the *no reasons objection*.[7] The objection highlights the unintuitiveness of the voluntarist claim. Even if God prohibits or wills against, say rape and other sexual abuses, surely there are justifying reasons for why such actions are wrong other than simply that God prohibits or wills against them. A related objection notes that a voluntarist theory of moral goodness seems to imply that since moral goodness is purely a matter of God's commands or will, then God could have counterfactually commanded or willed what we take to be clearly morally abhorrent actions. On this view, if God had commanded or willed rape or genocide, then according to this option such actions would then count as morally good. But this seems obviously and clearly wrong. Call this the *abhorrent command objection*. In essence, this objection is pointing out that the voluntarist option makes morality a completely arbitrary matter, which is, to say the least, highly unintuitive as well. Another related problem for the voluntarist position is how it affects ascriptions of moral goodness to God. For example, when someone references God as morally good (or some similar normative notion), a person tends to think that such an ascription is meaningful. But if this ascription is consistent with God being able to command or will obviously horrible actions as morally good (i.e., as the abhorrent command objection points out), then the attribution of goodness to God appears vacuous. Call this the *vacuity objection*. To my knowledge, a voluntarist divine command theory is unable to answer these objections in any adequate way and still maintain the voluntarist position. Therefore, the voluntarist option of divine command theory seems fairly hopeless.

---

7. The objections and their names come directly from chapter 7 of Baggett and Walls, *Good God*.

However, what we're calling the non-voluntarist position offers little better to the divine command theorist either. For it presents another problem that, from the divine command theorist's perspective, is equally unattractive. To embrace a non-voluntarist theory of moral goodness is to locate the standard of morality in a position independent from God. On this option, God must consult what the standard of morality normatively dictates before commanding or willing it. Thus, for example, God prohibits or wills against murder because he has discovered that murder is immoral—prior and independently of his commands or will.[8] Though this gets around all of the criticisms against the voluntarist, this is a serious problem for divine command theorists who identify themselves with the Western religious perspective. Why? God is normally conceived in this tradition as the only completely self-sufficient and independent entity that exists. Thus, all entities, other than God, depend in some way upon God for their nature and existence. But the non-voluntarist option of divine command theory makes the nature and existence of morality completely autonomous from God. In other words, God is completely superfluous or unimportant to the nature of morality—moral goodness is what it is completely apart from God. And this is a consequence that few theists (if any) in the Western tradition of religion will accept. Thus, the non-voluntarist take on divine command theory seems also to be an unacceptable option for divine command theorists.

To briefly summarize this section (§2.1.2), Socrates' original (and updated) question to Euthyphro gives a dilemma that implies that the divine command theorist has only two choices, both of which are taken to have seemingly insuperable problems: either God's relationship to morality makes morality a completely arbitrary affair (i.e., voluntarism) or God's relationship to morality leaves God superfluous to the nature of morality in any essential, special, or interesting way (i.e., non-voluntarism).

Remember that our main concern here is not to attempt to investigate and vindicate some ethical theory, but to be introduced to this ancient question and dilemma in order to see if it might give us any help us in our own investigation. Now that we've investigated the original (and updated) Euthyphro dilemma, let's now see whether this picture can help in our own investigation of God and logic.

---

8. I am being a little tongue-in-cheek when I use the word "discovered." I am not, of course, suggesting that non-voluntarists believe that there was a time when God did not know that murder was wrong. Thanks to Robin Parry for pointing out this issue.

THE *LOGICAL* EUTHYPHRO DILEMMA

2.2 EXTENDING THE EUTHYPHRO STRUCTURE

2.2.1 Motivating the Euthyphro Approach

Can the original Euthyphro question and dilemma serve as a profitable example or a suggestive way of how to begin thinking about the relationship between God and logic? Since I've spent several pages investigating the original Euthyphro dilemma, I of course am going to be arguing that this is indeed the case. This isn't an arbitrary proposal on my part, nor will I simply be trying to shoehorn our investigation into this particular mold. Rather, I think there are good reasons to think that a Euthyphro-like structure will be helpful and that it will naturally lend itself towards our goal of trying to understand the relationship between God and logic.

One reason to think that a Euthyphro-like structure will be helpful to our investigation is noticing how often the argument or dialectical structure of the Euthyphro dilemma, or something close to it, comes up in various other philosophical contexts. For example, note the following quote from political philosopher David Estlund:

> In Plato's dialogue *Euthyphro*, the question is raised whether something is pious because it is loved by the gods, or whether the gods love it because it is pious. The "Euthyphro question" has a form that crops up all over philosophy, and democratic theory is no exception. Many people today think that, at least under certain conditions, good political decisions are those that are democratically made. We do not have to accept the old slogan that *vox populi, vox dei* (the voice of the people is the voice of God) to see the parallel to the Euthyphro question: are good (or just, or legitimate) democratic outcomes good because they are democratically chosen, or are democratically chosen because they are good?[9]

As we see here, Estlund observes that the Euthyphro question (or better, the Euthyphro structure) seems to appear all over philosophy, including philosophical democratic theory. But why is the Euthyphro structure supposedly so common throughout philosophy? As I think Estlund's example shows, a Euthyphro structure seems particularly helpful in highlighting the pros and cons of representing a particular philosophical phenomenon as being either constructed (i.e., being the result of human activity in some way) or being non-constructed (i.e., existing completely apart from any sort of human activity). In this sense, the Euthyphro serves as a very helpful, as

---

9. Estlund, *Democratic Authority*, 65.

well as versatile, philosophical tool. Another example from the world of meta-ethics also helps to make this point.

Consider the position of moral constructivism, which claims that the reality of the moral domain is a constructive function of humans. Russ Shafer-Landau brings up the following criticism against moral constructivists who import certain moral constraints, which are evidently not humanly constructed. He complains:

> These constraints are not themselves products of construction, and so there would be moral facts or reasons that obtain independently of constructive functions. This is realism, not constructivism.
>
> If this is sounding a familiar note, it should. The dilemma pressed against the constructivist is a variation of one first found in the *Euthyphro*.[10]

Shafer-Landau is pushing a criticism here against moral constructivists, one that he claims bears strong similarity with the Euthyphro dilemma. Towards such constructivists the implied question, I take it, is something like the following: Are morally good actions morally good simply because humans construct or sanction them to be so? Or do humans sanction actions as moral because they are—independent of their construction—morally good in some way? Shafer-Landau is claiming that the moral constructivists in question, who seem to hold a voluntarist position of sorts since they seem to give an affirmative answer to the first question, are also inconsistently affirming a non-voluntarist position implied by the second question. The Euthyphro structure helps Shafer-Landau to clarify this critical point.

I think these examples give good evidence that the Euthyphro structure—i.e., the Euthyphro dilemma with its challenging question and attending options—is not only perhaps a common philosophical phenomenon; but also (and perhaps because of it being so) it seems to be an argument structure that is fairly versatile and helpfully highlights key issues to which it is applied.

However, the original Euthyphro structure was given as a way to think about a certain *theistic* philosophical position. This highly suggests that this versatile tool will most naturally extend to examining other similarly theistic philosophical positions. Indeed, note the following proposal from philosopher William Mann:

---

10. Shafer-Landau, *Moral Realism*, 42.

THE *LOGICAL* EUTHYPHRO DILEMMA

> It is useful to consider the [Euthyphro] dilemma in tandem with another theistic conundrum—whether God is the author of necessary truths, or whether they have their modal character independently of him. One might expect that a resolution to that conundrum would shed light on the *Euthyphro* dilemma.[11]

Mann is proposing here a Euthyphro-like investigation of the relationship between God and certain modal (i.e., necessary) truths. He speculates that a philosophically adequate resolution to that investigation would perhaps given an equally satisfying outcome, due to its analogous nature, to the original Euthyphro investigation concerning God and morality. I'm not so much concerned here with Mann's latter claim; but his initial idea is, I think, highly suggestive. In essence, Mann is proposing that a Euthyphro structure could be used to investigate other realities or phenomenon—besides just morality—in relation to God. This makes sense to me. Originally Socrates applied the Euthyphro structure to God and piety. Later, others naturally extended this by applying it to God and morality. Mann is suggesting we apply it to God and modality. And so I think a Euthyphro structure can be naturally extended to God and logic as well, or more precisely, to God and logical consequence.

Therefore, given the versatility and naturalness of extending its application to other questions concerning God's relationship to other realities, I will investigate the relationship between God and logic by applying a question and dialectical structure analogous to Socrates' original dilemma presented against Euthyphro's view of God and piety. As I believe we'll see, this will give us a very fruitful starting place for thinking about our subject. Let's see how this might go.

2.2.2 The Logical Euthyphro Dilemma

In order to propose a question analogous to Socrates' original Euthyphro question, or more particularly our updated Euthyphro question, let's first imagine that we have an individual who holds a position similar to the religious devotee Euthyphro in Plato's original dialogue. Let's call this individual Logiphro (pronounced LOJ-i-phro). We'll understand Logiphro to be a devoted monotheist who conceives of God broadly in line with the Western theistic tradition of classical theism as laid out in chapter 1. Logiphro thus generally thinks of God as the creator and sustainer of everything, apart

---

11. Mann, "Modality, Morality, and God," 83–84.

THE LOGIPHRO DILEMMA

from himself. Thus, the nature and existence of anything apart from God must be explicated, ultimately, in relation to God. How exactly, then, does Logiphro conceive of the relationship between God and logic? In response to this Socratic question, let's imagine that Logiphro makes a statement similar to Euthyphro's original: "If God favors some sequence of claims that we recognize as a logical argument, then it is a valid argument; if God disfavors some sequence of claims that we recognize as a logical argument, then it is an invalid argument."[12] As with the earlier Euthyphro position, this latter statement assumes that God only commands or wills that which he favors. Understood in this way, Logiphro is claiming that logically evaluable entities (whatever these entities may be) have their validity statuses in virtue of God's favor (i.e., commands or will). This sounds suitably similar to the original Euthyphro claim: an entity has its particular sort of status in virtue of the divine commands or will.

However, as we saw with the original Euthyphro position, Socrates asked a question that challenged Euthyphro to clarify and explain how piety is related to divine commands or will. In a similar vein, we can imagine a Socrates-like critic asking an analogous sort of question challenging Logiphro's claim above. Wording it as closely as possible to the original updated question, our new question to Logiphro would be something like the following: Do logically valid arguments have their validity simply in virtue of God's favoring them? Or does God favor them because they are—independently of his favoring them—logically valid?

This analogous Socratic question seems to push Logiphro to face a familiar sort of dilemma for clarifying and explaining his position. The question implies that there are at least two horns, or two options, for understanding Logiphro's suggested logical theory. We'll call this the *logical Euthyphro dilemma* or just the *Logiphro dilemma* for short.

The first horn of the Logiphro dilemma is the following: logically valid arguments are valid simply in virtue of God's favoring (i.e., commanding or willing) them. This option suggests that God's commands or will determine what counts as valid, and God's prohibitions or will against such determine what is invalid. Thus, concerning any sequence of claims (or in the limiting case where there is only a single concluding claim without premises), God has the ability to make the logical supporting relation between such claims valid or invalid. For example, this option claims that God could command

---

12. Again, see chapter 1 for an explication of what counts as an argument, and what constitutes logical validity and invalidity.

THE *LOGICAL* EUTHYPHRO DILEMMA

or will it to be the case that modus ponens (i.e., $p, (p{\rightarrow}q) \vdash q$), as well as any other generally recognized valid argument,[13] be invalid if God were to decide to make it so. Likewise according to this option, affirming the consequent (i.e., $q, (p{\rightarrow}q) \vdash p$), as well as any other generally recognized fallacy (i.e., an invalid argument), could be made into a logically valid argument if God commanded or willed it to be so. To be clear and emphasize the radical nature of this option, we need to see that this view is claiming in those cases where a concluding claim has no related premise claims, and thus logically true, then God could command or will these logical truths (i.e., $[\emptyset] \vdash \Phi$) to be invalid. Likewise with logical falsehoods—such as logical contradictions—God could command or will such claims to be valid.[14] To affirm this option clearly embraces a voluntarist theory of logical validity. Thus, let's call this first position *logical voluntarism*.

The second horn of the Logiphro dilemma is the following: God favors (i.e., commands or wills) valid logical arguments because they are— independently and antecedently of his favoring them—logically valid. This second option suggests that God's logical commands or will are what they are in virtue of what is already valid or invalid. On this view the validity status of a sequence of claims is a feature independent of, and antecedent to, God's commanding or willing it. As with the similar moral position, this view suggests that God, being a logical being himself, is only interested in commanding or willing that which is already valid. It seems to me that to

---

13. By "generally recognized valid implications" I am neither ignoring the different validity judgments amongst formal logical systems nor pre-judging a case between monistic and pluralistic conceptions of logic. Rather, the simple idea I'm appealing to here is that there are some implications that most logicians (and presumably most people in general) would agree as recognizing as valid. A similar point goes for the phrase "generally recognized fallacy."

14. "God could command or will logical falsehoods to be true" can be delineated in several different ways: (1) It's not possible that (p & $\sim p$) and yet God is able to make it the case that (p & $\sim p$); (2) It's not possible that (p & $\sim p$) *and* it's possible that it's possible that (p & $\sim p$); or (3) It simply claims that it's possible that (p & $\sim p$). I'll be interpreting "God can make logical falsehoods true" along the lines of (3). As I'll explain in chapter 3, I believe (1) and (2) are representatives of a *limited possibilism* reading of logical voluntarism while (3) is a stronger reading of logical voluntarism called *universal possibilism*. As I'll argue in chapter 3, I believe that limited possibilism reduces to universal possibilism. Position (1) can be found in Conee, "The Possibility of Power Beyond Possibility," 447–73. Position (2) can be found in Curley, "Descartes on the Creation of the Eternal Truths," 569–97. And though Graham Priest in his *In Contradiction* does not present a view of God and modality, his view of modality ends up being essentially similar to position (3).

affirm this view is to embrace a non-voluntarist theory of validity. So let's call this second position *logical non-voluntarism*.

2.2.3 Initial Problems for the Logiphro Logician

So given our initial setup here with our Euthyphro structure, anyone, like our imaginary Logiphro, who seeks to explain the relationship between God and logic in terms of God's commands or will has at least these two options to choose from. As our new dilemma puts forward, it seems that Logiphro must endorse either logical voluntarism or logical non-voluntarism. However, just as we saw how the Euthyphro ethicist is faced with difficult problems on either option, it seems to me that in very similar ways the Logiphro logician must also face analogous troublesome problems: he seems forced to hold that either the validity of logical arguments is completely arbitrary (i.e., logical voluntarism) or hold that the nature and existence of valid logical arguments is superfluous to the existence of God (i.e., logical non-voluntarism).[15] However, I believe the Logiphro logician is in even a worse situation than the Euthyphro ethicist. For along with the objections that are analogous to the moral case, the Logiphro logician has several additional problems that complicate his position even more than the Euthyphro ethicist had to deal with. I'll lay out these problems in more detail in later chapters. But let me briefly list a few of the problems here to give a flavor of the morass for the one who wants to explain the relationship between God and logic in terms of divine commands or will.

Concerning logical voluntarism, at the very least, it seems quite bizarre to even consider that logical arguments can change their validity status simply in virtue of God's commands or will. What would it even mean to say, for instance, that the law of non-contradiction is false, or that modus ponens is invalid? Questions of this sort seem to invite only chaos and puzzlement. There are a host of worries to bring out here, but we can summarize, in brief, that there is a serious doubt as to whether logical voluntarism is a coherent or even an intelligible position to make out. In addition, there is an even a bigger problem for logical voluntarism given that Logiphro is a member of the Western tradition of religion. As laid

---

15. As I'll argue in chapter 5, I believe the Logiphro dilemma (as well as the original Euthyphro dilemma) is a false one. The dilemma assumes that the *only* thing God can and does contribute to logical consequence is his commands or will. I believe this assumption is false.

THE *LOGICAL* EUTHYPHRO DILEMMA

out in chapter 1, claims about God in this tradition are usually taken from what are considered to be trustworthy testimonial accounts (i.e., Scripture) whose own origins are supposed to trace back to God's self-revealing claims about himself. But if logical voluntarism is correct, the view implies that any claim God may have communicated could not be understood by us in any usually straightforward way. For any kind of communication relies upon certain assumptions about logical inferential connections to other claims—what is included or excluded—at least to some degree. If logical voluntarism is true, then one could never be sure what this divine supra-logical being of logical voluntarism means when he communicates anything to humans. And given that many of those who operate in the Western religious tradition take Scripture to be the primary evidence for their claims about God, logical voluntarism calls this whole edifice into question. The sort of "possibilities" logical voluntarism avails itself of would make theistic philosophical formulation and theological discussion essentially pointless, for one could not take any claims about God in any usually understood way. In chapter 3, we'll address in detail the position of logical voluntarism along with these problems it appears to face.

Concerning logical non-voluntarism, this view presents a problem quite similar to the one we saw for the moral non-voluntarist position earlier. Again, the Western religious perspective normally conceives of God as the only completely self-sufficient and independent entity that exists. Thus, all entities, other than God, depend in some way upon God for their nature and existence. But adherents of logical non-voluntarism hold that the nature and existence of logical validity (whatever metaphysically constitutes it) is completely autonomous from God. Thus, God seems to be completely unneeded to explain the nature and perhaps the very existence of logic. Since such consequences seem to be unacceptable to theists in this tradition, it seems logical non-voluntarism is an untenable position for such theists to hold. In chapter 4, we'll clarify what the position of logical non-voluntarism amounts to along with addressing this problem and whatever other problems it may also face.

But let's put all of these problems to the side now and note what we've accomplished in this chapter. In §2.1 we investigated Socrates' original (and updated) Euthyphro dilemma, which included its challenging question and the presented options for the pietist (or ethicist) who wishes to draw a strong connection between God's commands or will and the nature of piety (or ethics). In §2.2 we also saw that the dialectical structure of the Euthyphro dilemma seems to arise in various philosophical contexts showing it to be a versatile and helpful philosophical tool. Given that the original Euthyphro was presented in the context of challenging a theory that made a strong connection between God and moral reality, I suggested that we could naturally extend the Euthyphro dialectical structure—in a roughly analogous way—to serve in our investigation of God and logic. Thus, we suggested a question analogously similar to Socrates' original question to Euthyphro to our imaginary Logiphro. This question presented a dilemma that implies at least two choices for our imaginary Logiphro: logical voluntarism or logical non-voluntarism. Thus, we have two fairly clear delineated options that help us to begin to consider how God and logic might be related.

2.3 AN OBJECTION TO ADOPTING THE EUTHYPHRO STRUCTURE

Though I believe the above has shown that the Euthyphro structure gives us a nice starting point for our investigation of the relationship between God and logic, one might think that this suggestion is actually pretty useless. Even assuming that one finds the primary question important or philosophically interesting—How are God and logic related to one another?—I can think of at least one objection that might be put forward to the Euthyphro structure approach that I am adopting here.

We saw how the original Euthyphro dilemma left us with only two options: moral voluntarism or moral non-voluntarism, both of which seemed plagued with difficulties. It must be pointed out that even a cursory knowledge of the philosophical literature on ethics seems universally united in claiming that these difficulties cannot be overcome. Thus, the Euthyphro dilemma is taken to be a damning critique of trying to explain morality in terms of God's commands or will.[16] But, if this is so, why think that an analogous use of this approach has any better chance of showing anything profitable concerning attempts to explain some other reality in terms of God's commands or will? In other words, if the Euthyphro structure so successfully destroyed Euthyphro's theory of God and morality, doesn't it seem fairly likely that it will truncate any sort of similar theory concerning God and logic? Why use a dialectical structure that has shown itself to be able to roundly discard such a theistic position? To do so seems like

---

16. Just one example: Antony, "Atheism as Perfect Piety," 67–84 does little more than assume this is the case.

THE *LOGICAL* EUTHYPHRO DILEMMA

entering a horserace with an old nag that has proven track record of being a loser. Surely, if one wants to philosophically investigate the relationship between God and logic, there must be a better and more defensible method to begin with?

Perhaps there is a better starting point—though I do not know of it. Nevertheless, I believe that the original Euthyphro dilemma may not be as victorious in its critique of divine command theories, or theistic versions of ethics more generally, as it is popularly held to be. For example, there has recently been a strong and healthy flow of philosophical literature attempting to show that the supposed strength of the original Euthyphro dilemma is not as robust as usually thought.[17] These works have focused upon overcoming the problems that the Euthyphro has foisted upon divine command conceptions of morality as well as addressing problems associated with non-theistic conceptions of morality. With these published works in mind, it seems that the Euthyphro structure may not be in such completely bad shape after all.

Thus, the unified philosophical response that upholds the Euthyphro critique as thoroughly successful is, at the very least, overstated. And, if such is the case, then it seems that a Euthyphro-like approach still holds out the possibility of serving as a productive starting point for investigating the relationship between God and some other reality like logic. Besides, even if the Logiphro dilemma ends up being successfully damning of any philosophical theory that seeks to establish some close or interesting relationship between God and logic as the original Euthyphro is conceived to be, it seems to me that this would still be an interesting philosophical upshot to be learned.

Therefore, I believe we have some good reason to believe that a Euthyphro-like approach can serve as an interesting and helpful way of approaching a philosophical investigation of the relationship between God and logic. The Logiphro dilemma has given us two fairly clear and contrasting targets to focus upon. This seems to me, at the very least, to make it a good starting point for our investigation.

---

17. See Baggett and Walls, *Good God* as well as Copan, "God, Naturalism, and the Foundations of Morality," 141–61, and Milliken, "Euthyphro, the Good, and the Right," 145–55. I will return to and address the supposed success of the Euthyphro dilemma against theologically based ethics in more depth in chapter 5.

THE LOGIPHRO DILEMMA

2.4 SUMMARY

We began by looking at Plato's *Euthyphro* and saw how Socrates' challenging question to Euthyphro's divine command theory led to an attending dilemma. Given our imaginary interlocutor Logiphro's view of God and logic, which is analogously similar to Euthyphro's original view concerning God and morality, we saw how an analogous challenging question can also be raised that puts forward a similar sort of dilemma. Despite the unpopularity of divine command theories, evidently buttressed by confidence in the success of the Euthyphro dilemma, I have argued that this does not serve as a sufficient reason to *not* adopt a Euthyphro structure in investigating God and logic. Therefore, I believe this chapter has shown that my suggested Euthyphro approach is a very natural and productive way to begin thinking about the relationship between God and logic.

Let's now turn to the investigation of the two positions that this approach has given us. In the next chapter, chapter 3, we will begin by investigating the position of logical voluntarism.

3

LOGICAL VOLUNTARISM

As laid out in the last chapter, opting for logical voluntarism is the view that God's commands or will determine which arguments are valid. Conversely, God's prohibitions or will against determine which arguments are invalid. Thus, for any sequence of claims that constitutes a logical argument, God has the ability to make its logical connection valid or invalid. To be clear and emphasize the radical nature of this option, we need to see that this view is claiming in those cases where a valid concluding claim has no related premise claims (i.e., traditionally thought of as a logical truth), then God could command or will such a claim to be false, and likewise with a logical falsehood—such as a contradiction—God could command or will it to be true. To affirm this option is to embrace a voluntarist theory of logical validity.

I divide this chapter into two main sections. In §3.1 I will attempt to explicate and clarify what logical voluntarism amounts to. Given the rather bizarre possibilities the view puts forward, in this section I will also try to figure out what might motivate logical voluntarism, particularly by looking at a few historical figures that have been suspected of holding something like this view. Then in the second section, §3.2, I will look at objections to logical voluntarism. Particularly, in §§3.2.1 and 3.2.2 I will look at some objections that I think the logical voluntarist may be able to answer. But in §3.2.3 I will deal with a third objection, which I believe is a huge problem for logical voluntarism from the perspective of the theist in the Abrahamic or Western tradition. In §3.2.4 I will discuss the possibility of the logical voluntarist who wants to "bite the bullet" of the objection discussed in §3.2.3. I will argue that the suggested move requires too large of a cost for the one who wants to continue to adhere to traditional Western theism.

3.1 CLARIFYING LOGICAL VOLUNTARISM AND EXAMINING MOTIVATIONS FOR THE VIEW

3.1.1 Clarifying Logical Voluntarism

Prima facie, logical voluntarism is a difficult view to make sense of. What does it even mean to say that God could command or will a valid argument to be invalid or an invalid argument to be valid?[1] Moreover, it is very difficult to begin explicating logical voluntarism without begging a whole host of metaphysical questions related to logic. For example, if instances of valid arguments are composed of nothing more than linguistic entities, then it might seem rather trivial to say that God can change the validity of these arguments, for surely human beings, to some extent, have control over the linguistic components they use. In other words, if logic is just a matter of language, and humans seem to have some choice about what language means or implies, then it seems obvious that God could have a choice in this matter as well. However, if some sort of Platonic entities (e.g., propositions, sets of possible worlds, etc.) constitute logical arguments, then the logical voluntarist would need to explain what God exactly changes when he changes the validity status of arguments constituted by them. Yet, I believe, we can (again) largely sidestep these metaphysical issues because the logical voluntarist needs to first deal with what I see as objections that are preliminary to any such metaphysical details of his account. But before dealing with these objections, we first need to clarify the picture of logical voluntarism that we were introduced to in the last chapter with a little more detail.

In order to get very clear on what exactly logical voluntarism is asserting, let's examine just one claim of the logical voluntarist position that God could command or will invalid arguments to be valid. Remember that logical truths are just one subset of valid arguments. Likewise, we think of

---

1. In chapter 1 I demarcated the term "argument" as referring to a stretch of indicative discourse where one or more claims is intended to support another claim. See that chapter for further explanation and caveats.

any logical falsehood as an inconsistent, and so invalid, argument. Thus, the logical voluntarist seems committed to the following:

> (LV1): God could command or will logical falsehoods (arguments of the form (p & $\sim p$)) to be true.

How should we understand what (LV1) is claiming? For instance, Earl Conee[2] seems to explicate something like (LV1) as: It is not possible that (p & $\sim p$) and yet God is able to make it the case that (p & $\sim p$). In a similar fashion E. M. Curley, in explaining his interpretation of Descartes on the subject,[3] defines (LV1) as: It is not possible that (p & $\sim p$) *and* it's possible that God could make it possible that (p & $\sim p$). In addition, (LV1) could be understood in a stronger and more straightforward way as it simply being possible for God to make it the case that (p & $\sim p$).[4] If we take logical truths to be one category of necessary truths—and thus logical falsehoods to be necessary falsehoods—I think these different formulations can be assigned to either of two different modal ways of understanding (LV1). I believe Conee and Curley's different readings of (LV1) are both instances of what is often called *limited possibilism* in that both understand (LV1) as a claim that necessary truths (and necessarily valid arguments) are only contingently necessary for God. In relation to classical theism, limited possibilism is usually explicated in the following way:[5] at the moment of creation—before establishing the necessary truths (including logical truths)—God could have commanded or willed any "truth" (i.e., any claim) to be either a necessary (or contingent) truth or a necessary (or contingent) falsehood. Thus, God had the power to determine the modal status, as well as the truth-value, of any claim in the moment of creation. Since we understand logical truths to be one category of valid arguments, this view extends to the claim that God also had the power to command or will the validity status of any argument at the moment of creation as well. However, so the view goes, once God established all of the truths at creation, including the necessary truths and falsehoods (and also the validity statuses of all other arguments) these claims of necessity bind even his omnipotent power—they are now necessary even for God.

2. Conee, "The Possibility of Power Beyond Possibility," 447–73.

3. Curley, "Descartes on the Creation of the Eternal Truths," 569–97.

4. Though his view has nothing to do with God, Graham Priest, in *In Contradiction*, holds that there are "dialetheias," i.e., there are *true* contradictions.

5 For an example of this view, see Clouser, "Religious Language: A New Look at an Old Problem," 385–407.

The third (and stronger) suggested reading for (LV1) above is oftentimes called *universal possibilism* in that it understands (LV1) to claim that God has the power to command or will the modal status, as well as the truth-value, of any claim at any time, as well as the validity status of any argument at any time, including beyond the moment of creation. On this reading of (LV1) there is no claim (and literally no *thing*) binding upon God, nothing that can act as an impediment to God's omnipotent power. On the universal possibilism reading, for God there are neither any necessarily true claims, nor any necessarily valid arguments.

It's clear that the limited possibilism reading of logical voluntarism is more charitable, and thus more plausible. However, as I'll explain later in §3.2.4, I believe the limited possibilism reading ultimately suffers from what I take to be the same objection that the universal possibilism reading does. Nevertheless, I'll assume the weaker limited possibilism reading of logical voluntarism throughout this chapter: God commanded or willed the modal status (and thus validity status) of every argument at the moment of creation.

Now that we have a little clearer picture of logical voluntarism, why would a traditional Western theist hold such a view concerning God and logic?

3.1.2 Motivations for Logical Voluntarism

In order to understand what might count as an impetus for this view, in this sub-section I think it will be helpful to look at a few historical figures that have been thought to be representatives of logical voluntarism, or something very akin to it. We'll briefly look at each historical example and then attempt to inductively draw some motivations for logical voluntarism.[6] In addition, by the end of §3.1, I will suggest a different category of additional reasons that have nothing to do with religious or theological reasons that might also be appealed to as motivation for logical voluntarism.

A possible representative of logical voluntarism was the medieval bishop and prolific writer Peter Damian (AD 1007–72). His most famous work *De divina omnipotentia* (*On Divine Omnipotence*) has been thought to show that Damian denied the universal validity of the law of non-contradiction (LNC). The impetus for this supposed claim seems to have been

---

6. As far as I know, no one has ever been motivated to logical voluntarism, or anything like it, specifically because of the Logiphro dilemma I've presented here.

LOGICAL VOLUNTARISM

Damian's dissatisfaction with a statement made earlier by the Christian church father Jerome (AD 347–420), who claimed that even God could not restore virginity to a woman once she had lost it. Damian's reply to this view can be seen in the following:

> Let the quibbling of the impious question be once more put forth; let it also be seen from what root it was produced, for then the stream that ought to be engulfed by the ground lest it should flood and ruin the rich fruits of sound faith may just dry out with its source. For in order to prove that God could not restore a virgin after her lapse, they add, as if it were a consequence: for would even God be able to bring it about that what has been done, has not been done? As if ... it ever established that a virgin has been spoilt, it could not happen that she would be intact again. This is assuredly true as far as nature is concerned, and the opinion holds. Also, that something has been done and that the very same thing has not been done cannot be the case. These, to be sure, are contraries to each other in such a way that if one of them is, the other cannot be. For of what has been it cannot truly be said that it has not been, and the other way around, of what has not been it is not correctly said that it has been. For contraries cannot coincide in one and the same subject. This impossibility, then, is indeed rightly affirmed if it is attributed to the lack of means of nature, but on no account should it be applied to the divine majesty. For he who has given birth to nature easily removes the necessity of nature when he wills (611D–612B).[7]

In direct opposition to Jerome, Damian affirms that God *could* restore virginity to a woman who had lost it. But what exactly does this affirmation entail? For example, is Damian affirming that God can perform logically contradictory actions: that some action could be successfully done and yet undone in the sense as if the action had never been done? Since the seminal work of German scholar J. A. Endres,[8] it has been fairly common to interpret Damian along these lines. Endres believed various passages, like the above, showed that Damian denied that any laws (logical as well as physical) could bind God's omnipotent power, implying that God could perform logically contradictory actions. So if God is able to perform logically contradictory

---

7. From Peter Damian's *De divina omnipotentia*. English translation by and quoted from Toivo J. Holopainen, in *Stanford Encyclopedia of Philosophy*, accessed June 6, 2016, http://plato.stanford.edu/entries/peter-damian/.

8. Endres, "Die Dialektiker und ihre Gegner im 11. Jahrhundert," 20–33. Endres' scholarship had been the final word on Damian for over a century.

actions, then it seems that he can will that logical contradictions be true. Thus, Endres' interpretation of Damian shows him to be in line with logical voluntarism. The following argument I think represents this interpretation of Damian's divine virginal restoration view:

(1*) Damian maintains that God can restore virginity to a woman who has lost it.

(2*) But restoration of virginity consists in removing those events in the woman's past that are incompatible with her being a virgin.

(3*) Therefore, Damian has to maintain that God can undo what has been done.

(4*) But the undoing of what has been done involves a contradiction.[9]

(5*) Therefore, Damian has to claim that the LNC is not universally valid (if only for God).

If this interpretation is correct, it seems clear that Damian was clearly an advocate of what we're calling logical voluntarism.

For many years this had been the primary interpretation of Damian's view; but recent scholarship has argued that this interpretation is mistaken.[10] The main evidence against what I'm calling a logical voluntarist interpretation is that it fits badly with what Damian says elsewhere in his work *On Divine Omnipotence*. The primary evidence relevant here is Damian's view of divine providence. Following Augustine, Damian holds that God is immutable, both in himself and in relation to his creation. Augustine claimed that to God there is no past or future; everything is present to him in an eternal now. Therefore, the past cannot be changed (i.e., denial of (2*) and (3*) above) because past events are immutably present in the divine providential plan that is immutable (607A). Therefore, this seems to show that even though Damian plainly affirmed the possibility of God restoring

---

9. One might wonder whether this is really a contradiction if God could destroy past events. It would take me too far afield to address this objection thoroughly. However, even if God could destroy past events, it seems to me that this position might still not rule out logical voluntarism.

10. See Holopainen, "Peter Damian," accessed June 6, 2016, http://plato.stanford.edu/entries/peter-damian/; Knuuttila, *Modalities in Medieval Philosophy*; Resnick, *Divine Power and Possibility in St. Peter Damian's De divina omnipotentia*. I should also note that my colleague Professor Joe Rigney disagrees with the traditional interpretation as well. See his unpublished "Restoring Virgins and Changing the Past: Peter Damian on God's Power and Possibility."

virginity (i.e., claim (1*) above), it does not necessarily imply a logical violation of undoing what has been undone (i.e., claim (3*) above). In other words, it seems that Damian believed that God could do the physically impossible—for example, like restoring the hymen to a woman who had lost it—but not the logically impossible, like undoing what has been done. If this understanding of Damian is correct, then it seems that Damian did not believe that affirming claim (1*) implies that God could do that which is logically contradictory (i.e., claim (4*)).

However, I think there is reason to push back against this newer interpretation of Damian, for surely restoring a woman's hymen is not equivalent to restoring her virginity. Once that woman has had the experience of sexual intercourse with another person, regardless of whether the physical evidence could be undone, that woman is no longer a virgin. In other words, it seems to me that (1*) *does imply* (2*). However, rather than entering into an exegetical or historical debate over whether Damian was actually a logical voluntarist, it's enough for us to note why a logical voluntarist interpretation of Damian is a tempting and understandable reading. Given not only in what Damian claims in the above passage, but elsewhere Damian admitted that theists should be reticent in being fully forthcoming of an explication of divine power that admitted that God could not do certain things—like commanding or willing a logically contradictory claim to be true. Damian's fear seems to have been motivated by the possibility that this truth might shake the faith of the common Christian believer. He writes: "For if it should reach the common people that God is asserted to be impotent in some respect (which is a wicked thing to say), the unschooled masses would instantly be confused and the Christian faith would be upset, not without grave danger to souls."[11] As Holopainen explains, Damian's "delicate task in [*On Divine Omnipotence*] is to convince his readers of the view that divine omnipotence remains intact even though God cannot undo the done, without ever saying that God cannot undo the done because this is "a wicked thing to say."[12] Given this goal, it's understandable how Peter Damian could be interpreted (even if mistakenly) as a logical voluntarist, or how a theist in this tradition might be motivated to such a view.

Another possible representative of logical voluntarism is the medieval thinker and theologian William of Ockham (AD 1287–1347). As is

---

11. Quoted in Holopainen, "Peter Damian," accessed June 6, 2016, http://plato.stanford.edu/entries/peter-damian/.

12. Ibid.

well known, Ockham was a prolific writer on various philosophical issues, including those related to theology and logic. Many commentators have noted how the doctrine of divine omnipotence was often a major factor in much of Ockham's thought.[13] Let's look at a couple of examples that highlight this claim.

In reference to the account in Exodus of Israel leaving Egypt, Ockham claims that Israel's despoiling of Egypt (Exod 12:36) was *not* a mass occurrence of theft, and thus not to be considered morally objectionable, simply on the grounds that God commanded the Israelites to despoil the Egyptians.[14] In other words, Ockham seems to be claiming that God's command to do some action X is the very basis of the morality of X. Thus, Ockham appears here to have been an advocate of moral voluntarism—our straightforward moral divine command theory laid out in chapter 2.[15]

Another example, Ockham's emphasis upon divine omnipotence can be seen in other areas of his philosophical thought such as in his account of "intuitive knowledge." For Ockham, intuitive knowledge is the immediate apprehension of a thing as existent—what we might call sense perception or direct empirical input today—which justifies the said cognizer to form statements corresponding to the existence of that thing. For example, if I have intuitive knowledge of an apple, Ockham says this allows me to claim, "This apple is red," or "This apple is tasty," or whatever other statements may correctly correspond to that cognition. Ockham gives a striking addition to this account in famously maintaining that God could cause us to have intuitive knowledge of an object that did not objectively exist. Thus, God could cause one to have intuitive knowledge of, say, this book—such that you are reading, touching, and even turning the pages of this book—but in fact the book not really existing. Ockham denied that God actually did perform such deceptive acts but insisted only that God *could* perform such actions

---

13. Weinberg, *A Short History of Medieval Philosophy*, 237–41; Copleston, *A History of Philosophy*, 47–51, 57–59; and Robert Merrihew Adams, *The Virtue of Faith*, 1233–34.

14. Quoted in King, "Ockham's Ethical Theory," in *The Cambridge Companion to Ockham*, 239. To quibble, it seems clear to me from the context of Exod 12:36 that the Israelites asked for the Egyptians' possessions, not that they simply took them.

15. However, there is some question as to whether Ockham was *consistently* a divine command theorist concerning morality. In other places, he seems reluctant to claim that God's commands are the sole basis for the rightness of an actions. King, "Ockham's Ethical Theory," 227–44 highlights this point, while McGrade, "Natural Law and Moral Omnipotence," 273–301 calls Ockham's view an "implicit divine command" theory. For a detailed account of Ockham's moral views see Karger, "Ockham's Misunderstood Theory of Intuitive and Abstractive Cognition," 204–26.

LOGICAL VOLUNTARISM

in virtue of his omnipotent power. Frederick Copleston comments on the emphasis upon God's omnipotence in Ockham's epistemological account:

> What Ockham has to say on the [above] matter admirably illustrates his tendency, as a thinker with marked theological preoccupations, to break through, as it were, the purely philosophic and natural order and to subordinate it to the divine liberty and omnipotence. It illustrates too, one of his main principles, that when two things are distinct there is no absolutely necessary connection between them. Our act of seeing the stars, considered as an act, is distinct from the stars themselves: it can therefore be separated from them, in the sense that divine omnipotence could annihilate the latter and conserve the former. Ockham's tendency was always to break through supposedly necessary connections which might seem to limit in some way the divine omnipotence....[16]

If Copleston's assessment of Ockham's thought is correct, then one might suspect that Ockham was also a logical voluntarist. Since premises and conclusions are distinct, then Ockham would seem to have believed that the necessary connections between premises and conclusions could in no way limit divine omnipotence as well. However, despite sounding like a logical voluntarist at times, Ockham seems to have stood firmly against such a view. This comes up in various ways in Ockham's writings. For example, Marilyn McCord Adams highlights Ockham's commitment against logical voluntarism in his philosophical use of contradiction:

> Ockham, in effect, takes the Indiscernibility of Identicals—i.e., the principle that for every individual x and y and every property F, if x is identical with y, then x is F if and only if y is F—to be a necessary truth about and our primary criterion of distinction for real things. Thus, he says that contradiction is "the most powerful way" of proving a distinction among real things, and insists that if we allow one and the same real thing to have contradictory properties simultaneously, "every method of proving distinction or nonidentity between any entity whatever would perish." Further, Ockham seems to assume that . . . if x is really the same as y, x is necessarily identical with y; and if really distinct, necessarily distinct . . . . Thus, Ockham implies that if x and y are really the same, it is not logically possible that x should exist without y and vice versa, *even by divine power*.[17]

---

16. Copleston, *A History of Philosophy*, 66–67.
17. Adams, *The Virtue of Faith*, 16–17 (emphasis mine).

THE LOGIPHRO DILEMMA

So even though it seems clear that Ockham was *not* a logical voluntarist, it's important to note, as with Damian before, that Ockham's philosophical views were strongly motivated by an attempt to uphold a strong reading of divine omnipotence; that is, Ockham seemed to be reluctant to say anything that might appear to show that God was not omnipotent *simpliciter*.

Let's look at one further historical example. And it seems that if anyone deserves the title of logical voluntarist, it would appear that René Descartes (AD 1596-1650), the father of modern philosophy himself, deserves it. Though Descartes never explicitly appeals to or expounds upon logical voluntarism in any of his main works, he seems fairly adamant about this position in several of his letters. In a letter to Marin Mersenne he says:

> The mathematical truths which you call eternal have been laid down by God and depend on him entirely no less than the rest of his creatures. Indeed to say these truths are independent of God is to talk of him as if he were Jupiter or Saturn and to subject him to the Styx and Fates. Please do not hesitate to assert and proclaim everywhere that it is God who has laid down these laws in nature just as a king lays down laws in his kingdom.[18]

Notice that Descartes sees mathematical truths (e.g., $a + b = b + a$, $a^2 + b^2 = c^2$, etc.) as "laws in nature" and that he conceives of God's relation to these laws as akin to a monarch bringing legislation into being. The existence of any legal laws is obviously contingent upon the deciding power of some ruler or ruling body that makes them or brings them into being. Likewise, Descartes seems to have believed that mathematical truths are merely laws of this sort, solely legislated by God. Thus, the existence of all such truths and laws are completely dependent upon God's commands—in the sense that they were created and are still enforced by God. In a later letter Descartes adds:

> You ask me by what kind of causality God established the eternal truths. I reply: by the same kind of causality as he created all things, that is to say, as their efficient and total cause. For it is certain that he is the author of the essence of created things no less than their existence; and the essence is nothing other than the eternal truths. . . . You ask what necessitated God to create these truths; and I reply that he was free to make it not true that all the radii of the circle are equal.[19]

---

18. Descartes, *The Philosophical Writings of Descartes*, 23.
19. Ibid., 25-26.

LOGICAL VOLUNTARISM

Though Descartes gives the example of a mathematical truth here, it should be clear that he is calling a logical truth into question as well. For if God could make a circle, all of whose radii are not equal, then it seems we have a contradiction, for a circle just is a figure all of whose radii are equal. Thus, Descartes seems to be endorsing logical, as well as mathematical, voluntarism. Elsewhere, he is even more explicit on this point:

> For my part, I know that my intellect is finite and God's power is infinite, and so I set no bounds to it; I consider only what I can conceive and what I cannot conceive. . . . And so I boldly assert that God can do everything which I conceive to be possible, but I am not so bold as to deny that he can do whatever conflicts with my understanding—I merely say that it involves a contradiction.[20]

Thus, Descartes' view of divine omnipotence includes the possibility of God doing everything conceivable and also being able to do anything inconceivable, including performing outright contradictory actions. Since performing such an action implies that God willed a contradiction, it would seem that Descartes was indeed a logical voluntarist.

However, as we've seen with our prior historical examples, there are scholars who have argued that Descartes should either not be read as a logical voluntarist,[21] or at least not one of the universal possibilism variety.[22] As with Damian before, the actual historical verdict need not concern us here. Descartes may have been, or may not have been, a logical voluntarist. But, as with Damian and Ockham before, I am more interested in why Descartes has sometimes been interpreted as a logical voluntarist. And again, as with Damian and Ockham, Descartes seems to have been concerned with interpreting God's omnipotence in a very strong way.

I think the above is enough of a historical sketch to clearly suggest what might motivate logical voluntarism then. Even though Damian, Ockham, and Descartes may have not been true advocates of logical voluntarism (though this is debatable, especially concerning Damian and Descartes), I think it has been clear from our investigation of them that what mainly

---

20. Ibid., 363.

21. Eric Stencil, in "Cartesian Modality: Possibility and Essence in Descartes and Arnauld," specifically argues that Descartes should not be understood as a logical voluntarist of either a limited possibilism or a universal possibilism variety.

22. See Clouser, "Religious Language," 385–407 and Janowski, *Cartesian Theodicy*, chapter 3, both argue that Descartes should be given a limited possibilism reading. But Schrader, "Frankfurt and Descartes," 4–18, argues that Descartes can be given either a limited possibilism or a universal possibilism reading.

motivated their voluntarist-leaning views was a desire to give a strong interpretation of the traditional category of divine omnipotence. I think an argument that characterizes this connection between divine omnipotence and logical voluntarism might go something like the following:

(1#) If the truth-values of individual claims and the validity status of arguments were independent of God's will or commands, then these things would act as limitations to God's power.

(2#) But if these things were independent of God's will or commands, then God would not be truly omnipotent.

(3#) But God is omnipotent.

(4#) Therefore, these things cannot be independent of God's will or commands.

But why give divine omnipotence such a strong interpretation, which then implies construing God's power along unintuitive voluntarist lines? I think a couple of things can be suggested here.

First, there seems to be a concern on the part of Western theistic defenders that anything less than a full voluntarist reading of God's power (whether it actually implies voluntarism or not) might be seen as thinking or conceiving of God as less than the way he should be thought or conceived of. Recall how Descartes said that to say that something like logical arguments are independent of God's power is "to talk as if he were Jupiter or Saturn and to subject him to the Styx and Fates."[23] Descartes believed that God could not be subject to anything outside of himself and his power. The implication for Descartes seems to be that to believe so is to demote God to the status of something like the mythic gods of ancient Greece, who, though possessing characteristics and powers beyond that of common mortal human beings, Descartes took such "gods" to be obviously deficient to the omnipotent being of classical theism. For the devoted Abrahamic theist, such a suggested demotion of God is intolerable and so God must be defended accordingly. By way of a similar example, if I know my friend is consistently honest and someone claims that she lied, I obviously would want to argue in defense of my friend. Not only because I think it's true that she is honest, but I desire to defend her out of loyalty and affection.

A second reason for defending such a strong view of divine omnipotence seems to be more related to a concern for those who are less

---

23. Descartes, *The Philosophical Writings of Descartes*, 23.

educated in their respective religious communities. Remember that Damian's reluctance to be fully forthcoming about God's power being limited was motivated by the fear that "the unschooled masses would instantly be confused and the Christian faith be upset, not without grave danger to souls."[24] Damian feared that unless God was unequivocally proclaimed to be omnipotent, with no qualification, then the majority of "unschooled" Christian believers would have their faith in God diminished, frustrated, or perhaps even destroyed. This may seem a deceptive suggestion on the part of Damian, but anyone who has taught an introductory course on a subject, say in a college setting, should be able to relate, at least a bit, to this concern. In introductory courses instructors will often say things that are not strictly true. Practitioners of good pedagogy know that beginning students need to be given straightforward general claims in order to get an initial and easy grasp of the subject. Such claims can sometimes be over-simplifications that are not strictly true. But to continually correct and qualify the claims of a subject when it is being introduced to students would make such claims needlessly burdensome to beginning students—confusion by a thousand qualifications! Thus, in an attempt to not confuse beginning non-experts with sufficiently qualified (and thus strictly true) claims, instructors will many times supply more simple (though strictly false) claims concerning the subject. In a similar way, a simple-minded view of divine omnipotence may be an acceptable, and perhaps necessary, starting point for those less educated in a religious community. However, later, more advanced teaching could become more nuanced in its claims.

I think these two reasons give some explanation why defending such a strong interpretation of divine omnipotence is so important for thinkers like Damian, Ockham, and Descartes, and why they are often read—even if not correctly so—as logical voluntarists. Though I believe these suggested reasons would probably be the most common for motivating a voluntarist picture of God in relation to various domains, especially from a specifically theistic perspective, I think there could be other reasons offered to believe that logical arguments may not enjoy the sort of modal and alethic permanence that they have traditionally thought to have. As a purely philosophical issue, if it were true that valid logical arguments were *not* necessary, or not strictly necessary (i.e., that our belief in such may need to be qualified

---

24. Again, see Holopainen, "Peter Damian," accessed June 6, 2016, http://plato.stanford.edu/entries/peter-damian/.

in some way), then this might motivate someone towards a voluntarist picture of God and logic. What might be some of these other reasons?

Philosopher Graham Priest has put forward the idea that at least some contradictions should be considered *dialetheias*,[25] his word for what he sees as *true* contradictions. As radical as this sounds, Priest has offered a book-length defense as to why dialetheias should be accepted as true existing realities. He argues that since some things, such as the semantic paradoxes,[26] seem to be true *and* false, thus showing that there are claims that prove the LNC (law of non-contradiction) is not universally valid, Priest concludes that we should deny holding the LNC as universally valid. Though this view has nothing to do with God, if Priest's radical conclusion is found convincing, then this would give impetus to a logical voluntarist's picture.

Another reason that might serve as a non-theistic motivation for logical voluntarism comes by way of the late W. V. Quine who also seemed to have been open to revising our understanding of logical possibility, at least in theory. A famous passage from Quine proclaims:

> Any statement can be held true come what may, if we make drastic enough adjustments elsewhere in the system. Even a statement very close to the periphery can be held true in the face of recalcitrant experience by pleading hallucination or by amending certain statements of the kind called logical laws. Conversely, by the same token, no statement is immune to revision. Revision even of the logical law of excluded middle has been proposed as a means of simplifying quantum mechanics; and what difference is there between such a shift and shift whereby Kepler superseded Ptolemy, Einstein Newton, or Darwin Aristotle.[27]

In the above Quine states that none of our beliefs, including our beliefs about logic, are immune to revision. But if that is the case then our beliefs about what counts as valid logical implications are also open to revision, as Quine suggests with intuitionist logicians questioning the validity of the

---

25. To be clear, dialetheias are statements of the form (p & $\sim p$) that are true. See Graham Priest, *In Contradiction*. Priest is agnostic as to whether dialetheias are sentences, propositions, or statements. He claims that his theory is unaffected by the choice of truth-bearer.

26. Semantic paradoxes include statements like "This sentence is false" and someone who always lies saying that "All liars never tell the truth." Their paradoxical nature seems to derive from trying to determine whether such a statement is true or false. For in saying it is true, it seems to come out false and in saying it is false, it seems to turn out true.

27. From W. V. Quine, "Two Dogmas of Empiricism," 43.

LOGICAL VOLUNTARISM

law of excluded middle ($\vdash p \vee \sim p$). If Quine's right, then this would mean that even our belief in the universal validity of the LNC is also open to revision. However, some of Quine's remarks seem to recommend that we should be reticent to follow through on this idea.[28]

Note that the two non-theistically motivated reasons noted above are epistemic in nature. In other words, Priest and Quine are not necessarily claiming that logical validities are changeable (by God or anyone else), but that we may be mistaken in our beliefs about which arguments are valid or invalid. Nevertheless, it seems to me, that these epistemological points could serve as motivations for logical voluntarism. For if we mere mortals can modify our beliefs about the validity status of logical arguments (as Quine so claims) or if certain long-held logical arguments do not have the status of validity that we thought them to have (as Priest so claims), then it might not be so crazy to believe that an omnipotent being can change the validity or truth-status of logical arguments (as logical voluntarists so claim).

So summarizing §3.1, I think I've clarified that logical voluntarism is the view that God determined the modal status, as well as the validity status, of every argument at the point of creation, thus assuming a limited possibilism reading. Moreover, we've seen some historical and late examples of theistic as well as non-theistic reasons that suggest why someone might be motivated to the logical voluntarist position.

However, as was introduced in chapter 2, it should be clear that the highly unintuitive nature of this view encumbers it with a host of objections and problems. It's to these that we will now turn our attention.

3.2 OBJECTIONS TO LOGICAL VOLUNTARISM

Obviously, various objections can be raised against the logical voluntarist view—objections that I believe largely mirror those leveled against the moral voluntarist view. In this section I will examine these objections. And, as I will explain, I think that the logical voluntarist might be able to answer some of these objections. But I believe there is one objection that the logical voluntarist cannot give a good answer to *and still consistently be a theist*

---

28. Quine, *From a Logical Point of View*, 80–94. Stewart Shapiro and Jack Arnold argue that despite such reticence, Quine (what they call the radical Quine) seems forced to take dialetheism seriously. See their "Where in the (World Wide) Web of Belief is the Law of Non-contradiction?" 276–97.

in the Western tradition of religion. I will conclude this chapter in §2.4 by addressing the attempt of trying to make logical voluntarism cohere with traditional Western theism in spite of this last objection—the "biting the bullet" option. I will argue that this option comes at too large a cost for the traditional Western theist.

In the previous chapter we briefly listed several objections to moral voluntarism. I think it will be helpful here to revisit these objections again, in a bit more detail this time, in order to see how they might also operate as similar objections against logical voluntarism.[29] I will list these objections against moral voluntarism in what I take to be their order of strength, from weakest to strongest.

One objection we previously listed against moral voluntarism was called the *vacuity objection.* This objection can take a couple of different forms. The first form goes like this: If God is the source of morality, then saying "God is moral" expresses a trivial truth. It is a mere tautology and not substantively or informatively true. If God merely determines what is morally good, then "God is good," just means "God is what God determines"— a pretty uninformative claim. However, a more interesting version of the vacuity objection takes the following form: If God defines morality, then calling God's actions right lacks determinate content. When theists claim God is good—that his actions are those that are good and moral—they usually take such claims to have determinate content; i.e., they take them to mean something informative. But if God's commands are the sole basis for the morality of an action, then the truth of "God is good" or "God's actions are moral" could be consistent with God being, to all appearances, bad. The basic point of the vacuity objection, regardless of its form, is that any theory that results in such obviously vacuous moral language should be considered a failed theory.[30] Though our moral concepts are surely far from perfect, the vacuity objection points out that by the moral voluntarist's pic-

---

29. As stated in the last chapter, these objections come from Baggett and Walls, *Good God,* 129–31. Thus, this section is highly indebted to that work.

30. One could counter that the vacuity objection doesn't necessarily follow for moral voluntarism. God need not be inconsistent in accordance with every command he might give. For instance, God might command "Always tell the truth" and yet refrain from telling the truth about some things; or he might command "Don't eat meat and milk together" but of course—assuming God neither eats nor drinks—this is something that he cannot violate. So, I admit, there is some slippage here that the moral voluntarist may squeeze out from under the vacuity objection. Nevertheless, as we'll see in a bit, the logical voluntarist has no such wiggle room. Thanks to Stewart Shapiro for pressing this point.

LOGICAL VOLUNTARISM

ture, our moral concepts and language are fairly useless! That seems far too strong of a claim.

Another objection to moral voluntarism we previously saw was the *no reasons objection*. This objection pointed out that if God's say-so is the sole reason for the morality of an action, then there seems to be no other reason why, for instance, human slavery is wrong. But surely there are many other reasons, apart from God's commands, for holding that such a practice is immoral. Just to name a few, human slavery seems to be a violation of basic human rights, it leads to other bad and undesirable consequences, and it seems to violate other ethical principles that we take to be intuitively and clearly correct. Surely these things have something to do with the moral status of human slavery. This objection further points out that if morality is not based upon reasons, then it seems that God's commands are not based on reasons either. And thus our obedience to these commands is nothing more than simple-minded deference to his authority and caprice.

The conclusion of the no reasons objection seems to naturally lead to what I believe is the strongest objection against moral voluntarism, what we labeled the *abhorrent commands objection*.[31] This latter objection points out that if God's say-so is the sole reason for the moral goodness of an action, then it seems to follow that God could make any action good simply by his declaring it so. Thus, slavery, genocide, rape, pedophilia, etc., would count as morally permissible actions if God had decided that they were to be so. But surely this is wrong. The abhorrent commands objection contends that we have good reasons to believe that things such as slavery, genocide, and the rest are morally problematic regardless, or in spite of, what God may command. In essence, both the no reasons objection and the abhorrent commands objection point out that moral voluntarism makes morality, in effect, completely arbitrary upon God's caprice, which seems clearly incorrect. Since the no reasons objection and the abhorrent commands objection are closely related, we can see them jointly as the *arbitrariness problem* for moral voluntarism.[32]

---

31. More accurately, this is what Baggett and Walls labeled it as.

32. Baggett and Walls interestingly observe that the arbitrariness problem and the vacuity objection are the "flip side" of one another. They write:

> So long as there are no constraints on God's will, and it's God's will that constitutes the standard for morality, then both of these implications follow: morality is whatever God says it is, no matter what, which introduces an arbitrariness problem; and God is good and right no matter what, which empties such terms of the determinate content they're thought to

3.2.1 Vacuity and Arbitrariness for Logical Voluntarism

Now that we've reviewed these objections to moral voluntarism in a little more detail, I now want to show how the objections to logical voluntarism can be analogously drawn from the objections to moral voluntarism. In addition, I will show how logical voluntarism suffers from a trouble not shared by moral voluntarism. I'll draw the analogous objections first in this section, and then in the §§3.2.2 and 3.2.3 go on to the additional problem that logical voluntarism suffers from.

I'll start with what seemed to me to be the weakest objection for moral voluntarism: the vacuity objection. As I explained for the moral voluntarist, the vacuity objection can take a couple of different forms. Likewise, I think a similar vacuity objection can be stated a couple of different ways against the logical voluntarist as well. The first form: If God is the source of validity, then saying "God is logical" expresses a trivial truth. But, as with moral voluntarism, I believe the more interesting form of this objection against logical voluntarism goes something like this: If God's commands or will solely determine what arguments are logically valid, then calling God's actions logical or rational (i.e., that his actions follow some identifiable set of logical rules) does not have any determinate content for his actions could then be consistent with anything. Suppose we actually had an observable example of God performing what we would normally take to be a fallacious move (e.g., from the assumed truths of q and $(p \rightarrow q)$, God inferred or moved to perform p). According to the logical voluntarist, the move in question could still be an example of a valid logical argument if God commanded or willed that argument to be valid. But this means that the truth of "God is rational" or "God is logical" could be consistent with anything, including to all appearances that which is irrational and illogical. If so, then logical voluntarism could make out many possibilities as "valid," though only vacuously so. In sum, the vacuity objection's basic critical point is that the logical voluntarist theory of God and logic should be considered a failed theory since it would result in making language vacuous.

I think the vacuity objection is a definite problem for logical voluntarism. But we should note here that this objection does not seem to have the same sort of punch that it delivers with moral voluntarism. It seems that pointing out that "God is good" is a vacuous claim is much more of

---

possess, rendering them vacuous in the sense that they are consistent with anything at all. (*Good God*, 242.)

LOGICAL VOLUNTARISM

a problem for the traditional Western theist than pointing out that "God is logical" is vacuous. I think this is so because the claim "God is good" is taken to be more central or more important to traditional Western theism's conception of God than the claims that "God is rational" or "God is logical." I don't think this is because these latter claims are held to be untrue or unimportant by such theists. Even though God is taken to be unequivocally good by theists, and God's rationality can seem fairly queer at times, I'm sure that many theists are confident that God has a rational and logical basis for all that he does, even when humans can't understand those reasons and his basis for action is not so clear. Nevertheless, despite this *prima facie* lessening, I think the vacuity objection is actually much stronger against the logical voluntarist than the moral voluntarist. I'll return to this and explain why this is so in §3.2.3. Let's go on to our other possible objections.

We were introduced to the "no reasons" objection to moral voluntarism. I believe that this objection can be posed towards logical voluntarism in the following way. One may object to logical voluntarism in that if God's commands or will are the sole basis for the validity of any valid argument, then there seems to be no other reason to believe that, say, modus ponens is valid or why the LNC is necessarily true. But surely there are other reasons to believe that such arguments are valid or necessary that have nothing to do with God's commands or will, and it's tempting to believe that those reasons should be God's reasons as well. Obviously there are non-theists who hold to these traditional claims of validity on grounds that make no appeals to God's existence, much less his commands or will. And if there are other reasons for justifying our beliefs about valid arguments, then it seems that God's commands or will could not be the *sole* basis for why we should believe logical arguments have the validity status that they do. Moreover, if God's commands or will were the sole basis for the validity status of every argument, then it seems to follow that God's commands or will are not based on reasons either. This is because we take our reasons to be why we think things are true. But, as proposed, God's commands or will would seem to be rooted in nothing more than his mere whims.

As with moral voluntarism, the no reasons objection also seems to naturally lead to what we called the abhorrent commands objection. For if God's say-so or will is the sole reason for the validity status of any argument, then it follows that God could command or will any argument to be necessary or contingent, true or false, simply by his declaring it so, which may not seem so "abhorrent"—a point that we'll return to briefly. We stipulated earlier that both of these objections could be grouped together as the arbitrariness problem for moral voluntarism. For it seemed that at bottom both of these objections were pointing out that morality appears to have a permanence or non-arbitrariness that moral voluntarism was denying. But, as we'll see later, the no reasons objection only serves as one motivation for the arbitrariness problem concerning logical voluntarism.

Returning to the abhorrent commands objection, and as we noted with the vacuity objection, this objection does not seem to have the same sting or punch for logical voluntarism as it does for moral voluntarism. For if the validity status of any argument can be changed merely by God's whim alone, then we only have the "abhorrent" possibility that logic does not have the sort of permanence that it is normally thought to have. These sorts of logical possibilities (e.g., the invalidity of modus ponens, the falsity of the LNC, etc.) may be undesirable or appear bizarre, but they hardly seem to have the intuitive gut-punch of the sorts of ethical possibilities that moral voluntarism suggests (e.g., that rape or genocide could be moral, that telling the truth or being kind could be evil, etc.). Point taken. But what I want to suggest here is that the abhorrent commands objection does carry over against logical voluntarism, but in a modified way. With moral voluntarism we seem to have the possibilities of wrongs that we intuitively think can't be made right. In a similar way, with logical voluntarism we seem to have the possibilities of a different sort of "wrongs" that we also have a hard time picturing as being made "right" as well. The difference for logical voluntarism is that the possibilities in question seem not wrong in a moral sense, but rather wrong in a logical or rational sense. For we must admit that it is hard to make sense of the claim that modus ponens could be invalid, or the LNC could possibly be false. In other words, the abhorrence being suggested here in the abhorrent commands objection is that of sheer incoherence or unintelligibility. I take this "abhorrence" to be a primary and highly intuitive objection against logical voluntarism: logical voluntarism is false because it is incoherent or unintelligible.

I think that these are actually two separate objections and in §3.2.2 I will address each objection in turn. Then I will return to the vacuity objection in §3.2.3 and show why, even though I take it to be the weakest objection for moral voluntarism, I believe this is actually the strongest objection against logical voluntarism.

LOGICAL VOLUNTARISM

3.2.2 The Incoherence and Unintelligibility Objections

We should be clear on what the objections of incoherence or unintelligibility amount to. Even though the word "incoherence" often serves as a synonym for "unintelligible" or "meaningless," I believe the notion of incoherence can actually be made distinct from the notion of unintelligibility. Therefore, I think it will serve us to get clear on each. First, let's clarify what incoherence is before framing it as an objection against logical voluntarism.

I think probability theory can help us here. In probability theory a set of probability assignments (percentages assigned or discovered for various situations or states of affairs) is usually considered incoherent if the set is an example of what is sometimes called a *Dutch book*.[33] This metaphor of a Dutch book refers to a set of probability assignments such that, if a person were to bet in accordance with those assignments, then he or she would lose no matter what the outcome. Thus, one could say, it would be *incoherent* for a person to bet on such a set of probability assignments. The charge of incoherence here is a judgment upon the act of holding a certain set of beliefs (i.e., a Dutch book) simultaneously. We can see an example of how this sort of criticism might arise with the following two claims:[34]

(a)   God transcends human experience.

(b)   None of our concepts applies to God.

Assume that a theist affirms both of these claims. An astute critic would point out that if God transcends human experience, then one cannot also claim that none of our concepts applies to God. Why? According to the above, it seems that one of our concepts is the following, i.e., "none of our concepts applies to God." And, laying Kantian worries to one side, we presumably know when our concepts do or don't apply to something. But, according to the claims above, one concept that seems to apply to God is, namely, none of our concepts apply to God. We seem to have a contradiction. Thus, we derive the verdict that one cannot *coherently* accept (a) as well as (b) simultaneously. Given this example, and similar Dutch book scenarios, I believe we can generalize to say that a set of reasonably investigable

---

33. This is an unfortunate designation used in probability literature. Though I can find no reliable source for the etymology of this name, it surely has some sort of racist connotation connected to it. If so, apologies to any Dutch reader here.

34. This example is taken, and modified, from Plantinga, *Does God Have a Nature?* 120.

claims[35] are incoherent for any agent A if by holding one of the claims in the set (say p), A should also be committed to denying (or qualifiying) at least one other claim in that set (for example $\sim p$). This definition assumes that an agent cannot be equally committed to two (or more) contradictory beliefs simultaneously. For if he were made aware of the contrary nature of the two (or more) beliefs in that set—if it was brought to his attention—then he would obviously reject at least one of them; or in the case where he is not sure which to reject, his commitment to both beliefs (or all beliefs in the set) would at least be greatly lessened or qualified.

But how would logical voluntarism count as incoherent according to this definition? To see how this objection goes, I think we can fairly characterize the logical voluntarist position with the following argument (LV2):

(1*) If God has power over all arguments, then he can command or will any valid argument to be invalid.

(2*) God has power over all arguments.

(3*) Therefore, God can command or will any valid argument to be invalid.

Now (LV2) is a valid argument. Therefore, given what (LV2) claims, the logical voluntarist should also be committed to the following claim,

(4*) God can command or will (LV2) to be invalid,

since (4*) is just one instance of the universal claim (3*). The logical voluntarist is thus committed to claims (1*) through (4*). But if (4*) were made true by God, then the logical voluntarist should not hold (LV2) as valid since it would then be invalid. But (LV2) just is a summary of the logical voluntarist position. Therefore, it seems the logical voluntarist must deny (4*) instead. But in denying (4*) the logical voluntarist would then be committed to denying (3*), and claim (3*) is a central belief for logical voluntarism. Therefore, it seems that logical voluntarism is *incoherent* on this characterization since an advocate of this view could not simultaneously hold both claims (3*) and (4*) as true, even though both seem to be central

---

35. By "set of reasonably investigable claims" I mean only those sets of beliefs that are reasonably within an agent's abilities and limitations to investigate. If this qualification were not included we would have a definition of incoherence that would only apply to an omniscient being.

LOGICAL VOLUNTARISM

to the logical voluntarist position.[36, 37] I call this the *incoherence objection* against logical voluntarism.

Nevertheless, in favor of the logical voluntarist, it seems to me that this incoherence objection might not bother the voluntarist Logiphro. For even if logical voluntarism *is* incoherent, that doesn't mean, by the logical voluntarist's own lights, that it is not true. Our definition of incoherence declared that any agent A could not simultaneously hold contradictory beliefs or at least hold them unqualifiedly. But the logical voluntarist might claim that God is not just *any* agent. If he is omnipotent in the way the logical voluntarist so says, then it is possible that God can change the validity status of arguments, and in limiting cases, the truth-values of logical truths and falsehoods. Therefore, according to the logical voluntarist, God could make it the case that (LV2) remains valid; thus claim (3*) would still be true *and* claim (4*) come out true as well, *simultaneously!*

However, if this is the response the logical voluntarist gives to the incoherence objection, I think many would be tempted to say, along with W. V. Quine,[38] that if the logical voluntarist claims (3*) and (4*) can be simultaneously true he does not really know what he is saying. For it seems

---

36. One might claim that you need not tease out divine omnipotence into the logical voluntarist position in order to attain the status of incoherence since J. L. Mackie, "Evil and Omnipotence," 200–12 simply claims omnipotence itself is incoherent. However, he argues for this by characterizing omnipotence as being unable to give a satisfactory response to (what he calls) the Paradox of Omnipotence: Can God make things that he cannot control?, which I take to be a version of the Euthyphro question and dilemma. Mackie's characterization of omnipotence is similar to that of logical voluntarism. Therefore, it seems to me, that claiming that omnipotence is an incoherent concept is just a more generalized criticism of the above claim that logical voluntarism is incoherent.

37. A counter to the incoherence objection I've given here might claim that our descriptions of God's actions need not deny that God is omnipotent, if such a description is of a "pseudo-task": that is, a self-contradictory act. George Mavrodes, "Some Puzzles Concerning Omnipotence," 221–23, coins this phrase and defends this position. According to Mavrodes, the failure to perform such a task implies no limit upon omnipotence since an incoherent description cannot be the description of a real or possible action. An omnipotent being should not be considered limited because it cannot simultaneously do X and not-X. But Harry G. Frankfurt, "Is Morality Logically Dependent on Religion?" 262–63, points out that this criticism relies upon the principle that an omnipotent being need not be supposed capable of performing tasks whose descriptions are self-contradictory. But this seems like a principle that the logical voluntarist would deny (Frankfurt claims that Descartes would deny it). Therefore, an appeal to the concept of pseudo-tasks does not succeed in provide an objection against logical voluntarism since it is apparently question-begging.

38. Quine, *Philosophy of Logic*, 80.

that no one can imagine what it means to say that "affirming the consequent is valid," or "modus ponens is invalid," or "the LNC is false," or that "some contradiction is true." In other words, if the logical voluntarist claims that the incoherence objection is unproblematic, then it appears his view has a further problem in that it seems unintelligible. Call this the *unintelligibility objection*. For if God's omnipotence means he can make claims (3*) and (4*) true simultaneously, it's not at all clear what that means for it seems that the logical voluntarist is using language in ways that we normally do not use such language, i.e., in unintelligible ways.

In making this objection against logical voluntarism, we should be clear that we are not including or confusing the notion of contradiction with unintelligibility. Contradictory sentences or descriptions have an intelligible place in our language. If they did not, then commonly held valid logical arguments such as *ex falso quodlibet* (i.e., $(p \& \sim p) \vdash q$) or *reductio ad absurdum* (i.e., $(p \rightarrow (q \& \sim q)) \vdash \sim p$) would be unintelligible as well and thus we could not use them in our logical derivations. Rather, the unintelligibility objection being put here to logical voluntarism is a challenge to the validity-status assignments it gives to certain arguments and claims. We understand many fallacious claims. For example, we understand what affirming the consequent is q, $(p \rightarrow q) \vdash p$, and what it is attempting to affirm. But, we have no idea how such an argument could be valid. We understand claims of the form $(p \& \sim p)$. We just have no idea how such claims could be true.[39] Gijsbert Van Den Brink elaborates well the problem that the unintelligibility objection is highlighting:

> [I]n saying that it is *possible* for God to make contradictions true, i.e., to do the logically impossible, either we derive the meaning of "possible," from our standard framework of modal logic, in which case the claim is contradictory, or we equivocate upon the meaning of "possible," in which case it is unclear what we are saying. In

---

39. One suggestion for understanding what intelligibility might amount to is that by claiming for something to be the case means other things cannot be the case. In other words, meaningful statements rules things out. But take the following statement: "Everything is true." This is a statement that rules nothing out. But even though this statement is presumably false, we understand what the statement is claiming, namely every statement there possibly is, is true. Thus "Everything is true" is meaningful even though it rules nothing out. Therefore, the intuition that the meaningfulness of a claim must rule out things does not seem to be a necessary condition for meaningfulness. See Priest, *In Contradiction*, 28 for a fuller discussion.

both cases, we would be flouting our ordinary standards of speech and thought if we held that the claim is nonetheless true.[40]

Nevertheless, the logical voluntarist may point out that our inability to understand or even imagine things like contradictory states of affairs only emphasizes the limitedness of our mental capacities.[41] It does not show that logical voluntarism is false. In fact, given the sort of motivations we saw with Peter Damian, William of Ockham, and Descartes, the logical voluntarist may claim that this observation only shows just how great and inscrutable God's omnipotence is, especially in comparison to our own limited abilities. Why believe that only those utterances that are conceivable or meaningful to us are the only ones that are true or capable of being true for God? As much as we may firmly believe this is the case, it seems presumptuous to think that this *must be* the case. This line of argument actually leads naturally back to the vacuity objection against logical voluntarism, which, again, we will return to in the next section.

But concerning the incoherence and unintelligibility objections, we need to see the force of the sort of responses that I've suggested that logical voluntarist can offer us here. For both objections it should be obvious that appealing to our commonly held views concerning logical validity—whether formal or informal—or appealing to commonly held views concerning truth and meaning, which also rest upon our views of logical validity, cannot refute logical voluntarism since this position questions the very status of such views. And this should be no surprise, for how could one argue for the validity of an argument—like the LNC or modus ponens—without assuming the validity of that argument? Stating this point more generally: An advocate of some logic L1 can only argue that some rival logic L2 is false or invalid while assuming L1. But of course the adherent of L2 will not accept arguments on the basis of L1 since this is the very point of disagreement.

---

40. Van Den Brink, *Almighty God*, 188.

41. Miller, "Descartes, Mathematics, and God," 451–65 agrees with this response arguing that Descartes' strong view of God's omnipotence undermines our ability to perceive necessary truths, like certain instances of valid logical arguments. He claims that if God could've made necessary truths differently, then we are being misled to believe they are necessary when they are not. Frankfurt, "The Logic of Omnipotence," 36–57, corroborates this interpretation claiming that Descartes held that our inability to conceive of true contradictions is merely a contingent fact about us. But Curley, "Descartes on the Creation of the Eternal Truths," 569–97, claims Frankfurt has misinterpreted Descartes. I'll leave this historical and exegetical debate to the Cartesian scholars. I only mention these references here to give credence to the logical voluntarist's response to the unintelligibility objection.

Thus, L2 cannot be refuted on the basis of L1. Obviously, this predicament is completely symmetrical for an advocate of L2 also could not argue that logic L1 is false or deductively invalid without assuming L2.[42]

What these responses show is that neither the incoherence objection nor the unintelligibility objection can deductively refute logical voluntarism. That is, we cannot give the logical voluntarist a successful valid deductive argument where the conclusion "logical voluntarism is false" comes out unabashedly sound (i.e., that the logical voluntarist will agree that the premises are true) and valid (i.e., that the logical voluntarist will agree that the conclusion is entailed by the premises). Thus, given these possible (and plausible by the logical voluntarist's lights) responses to the incoherence and unintelligibility objections, it seems that the logical voluntarist has a good case for believing that the validity status and truth status of each and every logical argument is whatever it is because God commands or wills it is to be the case.

3.2.3 The Vacuity Objection

Given the seeming failure of the incoherence and unintelligibility objections, it seems the logical voluntarist has a secure, even if bizarre, philosophical position. Nevertheless, from the perspective of the Western tradition of theism, I believe that logical voluntarism should still be rejected as the way of thinking about the relationship between God and logic. Even though logical voluntarism cannot be given a knockdown argument—it cannot be deductively refuted (see above)—I believe that one can still mount some very good justification for rejecting it.

One preliminary point I think should be noted here, and which was highlighted by the incoherence and unintelligibility objections, is that the logical voluntarist option seems highly incongruous with the commonly held intuition that logical arguments are independent of *human* language and thought. We usually believe logic is what it is despite how we humans think or how we talk. Logical voluntarism does not violate that intuition directly since it is God, not humanity, which has the ability to change the

---

42. Priest, *In Contradiction*, 170–71. Given such a debate one could say it's contingent that there are necessary truths for the logical truths that one believes. For to be necessary seems dependent upon the contingent choice of one's logical theory. I don't see this as a deep truth of metaphysics though. Rather, it's simply a common sense description of how one might arrive at the adoption of a logical theory.

LOGICAL VOLUNTARISM

validity statuses of arguments. Nevertheless, this independence of logic from humans is intuitive in the sense that arguments seem to have a permanence not enjoyed by many other things in our experience. To hold that God could change logic so effortlessly still pushes against this intuition. All philosophers know intuitions can sometimes be massaged away or modified, especially if they are incorrect. However, we should never *quickly* abandon our initial and deeply held inclinations. Claims that fly in the face of such deeply held intuitions need convincing argumentation. Though the logical voluntarist seems to have been able to answer our objections up to this point, I still don't believe we have any convincing argumentation that their view is true.[43] Nevertheless, it would be nice to have a good argument against logical voluntarism.

Which brings us to what I consider to be the most pressing concern for a logical voluntarist, at least if he or she wants to remain within the tradition of Western theism. Earlier we placed the vacuity objection to one side, where I commented that though it is the weakest for moral voluntarism. I think that this objection is actually the strongest objection one can give against logical voluntarism. In the following I'll explain why I think this is the case.

I had claimed that the more interesting (and thus tougher) version of the vacuity objection for logical voluntarism was the following: If God's commands or will solely determine what arguments are logically valid, then calling God's actions logical or rational (i.e., that his actions follow some identifiable set of logical implications) does not have determinate content for his actions could then be consistent with anything. The problem for the logical voluntarist is that the belief that God is logical or rational is consistent with God being, to all appearances, irrational or illogical. As pointed out before, the vacuity objection's basic point is that any theory should be considered a failed theory if it results in such obviously vacuous language. I now want to tease out why this is actually a substantial problem for the logical voluntarist from within the Western religious perspective, that is, if he or she wants to remain consistent with that tradition of theism.

---

43. Against a claim like mine Conee, argues: "It is nonetheless clearly intelligible to claim that someone has an ability to do something that is not done. This is to claim that someone has of an ability that is not exercised. It is equally intelligible to claim that someone has an ability to do the impossible," Conee, "The Possibility of Power Beyond Possibility," 456. However, it is far from clear to me that this is *equally* intelligible. I don't see how this is an intuitive or obvious move and so I believe Conee owes us more of an argument for why we should believe it.

THE LOGIPHRO DILEMMA

I will argue here that the vacuity objection, as it applies to logical voluntarism, shows more than just that the domain of logical language would be vacuous, it shows how all language as it applies to God, or is revealed by God, comes out vacuous, and thus makes such language malfunction for its usual intended communicative purposes. I will explain why this is so and why this would be such a huge problem from the perspective of the Abrahamic tradition.

As we previously specified in chapter 1, the tradition of theism we are working with in this work holds that God has revealed himself to human beings throughout history (i.e., revealed theology). Because such encounters with God are believed to have been rare, this tradition has usually focused upon the oral or written testimonial accounts of those who have claimed to encounter God. This is the reason why sacred texts, or Scripture, hold such primacy within this tradition. Scripture is believed to contain, among other things, claims from God communicating true data about God. To name just a very few key claims, Scripture declares the following:

(1) God is good.[44]

(2) God only tells the truth.[45]

(3) God does not change.[46]

These sorts of statements, and others, are the foundation upon which many theists within the Western tradition of religion build their religious beliefs, and thus from which reasoning concerning God, religion, and moral

---

44. "For the LORD is good; his steadfast love endures forever, and his faithfulness to all generations" (Ps 100:5). "Praise the LORD! Oh give thanks to the LORD, for he is good, for his steadfast love endures forever" (Ps 106:1). The New Testament also contends that "No one is good except God alone" (Mark 10:18).

45. "Know therefore that the LORD your God is God, the faithful God who keeps covenant and steadfast love with those who love him and keep his commandments, to a thousand generations" (Deut 7:9). "God is not man, that he should lie, or a son of man, that he should change his mind. Has he said, and will he not do it? Or has he spoken, and will he not fulfill it?" (Num 23:19).

46. "[The earth and the heavens] will perish, but you will remain; they will all wear out like a garment. You will change them like a robe, and they will away, but you are the same, and your years have no end" (Ps 102: 25–27). "For I the LORD do not change" (Mal 3:6). The New Testament also claims "So when God desired to show more convincingly to the heirs of the promise the unchangeable character of his purpose, he guaranteed it with an oath, so that by two unchangeable things, in which it is impossible for God to lie, we who have fled for refuge might have strong encouragement to hold fast to the hope set before us" (Heb 6:17–18).

LOGICAL VOLUNTARISM

actions are made by such theists. But the vacuity objection highlights that if logical voluntarism is true, then none of the above statements—nor any statements concerning God inferred from the above—can be taken at their usual face value. For logical voluntarism implies that any claim God may have communicated, or is taken to be a true claim about God, cannot be understood by us in any usually straightforward way. For any kind of communication relies upon certain assumptions about inferential connections to other claims—what is included or excluded—at least to some degree.[47] Linguistic communication relies upon and assumes certain inferential rules, presumably both conceptual and logical. So when someone attempts to communicate with us, or us with them, it seems that we need to assume a certain minimal amount of logic—at least rules that operate in the sort of deductive ways logic is usually taken to operate. However, if our interlocutor is a being that may not only not assume standard logical rules, but has the ability to change such rules, then it does not seem that we could truly understand what such a being meant when he communicated to us. Let's tease this out some to see this point.

When God reveals, say, claim (1) as true, on the logical voluntarist picture the vacuity objection points out that the following claim could be true as well:

(1a) God is not good.

But (1) and (1a) are obviously contradictory. God cannot be good and not good, at least not at the same time and in the same way. But on the logical voluntarist picture, such claims could be simultaneously true if God commanded or willed them to be so. Due to this voluntarist possibility, if God revealed (1) as true about himself, it could very well be the case that God was also not *not good*. In other words, the truth of (1) is consistent with God being evil (i.e., (1a)) by the logical voluntarist's own lights.

But a traditional Western theist sympathetic to logical voluntarism might object that (1a) is not a *real* possibility because God has revealed not only (1) to be true about himself but God has also revealed that:

(2) God only tells the truth.

---

47. Shapiro, "Simple Truth, Contradiction, and Consistency," 336–54, brings up a similar problem for Graham Priest's view of dialetheism. In sum, Shapiro argues that there are certain notions and concepts that the dialetheist invokes (informally) that cannot be adequately expressed unless his attendant meta-theory is completely consistent. I'm making a somewhat similar point here: God cannot be understood to be expressing the notions and concepts we think he is expressing unless logical voluntarism is false.

Thus, so this argument would go, (1a) could not be true along with God's revelation of (1) for that would contradict the truth of (2). Thus, the logical voluntarist pushes, even according to logical voluntarism it follows that we can and should understand (1) as we normally would understand this scriptural claim.

But hold on. The logical voluntarist holds that God has complete control over the validity relations between any claims. Thus, if logical voluntarism is true, the following could be true as well:

(2a) God sometimes fails to tell the truth.

By the logical voluntarist picture, God could make (2) and (2a) simultaneously true—though these are normally understood as contradictory to each other. Given this possibility on the logical voluntarist picture, one could then not take claim (2) as we normally would understand such a concatenation of words put together: that God only tells the truth without exception. Thus, appealing to claim (2) does note protect the truth or meaning of claim (1). But again, the logical voluntarist may further object that (2a), as well as (1a), are not real possibilities because God has also revealed the following scriptural truth:

(3) God does not change.

Therefore, claims the logical voluntarist, if God does not change (i.e., (3) is true), and he reveals himself as being good (i.e., (1) is true), and reveals that he always tells the truth (i.e., (2) is true), then it follows that neither (1a) nor (2a) could ever be true. Thus, the vacuity objection fails to make special revelation vacuous.

But, unfortunately, appealing to (3) does not get logical voluntarism off the vacuity objection's hook either. For if logical voluntarism is true—that God could change the truth status of any claim or change the validity relation between any claims—then (3) could be simultaneously true along with

(3a) God sometimes changes.

In fact, within logical voluntarism (3) could be simultaneously true with

(3b) God *always* changes (!).

Therefore, by logical voluntarism's own picture, claims (1), (2), and even (3)—all statements that Western theists believe are true because God has revealed them about himself—could not be understood in their usual way.

LOGICAL VOLUNTARISM

That is, we cannot justifiably believe that God never changes without exception as (3) would normally be understood; we cannot justifiably believe that God only tells truth as (2) would normally be understood; and we cannot justifiably believe that God is good as (1) would normally be understood. Moreover, we should be able to see how this result generalizes to all claims concerning God (those revealed and those inferred from special revelation) since no claims about God on the logical voluntarist picture could be taken to clearly mean what we would normally take them to mean.

This inability to take God's own revelatory claims, and other inferred claims about God, in a usually understood way as pointed out by the vacuity objection is a serious problem for theists in Western tradition since they hold that the main datum for thinking and theorizing about God is God's self-revelation. But, as I believe we've seen above, if logical voluntarism is true, then it follows that this datum is a completely vacuous and thus an unreliable source of information for we cannot justifiably believe that what is being communicated by this datum is what we think is being communicated. The "possibilities" that logical voluntarism avails itself of makes theological discussion and philosophical formulation from special revelation essentially pointless. If logical voluntarism were adopted, there would need to be a massive overhaul—to say the least—of all of the traditional claims about God in the Abrahamic tradition. For none of those claims would necessarily mean what they've been thought to mean. It would be as if humans on earth had been receiving messages from aliens in outer space for decades. Imagine that over this time some people (say scientists and other academics) thought they had deciphered this alien language—what its grammar and vocabulary consisted in. Based upon this datum, a detailed account of what these aliens were likely developed: their thought and civilization, including their science, economics, philosophy, political thought, sociology, etc. But then imagine that this academic community eventually discovered that these aliens had actually been operating according to a logic that was utterly and completely "alien" from our own understanding of logic. This discovery would bring the whole edifice and discipline of "alien studies" into question. For these scientists could not justifiably believe that all that they had thought they had understood and learned of these beings was what they had thought or was in fact true.[48]

---

48. This point is similar to Quine's notion of "radical translation" illustrated most memorably in his famous "Gavagai" thought experiment. See Quine, *Word and Object*, chapter 2.

In sum, the vacuity objection shows that if logical voluntarism were true, all language as revealed by God or supposedly applying to God is *utterly useless*, which calls the primary source of datum (i.e., special revelation) of the Western theistic tradition into question. Therefore, the vacuity objection shows that logical voluntarism is an unacceptable picture of the relationship between God and logic for those in the Western tradition of theism who primarily rely upon Scripture as their main epistemological source of information concerning God.

But one might object that I've moved too quickly here. Supposing logical voluntarism is true, why can't the Western theist go on to claim that God simply doesn't, and furthermore won't make contradictions true? In the same way that a libertarian about freewill might claim that moral praiseworthiness is dependent upon the ability to do otherwise. Perhaps the praiseworthiness of God—which is tied to his consistency in character and action—is dependent upon his ability to do otherwise (i.e., that he could make contradictions true). What this view is suggesting is that we read logical voluntarism only according to the limited possibilism reading, rejecting the universal possibilism reading as implausible or too strong, too straw-mannish of a reading of logical voluntarism. However, I don't think this helps the logical voluntarist at all against the vacuity objection.[49]

There's a couple of different ways to understand the limited possibilism reading. One: God once had the ability to change the truth status and validity status of every claim and argument at any time; but once he decided upon the truth and validity statuses of these claims (presumably at the time of creation), then these statuses remained fixed—God cannot now change them; he no longer has the ability to do so. Limited possibilism understood this way can be summarized:

> (LP1) God has the ability to determine the truth and validity status of any claim at any time, before creation.

A second way: God still has the ability to change the truth status and validity status of every claim at any time; but God never follows through on his power to make such changes. Limited possibilism understood this way can be summarized:

> (LP2) God has the ability to determine the truth and validity status of any claim at any time, but he will never do so.

---

49. I remind the reader that I have only assumed the limited possibilism reading of logical voluntarism throughout.

LOGICAL VOLUNTARISM

I think (LP1) would be the most natural way to apply limited possibilism to logical voluntarism. But I don't think it has any philosophical advantages over (LP2). Either seems like a perfectly legitimate way of trying to characterize logical voluntarism. But I don't think either helps the logical voluntarist. Why not? Doesn't it get the logical voluntarist around the vacuity objection? I don't think so, and for two reasons.

First, I don't see any merit in the claim that God's praiseworthiness is dependent upon his ability to do otherwise, at least not in many cases. People are sometimes considered praiseworthy for things that are beyond their control or power. For instance, a person could be praised for his or her natural beauty. The person obviously did not have control over this aspect of himself or herself yet we consider it something worth praising. In the same way, it seems to me that God could still be praiseworthy for something that is beyond his control or power.

Second, the limited possibilism suggestion (on either (LP1) or (LP2)) still gives away too much for it still delivers the same consequences as an unvarnished universal possibilism reading of logical voluntarism. In other words, universal possibilism is not ruled out by either characterization of limited possibilism. For if (LP1) were true, by the logical voluntarist's own picture, the following could be true as well:

(LP1*) Before creation, God decreed (LP1) to be necessarily false.

If (LP1*) was made true by God before creation, then we could not justifiably believe that (LP1) was true now. Therefore, this understanding of limited possibilism does not escape the vacuity objection. A similar problem holds for (LP2), for if it were true, by the logical voluntarist picture, the following could also be true:

(LP2*) God has the ability to determine the truth and validity status of any claim at any time, and he will do so.

In other words, what (LP1*) and (LP2*) are pointing out is that a limited possibilism reading of logical voluntarism in no way helps us to justifiably believe claims concerning God could be understood as they would normally be understood. On the logical voluntarist picture, we just could not know that predictions about how God would or should act would hold true. As Peter Geach points out, "we cannot say how a supra-logical God would act or how he would communicate anything to us by way of revelation."[50]

---

50. Geach, "Omnipotence," 11.

Therefore, since both limited possibilism readings deliver the same consequences of the universal possibilism reading, neither helps in defending logical voluntarism against the vacuity objection. In consequence, since the vacuity objection highlights that the primary source of datum for the traditional theist is called into question, the traditional Western theist should reject logical voluntarism. Regardless of how God and logic are actually interrelated, the price of logical voluntarism is too high for the theist in the Abrahamic tradition.

3.2.4 Biting the Bullet of the Vacuity Objection

Thus I've argued that even though logical voluntarism cannot be deductively refuted, the traditional Western theist has good reason to reject it in that its acceptance would make worthless the primary source of his information concerning God (i.e., special revelation or Scripture). All language revealed by God or applied to God would come out vacuously uninformative. But the logical voluntarist might still reply in the following way. Perhaps the Western tradition of theism should be given up, or modified. Perhaps the conviction that God's revelation is capable of being understood in any straightforward or regular way by human beings is a mistake or oversimplification. Maybe it is mere hubris to think that we finite mortals can come to even an approximation of understanding what an infinite being may communicate. In essence, this suggestion is claiming that we "bite the bullet," and accept the outcome of the vacuity objection: We cannot straightforwardly understand God's revelatory claims about himself, nor claims about God inferred from revelation, nor applied to God in any usually understood way of interpreting those same words as used in other contexts. In fact, there is a long tradition of theology that I believe is sympathetic to such a response.

The tradition I have in mind here goes back, at least, to the writings of an anonymous sixth-century Christian mystic who wrote under the name of one of St. Paul's converts, Dionysius (thus, scholars often refer to him as Pseudo-Dionysius). In his writings Pseudo-Dionysius distinguished between two different ways of doing theology: *kataphatic* or positive theology, which is constituted by affirming claims pertaining to God; and *apophatic* or negative theology, which is made up of negating claims pertaining to God. Vladimir Lossky, in his theology of the Eastern Christian Church, points out that Pseudo-Dionysius claimed:

LOGICAL VOLUNTARISM

> The first leads us to some knowledge of God, but is an imperfect way. The perfect way, the only way which is fitting in regard to God, who is of His very nature unknowable, is the second—which leads us finally total ignorance. All knowledge has as its object that which is. Now God is beyond all that exists. In order to approach Him it is necessary to deny all that is inferior to Him. It is by *unknowing* (*agnosia*) that one may know Him who is above every possible object of knowledge. Proceeding by negations one ascends from the inferior degrees of being to the highest, by progressively setting aside all that can be known, in order to draw near to the Unknown in the darkness of absolute ignorance. For even as light, and especially abundance of light, renders darkness invisible; even so the knowledge of created things, and especially excess of knowledge, destroys the ignorance which is the only way by which one can attain to God in Himself.[51]

Claiming agreement with Pseudo-Dionysius, Lossky claims that God is unknowable because he is "beyond all that exists." The idea seems to be that God's nature is such that we do not have categories of thought (and thus language) that corresponds to what God is like.[52] Therefore, according to Lossky, the most we can say about God is what he is *not* like. But I think it should immediately strike any clear-headed person that this apophatic approach to theology, at least as described here, is problematic. For is it not to affirm something about God to claim that God is "beyond all that exists"? And even if God is "unknowable," don't we know at least know one thing about him then, namely, that he is unknowable? This sort of talk seems to put the advocate of apophatic theology in a pretty pickle: affirming contradictory claims. Or perhaps, and this could very well be true, I'm not quite grasping what the apophatic theologian is up to.

In his book *Mystical Languages of Unsaying*, Michaeal Sells gives perhaps the clearest, and seemingly sympathetic, exposition of what theists like apophatic theologians are attempting. He calls such attempts examples

---

51. Lossky, *The Mystical Theology of the Eastern Church*, 25.

52. I think some of the reasons for motivating logical voluntarism we saw earlier (§3.1.2) fit well with this picture. Remember the quote we saw from Descartes earlier: "For my part, I know that my intellect is finite and God's power is infinite, and so I set no bounds to it; I consider only what I can conceive and what I cannot conceive. . . . And so I boldly assert that God can do everything which I conceive to be possible, but I am not so bold as to deny that he can do whatever conflicts with my understanding—I merely say that it involves a contradiction" (Descartes, *Philosophical Writings*, 363).

of the *aporia*, or the unresolvable dilemma of transcendence. He attempts his own explanation of such with the following:

> The transcendent is beyond names, ineffable. In order to claim that the transcendent is beyond names, however, I must give it a name, "the transcendent." Any statement of ineffability, "X is beyond names," generates the aporia that the subject of the statement must be named (as X) in order for us to affirm that it is beyond names.... This [sort of] discourse has been called negative theology. Denying what God is like, is affirming what God is; but this in turn must be denied—and this proceeds on to a linguistic regress. The regress is harnessed and becomes the guiding semantic force, the *dynamis*, of a new kind of language. This language is called *apophasis*.[53]

So Sells explains that apophatic language is more than just giving negating claims of God, but a series of claims that continue to negate. And furthermore, he explains that this is not a meaningless double-talk, but an entirely new type of language or discourse. He goes on to clarify what this new language is doing.

> Any [example of apophasis] saying (even a negative saying) demands a correcting proposition, an unsaying. But that correcting proposition which unsays the previous proposition is in itself a "saying" that must be "unsaid" in turn. It is the tension between the two propositions that the discourse becomes meaningful. That tension is momentary. It must be continually re-earned by ever new linguistic acts of unsaying.[54]

I think the idea that Sells is gesturing at is something like the following. Suppose the apophatic theologian claims that "God is not finite." This implies then God is infinite, right? "Not quite," claims the apophatic theologian. "God is also not infinite either." So God is neither finite nor infinite? "Correct," replies the apophatic theologian, "though this claim must also be further negated." Now I don't claim to understand what something like "God is neither finite nor infinite" amounts to; but I think the apophatic idea is that the "meaning" of such a claim (or eventual claim?), what Sells calls its "momentary tension," is not a straightforward assertion that is emphatically true or false. Rather, is it the sort of thing that we must revisit, or "re-earn" again and again through this sort of discourse in order to understand it, in

---

53. Sells, *Mystical Languages of Unsaying*, 2.
54. Ibid., 3.

LOGICAL VOLUNTARISM

some mystical way. As Sells explains, "Rather than pointing to an object, apophatic language attempts to evoke in the reader an event."[55]

Though I think Sells' above exposition is helpful here, I admit that I still struggle to grasp exactly what apophatic language is attempting to accomplish. Do the notions of "meaning" or "truth" or "falsehood" have any corresponding notions in apophatic language? If not, what exactly is being "communicated" to the listener? Concerning our discussion though, the more apt question is what the upshot of this apophatic approach to theology is for the logical voluntarist who wants to escape the brunt of the vacuity objection? Sells makes a comment that I think is apt here: "For the apophatic writer, the logical rule of non-contradiction functions for object entities [i.e., understood as everything other than God]. When the subject of discourse is a non-object and no-thing [i.e., God], it is not irrational that such logic be superseded."[56] Therefore, a logical voluntarist who is sympathetic to this apophatic approach to theology might utilize it to reject the vacuity objection above. Such a response might go: Since God is beyond our intellectual ability to comprehend we cannot justifiably believe that the valid arguments of our cherished logical systems apply to him. In fact, it seems that logic, as we see it, requires kataphatic (i.e., clear assertive) claims in relation to God—even in its use of negation. Therefore, given the perspective of apophatic theology, the vacuity objection concerning logical voluntarism (i.e., all language applied to God is vacuous) is just an unsurprising result given the kind of "no-thing" God is.[57]

However, I don't think appealing to apophatic theology lets the logical voluntarist get away so freely. There is still a stiff price to pay for opting for this position. I think this will become apparent in the following three responses to the apophatic view.

First, I want to push back against the conception of God the apophatic view presents. Why believe that God is transcendent to the point of requiring apophatic theology? Most advocates of the Western tradition of religion have gladly affirmed that God is transcendent and mysterious: there are things about God that we cannot fully understand or know, now or perhaps

55. Ibid., 10.
56. Ibid., 4.
57. One may object that I've subtly shifted from talking about what God can or can't do to what God is or is not. But I think the distinction is closely related. It seems intuitive to me that if we cannot say what God is like, then we more than likely cannot say what he can do or not do. Therefore, I do not believe I've shifted to an unrelated subject. Thanks to Stewart Shapiro for pressing this point.

ever. Scriptural passages like the following have often informed such a view: "For my [i.e., God's] thoughts are not your thoughts, neither are your ways my ways, declares the LORD" (Isa 55:8).[58] But, as Michael Rea highlights, most Western theists, including analytic philosophers of religion "typically share the supposition that we can arrive at *clear* knowledge of God, even if that knowledge is not *complete* and some mysteries remain."[59] Put simply, believing that God is transcendent is consistent with denying apophatic theology as the only or best way to make claims about God. Affirming that God is transcendent does not require denying the legitimacy of positive affirmations concerning God. Thus, I do not see why believing that God is transcendent gives any credence to upholding apophatic theology, and so I don't see this as a good reason to uphold logical voluntarism either.

Second, it seems to me that the advocates of apophatic theology want to have their cake and eat it too. Even though they claim that God is not bound by what we perceive as rational, apophatic theologians are usually adamant that their position does not entail irrationality. As we've seen with Lossky, Eastern Orthodox Christians traditionally uphold the apophatic approach to theology. In addition, this tradition also emphasizes personal experience as a primary means of spirituality. But, traditionally, members of this church believe that the dogmas of the Eastern Church must act as a corrective to subjective mystical experience. Any interpretation of such experience must cohere with their official teachings. Lossky comments: "Outside the truth kept by the whole church personal experience would be deprived of all certainty, of all objectivity. It would be a mingling of truth and falsehood, of reality and illusion: 'mysticism' in the bad sense of the word." He re-emphasizes this point: "For the inner experience of the Christian develops within the circle delineated by the teaching of the Church: within the dogmatic framework which moulds his person."[60] Christos Yannaras, another Christian writer in the Eastern Church, says things similar to Lossky here. "The priority of empirical participation in relation to the intellectual approach to ecclesial truth means neither cloudy mysticism and refuge in emotional exaltations, nor to overlook and devalue logical thought."[61] But how did the Eastern Church come to their official dogmas?

58. Traditional Western Christians affirm New Testament passages like the following to uphold God's transcendence: "For nothing will be impossible with God" (Luke 1:37).

59. Rea, "Introduction," in *Analytic Theology*, 9.

60. Lossky, *The Mystical Theology of the Eastern Church*, 9 and 21, respectively.

61. Christos Yannaras, *Elements of Faith*, 18–19.

LOGICAL VOLUNTARISM

It seems to me that they relied upon the experiences of the first Christians, including their written Scripture concerning these experiences. The outcome, claim advocates of the Eastern Church, is the dogma of their church. Yannaras writes: "The result was an excellent achievement of Greek reason which, without betraying Christian truth and the *apophatic* knowledge of this truth, remained absolutely consistent with the demands for philosophical formulations."[62] We see here that Yannaras is quite explicit in claiming that the official apophatic claims of the church are *logically consistent* with other philosophical claims, presumably among these claims are the valid arguments of logic. So here, along with Lossky, Yannaras affirms that apophatic theology does not imply irrationality, or an "anything goes" result. Claims of spiritual experience must be consistent with the claims of the church, which are the result of apophatic theology.

But, it seems to me, given the commitments of apophatic theology, too much rope has been given up to still have the intellectual grip on theology that apophatic theologians claim they have. Yannaras cannot claim, for example, that our knowledge of God is totally incomprehensible *and* simultaneously claim that our theological formulations are "absolutely consistent" with other philosophical claims. Take X to be a placeholder for some piece of apophatic knowledge concerning God and take p to be some clear affirmation. Thus, an instance of Yannaras' general claim is the following:

(A1) (X & p) is true.

But the apophatic theologian cannot affirm (A1) as true without knowing that both sides of the conjunction are true. Given the nature of apophasis—as laid out earlier by Sells as a "tension" or "event"—one cannot affirm (A1) because X may contain (for all we know) $\sim p$, or perhaps X doesn't contain the kind of thing that we can call "true" or "false." Thus, despite affirming that apophatic theology does not entail irrationality, there's nothing to prevent what we normally take to be irrational here. Despite assuring us to the contrary, apophatic theologians do not give us, nor can they give us it seems, any reason to justifiably believe that irrationality is not so entailed. Therefore, again we have a reason to avoid apophatic theology and thus another reason not to use it as a defense of logical voluntarism.

Third, the Western tradition of theology has long affirmed the transcendence of God without the costs of apophatic theology in that it has long held what is often called the *doctrine of analogy*, which Thomas Aquinas

---

62. Ibid., 19.

THE LOGIPHRO DILEMMA

(AD 1225–74) is usually credited with developing. Aquinas held that when a word is applied to both a created being and to God, it is not being used *univocally* (i.e., with exactly the same meaning) in the two instances; yet neither is the word being used *equivocally* (i.e., with two completely different meanings) as when "bank" is used to apply to the land next to a river or the place where you deposit your paycheck. Rather, when a word is applied to both a created being and God (e.g., Sally is *good* and God is *good*.), then the word is being used *analogously* (i.e., with some overlap of meaning). Theologian Michael Horton explains the motivation for this view:

> When we say that God is good, we assume we know what *good* means from our ordinary experience with fellow human beings. However, God is not only *quantitatively better* than we are; his goodness is *qualitatively different* from creaturely goodness. Nevertheless, because we are created in God's image, we share this predicate with God analogically. *Goodness*, is attributed to God and Sally, is similar but with greater dissimilarity.[63]

Given this motivation to see God as qualitatively different from all created things (i.e., transcendent), the doctrine of analogy should be seen as a theory of how to understand predication concerning claims about God. Again, the Western theistic tradition has long affirmed this theory as a part of how to understand God's revelatory claims about himself, and claims made about God inferred from his revelation.

But the apophatic thinker may claim that the theist who adheres to the doctrine of analogy is being disingenuous for pushing the vacuity objection against logical voluntarism as being problematic for understanding religious language. In other words, by being committed to the doctrine of analogy he is already claiming that statements about God cannot be understood in a usually straightforward (i.e., univocal) way. Therefore, the traditional Western theist is being inconsistent in rejecting logical voluntarism on the basis of the vacuity objection.

However, I think that there is wiggle room for the Abrahamic theist to explain his commitment to the doctrine of analogy while still justifiably rejecting logical voluntarism on the grounds that it obliterates the means of understanding God's revelation. I think the traditional theist must admit there is a limit to the application of the doctrine of analogy when it concerns claims about God and logic. I know of no particular claims from Scripture that specify that "God is logical" or "God is rational." Nevertheless, it seems

---

63. Horton, *The Christian Faith*, 55.

LOGICAL VOLUNTARISM

clear that many theists want to affirm such claims as inferences from other revelatory claims concerning God. Of course, it is obvious that God's logical acumen far outstrips even the most brilliant minds among us humans. So Sally's mind can't be as rational or as intellectually acute as an omniscient mind such as God's. But surely such claims as "God is logical" or "God is rational" cannot be understood analogically in the sense that when the premises are true of some valid logical argument, then the conclusion must be true *for us*; while also claiming that for the same argument that somehow the conclusion does not have to be true *for God*. Thus, I'm suggesting that the doctrine of analogy has some limitation of application: it cannot be fully applied to claims about God and logic. If such claims are not understood univocally, then it seems we have—if not logical voluntarism—something akin to it lurking close behind. So it seems to me that the traditional theist can non-hypocritically adhere to the doctrine of analogy (in the modified form I've suggested here) while still rejecting logical voluntarism and its apophatic interpretation.[64]

Given these three responses it seems to me that appealing to apophatic theology does not get the logical voluntarist out of the problems concerning God and language that the vacuity objection points out. If the apophatic perspective is adopted, then I don't see how any substantive philosophical reasoning concerning God could be done—the kind done by most philosophers of religion, theologians, and even that which everyday theists do. I suppose the apophatic theologian could continue to talk and theorize as the traditional Western theist does, but always keeping in the back of his mind that none of these claims can be taken in any sort of usual fashion. But it seems to me that most traditional Western theists should find this cost far too high and very unsatisfying. When one makes a claim that he believes to be true, or an argument that he takes to be valid or cogent, there is some satisfaction based on the underlying assumption that his claims and arguments are matching up with the world—maybe not perfectly, but at least attempting to. It seems that language concerning (at least) most subjects should be more than a mere game. If my wife says "I love you," I personally would take no joy in this utterance if it did not mean what I normally thought it to mean, namely that my wife did indeed love me. If the

---

64. I'm fully aware that much more should be said here and that all I've really done is just gestured towards a call for a distinction. The doctrine of analogical predication is one that I believe needs much more refinement and clarification. But I'm convinced, at least at this point, that analogous predication needs some sort of limit if the vacuity objection is to be avoided.

theist adopts the apophatic interpretation of theism, then claims concerning God—e.g., "God [is] merciful and gracious, slow to anger, and abounding in steadfast love and faithfulness" (Exod 34:6)—cannot be taken too seriously either. But it seems to me that many Western theists usually take revelatory claims like these very seriously; and so if one wants to remain within this rational picture, then one should eschew logical voluntarism, as well as the apophatic theological suggestion.

3.3 CONCLUSION

In this chapter I clarified logical voluntarism more fully and looked at the motivations, even a few non-theistic motivations, for holding this view. I then examined how the objections often leveled against moral voluntarism carry over, for the most part, to logical voluntarism. We saw how the incoherence and unintelligibility objections were perhaps not fully successful in that logical voluntarism cannot be deductively refuted. Nevertheless, I argued that the traditional Western theist has justifiable grounds for rejecting logical voluntarism on the basis of the vacuity objection: logical voluntarism destroys the main source of datum concerning God for the traditional theist in that it implies that claims about God cannot be understood in any usual straightforward way of interpreting language. In the last section we investigated what would follow if the logical voluntarist "bit the bullet" and accepted the outcome of the vacuity objection by adopting the apophatic tradition of theology. I gave several reasons why the apophatic interpretation had too high of a cost for the traditional Western theist.

In conclusion, since logical voluntarism does not cohere with the commitment to the understandability of special revelation associated with traditional Abrahamic theism (i.e., it does not respect at least part of the notion of God as laid out in chapter 1), I believe logical voluntarism does not count as a good explanation of the relationship between God and logic. Therefore, we should reject logical voluntarism as an acceptable explanation of the relationship between God and logic.

We now move on to the second option of the Logiphro dilemma to see if it might be a better way of thinking about the relationship between the God of classical theism and logical consequence.

4

LOGICAL NON-VOLUNTARISM

To recount, we began our investigation of what relationship may exist between God and logic by following the infamous Euthyphro question from philosophical antiquity. As we saw, a good contemporary rendering of Socrates' original question to the religious zealot Euthyphro goes like the following: "Are morally good actions morally good simply in virtue of God's favoring them? Or does God favor them because they are—independently of his favoring them—morally good?"[1] For those who wish to establish a strong relationship between God's commands or will and morality, the question presents at least two problematic options, which has become known as *the* Euthyphro dilemma: either God's will or commands determine the nature of moral goodness (i.e., moral voluntarism) or God wills or commands that which is morally good, and yet the nature of moral goodness is something independent and antecedent to God's willing or commanding it (i.e., moral non-voluntarism). Suggesting that this ancient question and its attending dilemma are a natural and helpful way to orient our own investigation, I proposed a similar Socratic question concerning God and logic: "Are valid logical arguments valid simply in virtue of God's favoring them? Or does God favor them because they are—independently of his favoring them—valid?" Like the original Euthyphro question, this one also seems to give at least two options: either God's will or commands determine the validity of arguments (i.e., logical voluntarism) or God wills or commands what is logically valid, and yet validity is independent and

---

1. Antony, "Atheism as Perfect Piety," 71.

THE LOGIPHRO DILEMMA

antecedent to God willing or commanding it (i.e., logical non-voluntarism). I dubbed this the logical Euthyprho dilemma, or simply the Logiphro for short.

In the last chapter we investigated the voluntarist horn of the Logiphro and concluded that it demands too high of a price for the traditional Western theist. Thus, we concluded that logical voluntarism does not count as a good explanation of the relationship between God and logic. This now leaves us with the other horn of the Logiphro dilemma, logical non-voluntarism. This chapter will investigate whether logical non-voluntarism is a philosophically viable alternative to conceive of the relationship between God and logic.

In §4.1 I will clarify what the thesis of logical non-voluntarism is, and what advantages the view gives, especially in contrast to logical voluntarism. This section will first present logical non-voluntarism as a Platonist conception (i.e., a theory that appeals to abstract objects). Though I will also discuss a nominalist conception (i.e., a theory that does *not* appeal to abstract objects) of logical non-voluntarism in §4.3, there are three reasons for presenting the Platonist version first. One, as I'll explain in §4.1, a Platonist rendering of non-voluntarism most naturally suggests itself and it is historically the more influential interpretation of such a view. Two, logical Platonism (as well as other kinds of Platonism) is clearly more popular than nominalism among theistic philosophers and theologians today.[2] And three, given the problems for Platonist construals of logical non-voluntarism to be discussed in §4.2, this will naturally lead to discussing a nominalist understanding of logical non-voluntarism as a possible alternative in §4.3. Logical nominalism is a vast subject and deserves a full discussion in its own right. Richard Swinburne is the only theistic philosopher I know of who has developed a fully detailed nominalist account of logic. Therefore, I think his view will serve as the best representative for conceiving of logical non-voluntarism in a nominalist way. §4.3 mainly concerns his view and the various problems it incurs. But I'll also argue that these problems are most likely symptomatic of any nominalistic account of logic.

Like the last chapter, the overall conclusion of this chapter is negative. I believe we will see that both Platonist and nominalist accounts of logic are problematic for upholding logical non-voluntarism. Therefore, I will

---

2. Interestingly, Hans Boersma, *Heavenly Participation* makes the book-length case that theists must be Platonists in order to remain orthodox within the Western tradition. However, it seems to me that most theologians and theistic philosophers are motivated to Platonism on more philosophic, as opposed to religious or theological, grounds.

LOGICAL NON-VOLUNTARISM

conclude that logical non-voluntarism also does not serve as a good explanation of the relationship between God and logic. As with the voluntarist horn of the Logiphro dilemma, I'll conclude that logical non-voluntarism must be rejected as well.[3]

4.1 CLARIFYING LOGICAL NON-VOLUNTARISM

4.1.1 Robust Logical Non-Voluntarism

Throughout this work logical non-voluntarism has been characterized as simply the position that the logical validity of any argument is a feature that is independent of and antecedent to God's commanding or willing it. That is, on this view the notion of logical consequence has complete independence from divine willing or commands. Thus, unlike logical voluntarism, logical non-voluntarism claims that God does not, and cannot, command or will a change to the validity status of any argument.[4] So, for example, modus ponens is valid regardless of God's will or commands. And likewise, affirming the consequent is invalid despite God possibly willing or commanding to the contrary. Worded this way though, logical non-voluntarism is simply the negation of logical voluntarism. But, if that is all that logical non-voluntarism amounts to, then it is a broad position indeed.[5] For then *any* view of logic that rejects the logical voluntarist position would count as logical non-voluntarism. This would include any explicitly non-theistic view of logic as well as any view of logic that simply fails to reference God, which, I think should be obvious, would include *most* philosophers' views concerning logic. So we need to severely pare down logical non-voluntarism quite a bit and clarify our intended target.

---

3. In sum, I am arguing that the Logiphro is a false dilemma. I'll fully address this claim in chapter 5 where I will argue that there is at least one other legitimate option than just the two (logical voluntarism or logical non-voluntarism) that the Logiphro has presented to us.

4. Remember that in the last chapter I explored a more nuanced version of logical voluntarism (the limited possibilism reading) that claimed that even though God has the ability to change, by command or will, the validity status of any argument, one could assert that he never does so. In short, my criticism against that move was that if indeed God truly had the power to change the validity status of any argument, then we could never justifiably believe that he *never* does so or would *never* do so despite whatever assurances he might give.

5. Thanks to Chris Pincock for bringing this point to my attention.

THE LOGIPHRO DILEMMA

Obviously, the position of logical non-voluntarism we have in mind is an explicitly theistic position. The version of logical non-voluntarism we're targeting holds that God's will or commands have nothing to do with the logical consequence relation, particularly its validity status. But note that we've only been emphasizing logical non-voluntarism, up to this point, as being independent of God's will or commands. But, it seems to me, that logical non-voluntarism should also be understood more inclusively as not only independence from God's commands or will, but also to include that logic is also *ontologically independent* from God. That is, it's not only the case that logical validity is free from God's commands or will but that it's also the case that God's very being also does not ground, cause, or explain the existence of logical consequence. This is a very robust notion of independence. So much so, we can no longer remain metaphysically neutral in our stance towards logical consequence. We now need to be able to at least start explaining the ontological dynamics of this non-voluntarist relationship between God and logic. This being the case, how should we metaphysically conceive of logical non-voluntarism's claim of logic's independence?

I think the most natural way to conceive of a view like logical non-voluntarism, or at least the most historically influential way to conceive it, is suggested by Plato's dialogue called *Timaeus*. In this work Plato gives an account of the world as a creation of a Demiurge ("*dêmiourgos*," 28a),[6] sometimes translated as "Divine Craftsman." A traditional interpretation of the *Timaeus*[7] understands this Divine Craftsman as the being that created our physical world (the temporal and changing world of *becoming*) by using Plato's Forms (part of the eternal and changeless world of *being*) as exemplars or templates. However, so the usual interpretation goes, the Divine Craftsman did not create the Forms nor could he affect them in any way since they are eternal changeless entities like himself.

Logical non-voluntarism is, I think, easily conceived as following something akin to this picture. In the same way that Plato's Divine Craftsman has no power or control over the Forms—the Forms are independent of his will or commands—so the logical non-voluntarist's God has no ability to will or command differently what transcendent reality constitutes logical entailment—logical consequence is independent of God's will or

---

6. Parenthetical reference comes from Plato's *Timaeus* found in *Plato: Complete Works*.

7. For further details concerning the traditional interpretation see Armstrong, *An Introduction to Ancient Philosophy*, 44–52.

LOGICAL NON-VOLUNTARISM

commands. But in addition, on Plato's picture the Forms have an ontological independence as well. In other words, the Divine Craftsman does not create, ground, or explain the existence of the Forms. So, similarly, logical non-voluntarism could conceive logical consequence as being ontologically independent from God in a similar way. God does not create, ground, or explain the validity of logical arguments. For, like Plato's picture, the reason logic is independent from God and his considerable influence is because the reality that makes up logic seemingly shares features that God himself possesses such as eternality, immutability, etc. Thus, the entities that constitute logical consequence exist independently of God's ontologically creating or sustaining power as well as being independent of God's changing power, via his will or commands. Call the above picture *robust* or *Platonic* logical non-voluntarism.

But if this is the picture robust logical non-voluntarists have in mind, what exactly is the Platonic reality that constitutes robust logical non-voluntarism? Do Plato's Forms constitute logical consequence? There are various candidates that might fit the robust non-voluntarist bill, entities such as possible worlds,[8] propositions, relations, etc. Such entities are often referenced in the philosophical literature as *abstract objects* in contrast to the everyday concrete objects of our normal experience. Philosophers throughout history, including today, often appeal to abstract objects in their theorizing. But abstract objects are highly contentious things. Not only is their very existence debatable, the philosophical literature contains controversy over how to even satisfactorily characterize the distinction between abstract and concrete objects.[9] Nevertheless, many philosophers still appeal to abstract objects as an explanatory resource in their philosophical theorizing. One familiar example is the way that some philosophers of language explain the notion of meaning by appealing to propositions. They claim that a proposition is the object expressed by the utterance of a token indicative sentence. Thus, so the explanation goes, the proposition can become the object of thought or belief and thus becomes the common factor between different persons and languages. (Note that philosophical theories that appeal to abstract objects do not necessarily entail religious commitments or theistic implications. Many non-theistic philosophers have gladly

---

8. Possible worlds are not abstract objects on some views. Most famously, David Lewis argued that the best theory of modality must posit concrete possible worlds. See his historic *On the Plurality of Possible Worlds*.

9. See Rosen, "Abstract Objects," accessed June 7, 2016, http://plato.stanford.edu/entries/abstract-objects/ for a discussion of many such problems.

appealed to such objects. Despite their possible origin with Plato or his account of the Divine Craftsman, the notion of abstract objects is not necessarily theistically committing.)

For our purposes, I don't think we have to specifically pin down what sort of abstract objects robust logical non-voluntarism might appeal to. Our investigation only requires that we acknowledge that robust logical non-voluntarists appeal to abstract objects of some kind. Thus, we clarify that robust logical non-voluntarism is the view that the logical validity of any argument is a feature that is independent of God's ability to change (i.e., independent of his will or commands) and also that logical validity is ontologically independent of God's creating or sustaining power (i.e., ontologically independent). We offered the *Timeaus* picture as a natural way to conceive of robust logical non-voluntarism. With this picture in mind, robust logical non-voluntarism claims that logical consequence is ontologically independent and free from God's will or commands because logical validity is constituted by abstract objects (of some kind), which have features that make them independent in these ways.

What advantages does this view of logic offer in comparison to logical voluntarism?

4.1.2 Advantages of Logical Non-Voluntarism

For the one trying to understand and argue for what sort of relationship exists between God and logic, there are at least two major advantages for opting for robust logical non-voluntarism.

First, robust logical non-voluntarism neatly avoids all of the major criticisms we saw leveled against logical voluntarism. It does not suffer from the incoherence or unintelligibility objections that logical voluntarism immediately invites since it does not add to or subtract anything from our accustomed and seemingly effortless ways of comprehending logic or language. Thus, our usual ways of understanding logic remain intact. Similarly, robust logical non-voluntarism does not suffer from the vacuity objection against logical voluntarism that I argued plays havoc with humanity's ability to understand any sort of communication (i.e., special revelation) that God may give. Since by the robust logical non-voluntarist's lights the logical consequence relation is completely independent of God when he should choose to communicate with humans in some known language to them,

LOGICAL NON-VOLUNTARISM

then humans can straightforwardly take God to mean what such utterances would normally mean.

Nevertheless, the robust logical non-voluntarist could still stipulate that God has some sort of privileged epistemic access to logic due to his omniscience. This idea is similar to the way that a moral non-voluntarist might claim that even though God's commands do not establish what is morally right, he nevertheless is an authority on what is morally right in virtue of his superior character and omni-benevolence. As John Milliken suggests, God might "provide a nice shortcut for figuring out what agents could nevertheless come to on their own."[10] But beyond this suggestion of God being an excellent moral advisor though, the moral non-voluntarist maintains that God's commands or will are, for the most part, superfluous to the moral status of actions since the canons of moral rightness are independent of God's commands or will. Similarly, according to the robust logical non-voluntarist, even though the canons of logical validity are independent of God's commands or will, or his creating or sustaining power, nevertheless it could be that God might report to us facts concerning logic also in virtue of his superior knowledge. But even if this were the case, as with the moral non-voluntarist, the robust logical non-voluntarist also maintains that neither God's will nor commands has any bearing upon the logical knowledge revealed. I think this point bears fleshing out a little more.

Suppose God had given Moses, in addition to the familiar ten *moral* commandments, a list of ten *logical* commandments (e.g., "Thou shalt not equivocate," etc.). As the former commandments are supposed to be used by humans to judge the moral correctness of some action, suppose the latter could also be used to judge the inferential correctness of some bit of reasoning. Nevertheless, the robust logical non-voluntarist's position emphasizes that even if God had indeed given such commandments, this in no way would show that God's will or commands, or even his creating or sustaining power, is responsible for the validity status of logical arguments. Moreover, even if the class of all inferences that God sanctions (i.e., those sanctioned by the ten logical commandments and inferences from it) overlapped *exactly* with the class of all valid logical arguments, this still would not show that God's will or commands, or even his creating or sustaining power, is the cause of, or grounds for, the validity of these arguments. Just as the notions of creature with a kidney and creature with a heart overlap

---

10. Milliken, "Euthyphro, the Good, and the Right," 146.

exactly (as far as I know), nevertheless the notion of having a kidney has nothing to do with grounding, causing, or explaining the notion of having a heart. In the same way, the robust logical non-voluntarist claims God (his will or commands, or his creating or sustaining power) and logic are also completely distinct and unrelated. At most, claims the robust logical non-voluntarist, God might be the source of some (or even all) of our logical knowledge, but nothing more.

A second advantage of robust logical non-voluntarism is that it fits well with the widely shared intuitions concerning logical necessity. Earlier, in chapter 1, I argued for the following characterization of logical consequence:

> (LC) Φ is a logical consequence of Γ, if at every possible world in which the uniform substitution of the non-logical content in Γ and Φ renders every member of Γ true, then it also renders Φ true.

By using possible worlds language (LC) appeals to the common modal intuitions that logical consequence is a relation of necessity between conclusion and premise(s). The idea is that if an argument is deductively valid, then this means that if the premises (if any) are true, the conclusion is necessarily true as well. In addition, we also saw in chapter 1 J. C. Beall and Greg Restall characterize logical consequence in terms of universal applicability, another common intuition concerning logic:

> The fact that logical consequence is necessary means that logical consequence applies under any conditions whatsoever. If we consider what might happen *if* A were the case, and we reason from the premise that A, validly to a conclusion B, we ought, by rights, be able to conclude that if A were the case then B would be the case too. The applicability of logic is not a contingent matter; it works come what may, whatever hypotheses we care to entertain.[11]

Since it's widely held that logical consequence seems to hold "come what may," then the validity of an argument seems to be something that cannot be changed or modified. If a valid argument is indeed *necessarily* valid, then it seems that nothing—including the will or commands, or the creating or sustaining power of God—should to be able to change that. Robust logical non-voluntarism maintains such intuitions because this view holds that the validity status of arguments is a feature beyond God's creating or sustaining power, or his will or commands to alter in any way.

---

11. Beall and Restall, *Logical Pluralism*, 15–16.

LOGICAL NON-VOLUNTARISM

Since robust logical non-voluntarism avoids the seeming nonsense invited by logical voluntarism and respects the deeply held intuitions that many already hold concerning logic, this view seems to be an excellent way of construing the relationship between God and logic.

However, despite the above advantages, many theists will find this picture of robust logical non-voluntarism, with its commitments to abstract objects, to be an unacceptable explanation of the relationship between God and logic. In chapter 2 we were briefly introduced to this problem for moral and logical non-voluntarism. I now want us to see that this problem is nested in an overarching theistic worry. In recent years, there has been a growing body of literature among analytic philosophers of religion about issues related to God and Platonic entities (i.e., abstract objects) of all kinds.[12] There are a host of problems that have been alleged against positing the existence of abstract objects in relation to God. We'll now investigate those problems and see how they bear on the robust logical non-voluntarist picture we've presented above.

4.2 THE PROBLEM OF GOD AND ABSTRACT OBJECTS

In a recent article, Paul Gould lays out what many theistic philosophers consider to be *the* problem of God and abstract objects. In order to see the general nature of this problem, and how it might apply to robust logical non-voluntarism, we must first investigate and clarify a core doctrine of traditional Western theism, one which Gould dubs the *aseity-sovereignty doctrine*. He provides a brief synopsis of this doctrine with the following:

(i) God does not depend on anything distinct from himself for his existing; and

(ii) everything distinct from God depends on God's creative activity for existing.[13]

---

12. Not a comprehensive list, but the following are some key works in the debate. Plantinga, *Does God Have a Nature?*; Menzel, "Theism, Platonism and the Metaphysics of Mathematics," 365–82; Morris, *Anselmian Explorations*; Morris and Menzel, "Absolute Creation," 161–78; Copan and Craig, *Creation Out of Nothing*; Gould, "The Problem of God and Abstract Objects," 255–74; Leftow, *God and Necessity*. Not to be missed, one should definitely read Paul Gould's latest edited volume *Beyond the Control of God? Six Views on the Problem of God and Abstract Objects* (New York: Bloomsbury, 2014).

13. Gould, "The Problem of God and Abstract Objects," 256. See Copan and Craig, *Creation Out of Nothing*, chapters 1–3 and Craig, "Nominalism and Divine Aseity," 43–46

For the Western theistic tradition, claim (i) points out that God's existence is taken to be an *a se* existence. That is, God is understood to be a being whose existence is completely independent and self-sufficient. God neither relies upon anything for his existence nor has need of anything outside of himself for his continued existence. In addition, claim (ii) of this doctrine posits that all objects and realities distinct from God are taken to be dependent upon God's creative activity in some way, i.e., everything apart from God is created by God. Though Gould's wording does not make this explicit, this latter claim is also usually understood to include that all objects distinct from God are dependent upon God for their *continued* existence as well. So claim (ii) should be more correctly understood as, apart from himself, God created everything—I'll call this the *creation condition*; and in addition, God sustains everything's continued existence—I'll call this the *dependence condition*.[14] Furthermore, this clarification implies an added explicit condition to claim (i). Given that everything distinct from God depends on God, per claim (ii), it follows that God's *a se* existence displayed in (i) is an existence unique to God. In other words, God, *and God alone*, neither relies upon anything for his existence nor has need of anything for his continued existence. I'll call this the *uniqueness condition*. With these conditions made explicit, let's revise Gould's wording of the aseity-sovereignty doctrine to the following:

(a) God, *and God alone*, does not depend on anything distinct from himself for his existing; and

(b) everything distinct from God depends on God's creative *and sustaining* activity for existing.

I'll call claim (a) the *aseity intuition* (which includes the uniqueness condition) and claim (b) I'll call the *sovereignty intuition* (which includes the creation and dependence conditions). Since both of these intuitions and their included conditions are core to the traditional Abrahamic theism, few theists in this tradition will willingly, or at least quickly, surrender any part of the aseity-sovereignty doctrine.

---

for brief but good historical overviews as to why traditional Western theists have upheld the aseity-sovereignty doctrine.

14. In this work I will not be addressing the following question: "Did God create himself?" Given what I've written above, I think it's clear that my answer should be "no." But I'll not attempt to defend that answer here other than say that my stance corresponds with the general Western theistic tradition.

LOGICAL NON-VOLUNTARISM

With this revised doctrine in place we can now begin to see how any theory that posits abstract objects, like our current conception of logical non-voluntarism, is more than likely going to be problematic for such theists. In general, the problem seems to be that either (1) the existence of abstract objects end up making God dependent upon such objects in some way (i.e., it violates the aseity intuition); or (2) the existence of abstract objects implies they are uncreated (i.e., thus violating the creation condition of the sovereignty intuition); or (3) the existence of such objects implies that their continued existence is independent of God in some way (i.e., thus violating the dependence condition of the sovereignty intuition, as well as denying the uniqueness condition of the aseity intuition).[15] I believe that this also correctly characterizes the sorts of problems that our current proposal of robust logical non-voluntarism will run into. But let's investigate for ourselves how these problems might arise.

4.2.1 Practical Worries

Before going on to what I consider to be the more pressing philosophical problems pertaining to God and abstract objects, let me first address what seem to me to be more like a group of practical worries than actual philosophical problems. Some theists might worry that the existence of abstract objects does not sit well with traditional notions of God's sovereignty and omnipotence, and from their perspective in very practical ways. For example, if there exists some things that are resistant to God's power (his will, commands, creating or sustaining power), then this seems to imply that God is not really sovereign over *every*-thing, or that he is not truly *all*-powerful (i.e., omnipotent). A similarly related worry is the concern that the existence of abstract objects would operate as restraints against divine

---

15. Gould claims that the main problem with abstract objects, in relation to the aseity-sovereignty doctrine, is that they are *necessarily* existing objects. However, Kit Fine (among others) has pointed out that, in general, one cannot infer claims about independence from claims about necessity. For example, it's usually held that the set with the number 2, i.e., {2}, exists necessarily. Yet, {2} still depends for its existence upon something else, namely the existence of the number 2. See Kit Fine, "Essence and Modality," 1–16. But even though necessity may not be the source of the independence of abstract objects, everyone agrees that abstract objects, if they exist, are independent in some sense. (Though sets with contingent members may be an exception to this idea.) For my purposes, I don't think I need to identify what makes such objects independent, only that they are usually considered to be so. Thanks especially to Scott Brown, and David Blanks, for helping me to see this issue more clearly.

freedom. That is, there would exist entities that God could not affect, and thus could not freely act upon. If this were true, if God was not in control of all creation, or all-powerful, or completely free, then many theists fear that God could not be reliably depended upon. As theologian Michael Horton elaborates that if this were true of God, then theists "would have no confidence that [God] could overcome evil or rescue [them] from death."[16]

However, I believe these worries based upon the idea that God may be limited in some way are, at best, exaggerated. For they seem to me to be clear non-sequiturs. I would point out here that our investigation has already ruled out logical voluntarism as a viable possibility. Therefore, we've already accepted the idea that God is limited to some degree (i.e., he cannot do the logically impossible). Similarly, remember that one objection against the moral voluntarist was the abhorrent command objection: God cannot turn an obviously immoral action (e.g., rape) into a moral action by willing or commanding it to be so. Given that most theists accept this objection against moral voluntarism, and as I've argued they should also accept a similar objection against logical voluntarism, it seems to me that most theists already accept "limitations" of a sort on God. Similarly, I would conclude that the robust logical non-voluntarist position that claims God is completely unable to affect the entities that constitute the validity of any logical argument seems congruent with these notions that are already accepted by most theists. Thus, the "limitations" that moral non-voluntarism and robust logical non-voluntarism imply concerning divine sovereignty, power, and freedom do not really exacerbate any sort of practical worry that theists like Horton suggest. Rather, the fact that God *must be* logical (as well as the fact that God *must be* moral) should give theists more confidence towards God. So it seems to me that the above sorts of worries are really unfounded and thus not really problematic.

4.2.2 The Ultimacy Problem

Let's now turn to more substantive issues of how the problem of God and abstract objects might relate to robust logical non-voluntarism. For example, philosopher Brian Leftow contends that traditional Western theists acknowledge God to be the *ens realissimum*, i.e., "ultimate reality," or, as is sometimes said, God is "the universal ground of all being."[17] Though this

---

16. Horton, *The Christian Faith*, 235.
17. For a classic and extended treatment of this notion and the Platonic notion of

LOGICAL NON-VOLUNTARISM

may sound a bit vague or mystical, I think Leftow explains the intuition, and its appeal, very clearly:

> It is a common theistic belief that God's existence is not derived from anything else—that "God made the universe, but nobody made God." This belief is bound up, for example with the common theistic belief that God is the real source of the universe. For if something else created God, and then God created the universe, it would seem to most that this other thing was the *real* source of the universe, and God just an intermediary.
>
> Let us put this belief about God's existence a bit more formally: it is part of the ordinary theist's concept of God that no regress of true explanations can go past God's existence, i.e., that when one has traced some phenomenon back to the fact that God exists, one can go no further.[18]

So, following Leftow, holding that "God is the universal ground of all being," is, at the least, the claim that God is the ultimate explanation for *any* existing entity. Theists hold that God is not the intermediary source of just some entities but the "*real* source" of *all* entities. However, given the way Leftow has stated it, it's ambiguous whether this idea rules out the *Timaeus* picture we were presented with earlier.[19] For Plato seems to imply that even though the Divine Craftsman needed the Forms in order to make the physical cosmos, this Craftsman himself is still evidently eternal, i.e., he was not made by something else. So, in a sense, the Divine Craftsman is still the ultimate explanation for Plato's universe. However, in the *Timaeus* the Divine Craftsman still had need of the Platonic Forms as templates for creating the world. So to explain the universe one does have to, in a sense, "go past God's existence" as Leftow says, since the creation of the universe includes, along with the Divine Craftsman, the Platonic Forms as well. On this reading, and I'm sure that this is the worry Leftow has in mind, a *Timaeus*-like picture would be unacceptable to most theists in the Western or Abrahamic tradition. On Plato's account of the universe theists could only say, at the most, that the Divine Craftsman is just *part of* the ultimate explanation. Thus, the *Timaeus* picture contradicts the creation condition of the sovereignty intuition since the Platonic Forms are uncreated, and it

---

"chain of being" see Lovejoy, *The Great Chain of Being*.

18. Brian Leftow, "Is God an Abstract Object?" 584.
19. Thanks to Chris Pincock for bringing this point to my attention.

also contradicts the uniqueness condition of the aseity intuition since the Platonic Forms have *a se* existence in addition to God.

But I think Leftow is suggesting perhaps a deeper difficulty, one that is sometimes called the *ultimacy problem*.[20] This problem arises when the positing of (at least some) abstract objects implies that God's own existence is explained by such objects. To illustrate this problem, consider one kind of abstract object: properties. As we've seen the Platonist story go, abstract objects, like Forms, exist independently of God in a very robust way such that these abstract properties also exist independently of God. Note that God is usually conceived as having properties. He has, for example, the properties of being good, being powerful, being wise, among many others. But if these properties are abstract objects, as sometimes conceived, then God's being is grounded in something other than God, namely these abstract properties. And this would mean that God is not the ultimate explanation of his own self. But, as Leftow states, "theists want all explanations to trace back *to* God, rather than *through* God to some more ultimate context."[21] So the ultimacy problem points out that the existence of at least some abstract objects, like properties in the above example, not only violates the uniqueness of the aseity intuition, but it seems to also invite the idea that God's own being would be dependent upon these objects as well.

But does the ultimacy problem extend to all Platonist theories, including robust logical non-voluntarism? Perhaps the answer to this question depends on what sort of entities the robust logical non-voluntarist opts for here. Let's suppose, for illustration, that a robust logical non-voluntarist takes possible worlds as existing abstract objects in order to secure the fully independent relationship of logical validity. Thus, the logical entailment relation holds because there are an infinite number of possible worlds that make it so. In addition, note that in the Western theistic tradition God is usually taken to be a necessarily existing being. Combined with this possible world picture, this latter claim would mean that God exists at every possible world. In other words, God's necessary existence is explained by claiming that at any possible world that may obtain, God would exist there. But, as Leftow points out, this picture "threatens to make God's existence derive from items independent from Him: the worlds are there

---

20. Coined, as far as I know, by Gould, "The Problem of God and Abstract Objects," 258.

21. Leftow, "Is God an Abstract Object?" 587.

LOGICAL NON-VOLUNTARISM

independently, that He is in all of them entails God's existence."[22] So it appears that a robust logical non-voluntarism that posits possible worlds as abstract objects falls foul of the ultimacy problem. For according to this picture God's necessary being would be grounded by something other than God, namely the abstract possible worlds.[23]

But, despite this example, I believe the robust logical non-voluntarist may not in all cases be saddled with the ultimacy problem. For suppose he or she opts for another kind of abstract object such as positing propositions in order to explain the logical consequence relation. Thus, the robust logical non-voluntarist would claim that the logical entailment relation holds because there is an infinity of propositions such that whenever, for any $\Gamma \vdash \Phi$ (where Φ is some proposition and Γ some set of propositions), the uniform substitution of the non-logical content that renders every member of Γ true also renders Φ true. Does the ultimacy problem arise even here? One might think so if we consider ontological arguments for God's existence. There are many sorts of these arguments but all have the same general structure. Such arguments proceed from some purported logically necessary proposition and endeavor to show that it is a consequence of that proposition that God exists. But, as Richard Swinburne complains, if such an argument were sound, "God would seem less than totally supreme if he depended for his existence on something quite other than God—for instance, on such a general logically necessary principle."[24] Swinburne is suggesting here that if we did have a sound ontological argument for God's existence, and if the above robust logical non-voluntarist's picture were accurate concerning propositions as abstract objects, then this would imply that God's existence is a result of, and thus dependent on, the necessary proposition (or propositions) of this argument.

But I think Swinburne is mistaken and I think this example is unsuccessful in giving us an instance of the ultimacy problem. For one thing, it seems to me that the robust logical non-voluntarist may object there are any sound ontological arguments for God's existence. At the very least, there are surely no such arguments that are undisputed by a good number of philosophers. Ironically, this would be a plus for the *theist* who holds to

22. Ibid., 27.

23. I think it should be obvious that this same problem would arise even if possible worlds were concrete objects. In such a scenario God's necessary existence would be dependent on these concrete possible worlds and so his divine existence would still not be ultimate.

24. Swinburne, *The Christian God*, 145.

robust logical non-voluntarist; for if there are no sound ontological arguments for God's existence, then there is no possibility for God's existence to be dependent upon the proposition(s) of that argument and thus no ultimacy problem.

But if, for the sake of argument, there were a sound ontological argument for God's existence, I still don't believe the ultimacy problem arises here. For it's usually thought that theories that posit propositions see such entities as truth-*bearers*, not truth-*makers*. A typical feature attributed to propositions is that they correspond, in some way, to facts or states of affairs that give the propositions their truth-values. For example, the proposition *Columbus is the capital of Ohio* is true because it corresponds to the fact or state of affairs in the world that makes it true. The proposition does not make the fact or state of affairs true. Rather, the direction of truth-making is reversed: the fact or state of affairs makes the proposition true. Swinburne's complaint is guilty of getting this order backwards as well. If there was a sound ontological argument that necessarily implied the proposition *God exists*, the soundness of the propositions in the argument would only be true because of the facts or states of affairs that made them so. Thus, *God exists* would be true because God himself is the fact or state of affairs that makes that proposition true. So, God's existence would *not* be dependent upon the proposition *God exists* or any of the propositions that made up the supposed ontological argument in question.

So even though the ultimacy problem may arise for certain Platonist theories, it seems that the robust logical non-voluntarist may get around this problem depending on what sort of abstract objects he may posit. However, as we've seen, it's still the case that the existence of abstract objects, of any kind, still violates the uniqueness condition of the aseity intuition, as well as the sovereignty intuition. So let's return to these problems, for I think the robust logical non-voluntarist has larger difficulties than what the ultimacy problem has presented, or may present.

4.2.3 Problems Related to Creatio ex Nihilo

Probably the most outspoken critic of any view that posits abstract objects alongside of God is the theistic philosopher William Lane Craig. The following is a nice rundown of the biggest problems that Craig sees with such views:

LOGICAL NON-VOLUNTARISM

> The chief theological failing of Platonism [i.e., theories that posit the existence of abstract objects] and therefore for its unacceptability for orthodox theists is that Platonism is incompatible with the doctrine of *creatio ex nihilo* and so fundamentally compromises divine aseity. For Platonism posits infinite realms of being which are uncreated by God. The physical universe which has been created by God is an infinitesimal triviality utterly dwarfed by the unspeakable quantity of uncreated beings. Moreover, the metaphysical pluralism entailed by Platonism's denial of *creatio ex nihilo* robs God of His aseity. The divine attribute of existing *a se* is traditionally understood to be a unique perfection of God, the *ens realissimum* (ultimate reality). God alone exists self-sufficiently and independently of all things. All other beings exist *ab alio* and are contingent in their being. By contrast Platonism posits endless infinities of beings, each of which exists *a se* not *ab alio*. God Himself is reduced to but one being among many.[25]

There are at least two issues that Craig brings up here. First, Craig notes that the abstract objects usually appealed to by philosophers almost always imply an infinity of such objects. Craig has all sorts of Platonist theories in mind here, especially those that appeal to numbers or sets. But considering robust logical non-voluntarism alone, Craig's worry still applies since this view also implies an infinity of abstract objects as well. For example, most philosophers take the implication of double negation introduction to be clearly valid. Thus, for any claim *P* it validly implies ~ ~*P*. But if that's the case the following arguments are also valid:

$$
\begin{align}
&(1) &&\sim \sim p \vdash \sim \sim \sim \sim p \\
&(2) &&\sim \sim \sim \sim p \vdash \sim \sim \sim \sim \sim \sim \sim \sim p \\
&(3) \sim \sim \sim \sim \sim \sim \sim \sim p &&\vdash \sim \sim \sim \sim \sim \sim \sim \sim \sim \sim \sim \sim \sim \sim \sim \sim p \\
&\quad\cdot &&\quad\cdot \\
&\quad\cdot &&\quad\cdot \\
&\quad\cdot &&\quad\cdot
\end{align}
$$

As should be obvious, this chain of double negation introduction arguments extends indefinitely. Moreover, the premise of any one of these arguments also implies *every* conclusion in *all* of the arguments after it. Thus, we have several infinities of valid arguments here—and this is with just *one* claim (i.e., *p*) and *one* logical connective (i.e., negation)! Assuming the robust logical non-voluntarist picture, the above would imply that we have infinities of entities (be they propositions, possible worlds, or whatever)

25. Craig, "Nominalism and Divine Aseity," 46.

that make up these arguments. Craig is troubled by this picture claiming that it makes the created physical universe a "triviality" and elsewhere he exclaims that the "profligacy" of this picture "truly takes one's breath away."[26] However, it's not entirely clear to me what problem Craig is exactly pointing to here. As I think his next concern shows, it's not really the number or magnitude of abstract objects that's problematic for the traditional Western theist.

A bigger and clearer problem that Craig highlights is that the existence of abstract objects alongside of God is incompatible with the traditional doctrine of classical theism that God has created *ex nihilo*. The Latin phrase "*creatio ex nihilo*" literally means "creation out of nothing." This doctrine asserts that everything that is created by God, which traditional Western theists hold is everything apart from God, is created from absolutely nothing and thus not from some pre-existent matter or entities of any kind. Craig notes that theories that posit abstract objects usually hold that these objects are uncreated (like Plato's *Timaeus* picture), which also fits with our characterization of robust logical non-voluntarism thus far. So the incompatibility that Craig highlights here with the *creatio ex nihilo* doctrine is an incompatibility with what we've been calling the creation condition of the sovereignty intuition—that everything distinct from God depends on God's creative activity. But even more, Craig claims that the existence of abstract objects also "fundamentally compromises" or "robs" divine aseity. In particular, the worry Craig is pointing to here is that such objects would violate the dependence condition of the sovereignty intuition—such objects are not only not created by God, but also not sustained by him either. Moreover, Craig notes that if there are other entities existing independently of God's creating and sustaining power, then, like Leftow, Craig observes that this would deny the uniqueness condition of the aseity intuition—God is not the *ens realissimum*, or "ultimate reality." (Even just one such entity would count as a problem here; thus showing that Craig's first complaint seems to be beside the point.) Since theories that posit abstract objects violate the sovereignty intuition (i.e., the doctrine of *creatio ex nihilo*) and the aseity intuition, Craig urges that adherents of the Western tradition of theism should not hold such theories, which would include our current offer of robust logical non-voluntarism.

---

26. Copan and Craig, *Creation Out of Nothing*, 173.

I think Craig is accurate in his assessment here. But, given the problems he has pointed out for theists who opt for abstract entities, is there any way for robust logical non-voluntarism to get around them?

4.2.4 Absolute Creationism

Christopher Menzel and Thomas V. Morris are two theistic philosophers who take criticisms, like Craig's concerning God and abstract objects, to be very serious for traditional theism. They suggest a view, dubbed *absolute creationism*, that attempts to respect the traditional sovereignty and aseity intuitions by claiming that God has created *all* entities including even abstract objects.[27] However, this idea is not an entirely new one.

In his *On the Creation of the World*, the first century Jewish philosopher Philo attempted to meld the *Timaeus* account of creation given by Plato with the Genesis account of creation given by Moses. Philo claims that before creating any part of our current physical world God must have had a model for "there could not exist a good imitation without a good model."[28] As we've seen, this is similar to Plato's account of the Divine Craftsman looking to the Platonic Forms in order to create, as when an architect looks at blueprints in order to construct a building. However, Philo also sought to respect traditional commitments of classical theism such as the aseity and sovereignty intuitions. Therefore, he claimed that God first made the model, "conceived by God's intellect" before the imitation, or physical world, was made from the model.[29] So, according to Philo, before creating the world, God first created (i.e., "conceived") a model—something akin to Plato's Forms or something like what philosophers today reference as abstract objects. The consequence of this idea is that since the model is also created, like everything else other than God, it does not violate the sovereignty intuition (at least the creation condition) and since God alone exists independently (i.e., the model apparently does not) it does not violate the aseity intuition either.

---

27. Morris and Menzel, "Absolute Creation." The name "absolute creationism" is perhaps unfortunate given the connotations usually associated with "creationism." But Morris and Menzel's view has nothing to do with the age of the universe or debates about evolution. Rather, the name highlights that God is the ultimate explanation for the existence of anything apart from himself.

28. Philo, *The Works of Philo*, 4.

29. Ibid.

Menzel and Morris' absolute creationist view is very similar to Philo's account above. They write the following:

> [A]ll properties and relations are God's concepts [i.e., abstract objects], the products, or perhaps better, the contents of the divine intellective activity, a causally efficacious or productive sort of divine conceiving. Unlike human concepts, then, which are graspings of properties that exist ontologically distinct from and independent of those graspings, divine concepts are those very properties themselves; and unlike what is assumed in standard Platonism, those properties are not ontologically independent, but rather depend on certain divine activities.[30]

I'll summarize, in my own words, what I take Menzel and Morris to be claiming here. They identify a couple of different kinds of abstract objects as "God's concepts." What these exactly are is unimportant for our purposes. What is important is that Menzel and Morris claim such objects are products of a certain kind of divine creative activity. Unlike human concepts, which are merely "graspings" of abstract objects, Menzel and Morris seem to claim that God's concepts are identical to these abstract objects.[31] Thus, similar to Philo's account, absolute creationism appears to give an account of abstract objects that respects both the uniqueness condition of the aseity intuition—since these abstract objects do not exist *a se* like God—and it appears to respect both conditions of the sovereignty intuition—since these abstract objects are both created and seemingly continually sustained by God. So, *prima facie*, an absolute creationist account of abstract objects appears to overcome the various problems we've seen associated with philosophical accounts of God and abstract objects. Therefore, it seems that this account could be easily co-opted by robust logical non-voluntarism. In broad strokes, such an account would contend that all logical arguments hold their continued and permanent validity independently from God. And this would be so because such arguments are constituted by abstract entities (of some sort) that are identical to divine concepts, which are cre-

---

30. Morris, *Anselmian Explorations*, 166. There is some confusion in the literature whether this view counts as a version of *theistic activism*. In short, theistic activism holds that abstract objects (1) exist, (2) depend on God's creative activity, and (3) are identified with constituents of the divine mind. The question is whether (3) holds true for absolute creationism. Gould, "The Problem of God and Abstract Objects," 265–69 gives a good overall discussion of the moves surrounding this issue.

31. In the next chapter we'll see that there is more than one way to interpret Menzel and Morris' view here.

LOGICAL NON-VOLUNTARISM

ated by God thus getting around the sorts of worries that Craig and other theistic philosophers have put forward.

Overall, I think this is a very interesting view. But it's also interesting that few have been willing to follow Menzel and Morris (and Philo) in their suggestion. The reason being that various objections have been raised against such a view. One such objection is sometimes called the *bootstrapping objection*.[32] Simply stated, the bootstrapping objection points out that the absolute creationist account of God creating (at least certain) abstract objects presupposes that those objects already exist. For example, it doesn't seem that God can create the abstract property of *being powerful* unless he already has the property of *being powerful*. Bootstrapping objectors claim this problem generalizes to other (if not all) abstract objects on Menzel and Morris' view. Therefore, the problem for absolute creationists is to find a way out of this explanatory circle. Many see this as a completely damning problem. But Paul Gould suggests what he takes to be an obvious way out, at least concerning properties. He writes:

> Why not hold that it is only properties distinct from God that are created by God? On this suggestion, all of God's essential properties (that is, divine concepts) exist *a se* as a brute fact within the divine mind, and it is only those properties that are not essentially exemplified by God (that is, necessarily satisfied in God) that are created by God.[33]

This move seems simply *ad hoc* to me. Gould, however, proposes that this is only the case "if there were no independent motivations for thinking abstract objects exist."[34] Gould is suggesting here that there are other reasons sufficient for adopting a view of properties, distinct from God, as real abstract objects. Presumably these reasons are the sorts of theoretic ones shared with non-theistic philosophers who see explanatory power in appealing to abstract objects.

But even if this move is not *ad hoc*, another problem arises as it relates to robust logical non-voluntarism: If God created all abstract objects distinct from himself, including those that constitute logical consequence,

---

32. This problem has been pointed out in various places, such as Bergmann and Brower, "A Theistic Argument against Platonism," 357–86; Gould, "The Problem of God and Abstract Objects"; Craig, "Nominalism and Divine Aseity," et al.
33. Gould, "The Problem of God and Abstract Objects," 268.
34. Ibid.

couldn't God have created any sort of logic he wanted to?[35] In other words, the absolute creationist picture seems to question whether logical consequence is really independent in the way that robust logical non-voluntarism was supposed to preserve. In other words, an absolute creationist account of robust logical non-voluntarism seems to reduce to the position of logical voluntarism, with all its ensuing problems that we saw back in chapter 3. For if God created the abstract objects that constitute logical consequence, and presumably if God was free to choose to create whatever he wanted to create (i.e., his decision to create was a contingent matter), then logical consequence may have been different than what it is now. And as the vacuity objection pointed out in the last chapter against logical voluntarism, this means we cannot justifiably believe God operates in his revelatory communication with the same logic we do, thus calling the intelligibility of special revelation into question.

But perhaps the absolute creationist account of robust logical non-voluntarism could deny the presumption that God could create whatever he wanted to—at least in the domain of certain abstract objects.[36] For example, the absolute creationist might theorize that geometric objects are abstract objects created by God. So, for instance, the Euclidean triangle would be God's creation. Nevertheless, the absolute creationist might suggest that God could not fashion the Euclidean triangle in any old way he wanted to due to the fact that this object has a nature or structure that necessarily constitutes what it is. Thus, God could *not* have made, say, a Euclidean triangle with four sides, or whose inner angles summed to more than or less than 180 degrees. Again, if this were not so, we would be back to a sort of voluntarism and its ensuing problems.

So the absolute creationist rebuttal on offer here is an interpretation of robust logical non-voluntarism that claims God created the abstract entities that constitute logical consequence. But this does not entail logical voluntarism because God could not fashion these abstract objects, and thus the resulting logical consequence relation, in just any arbitrary way he might have wanted to choose. And this is due to the fact that such objects and the logical consequence relation have an intrinsic nature or structure that necessarily constitutes what they are.

Unfortunately, I think this move has its own problems. Foremost, it seems to me that we have a regress issue with this picture. Remember that

---

35. Thanks to Stewart Shapiro for highlighting this point.
36. Thanks to Tamar Rudavsky for pointing out this response.

LOGICAL NON-VOLUNTARISM

the absolute creationist, like Philo, says God must make a good model before being able to make good imitations. And the above suggestion claims that God is not free to make models in just any arbitrary way. Rather, models seem to have an intrinsic nature or structure that necessitates what sort of entities they may be. But this sounds like models (i.e., abstract objects) must follow the pattern of *other* models, or meta-models. For if abstract objects have a certain nature that they must have in order to coherently exist (i.e., to escape voluntaristic implications), then it seems there are other (abstract?) objects that they must be patterned after. And if this is so, we need an explanation of how these meta-models, these higher objects, have the existence and nature that they do. Thus, we have the original problem again that this suggestion was meant to overcome. And unless we're given a different answer, it just leads to a regress of the same.

In this vein, philosopher Greg Welty argues that whatever absolute creationists try to do to overcome this problem only invites other problems that are endemic to their project. For if abstract objects are created by God, one must ask "does God look to something *external* to himself as the exemplar for this particular act of creation? Or does something *internal* to God play this role?"[37] Of course, the absolute creationist believes that creation is not imposed on God from outside of himself. This was the main point of putting forward this view. But Welty clarifies that his question is of a different sort: not "'does something external to God *force God* to create the framework he does?' but rather, 'does something external to God *provide the model for the content of* the framework which God does in fact create?'"[38] Welty claims there are only three possible responses to this question and none of which are favorable to the absolute creationist project, and thus not favorable to the robust logical non-voluntarist picture either.

First response: the absolute creationist could claim that God creates the abstract objects and the model for this act of creation is something external to God. But this suggestion, as we've seen, is clearly a violation of the sovereignty intuition, as well as a violation of the uniqueness condition of the aseity intuition. By way of re-iterating why many traditional Western theists reject this, Alfred Freddoso comments:

> [S]omeone might point out that Platonic entities have traditionally been construed as exemplars (or paradigms or models) according to which created things are fashioned. But if such exemplars were

37. Welty, "Theistic Conceptual Realism," 198.
38. Ibid., 199.

wholly distinct from God and independent of God, then his creative activity would be constrained by standards which originate outside the divine intellect. In that case God in creating would be more like the imitator who copies an original painting than like the creative genius who produces the masterpiece "on his own."[39]

Given that absolute creationists like Menzel and Morris (and perhaps Philo) identify themselves as traditional Western theists, this first response is unacceptable.

Second response: the absolute creationist could claim that God creates abstract objects and the model for this act of creation is something internal to God. This seems to be closer to Menzel and Morris's view when they claim that "all properties and relations are God's concepts," or "divine concepts are those very properties themselves," or "we characterize properties as God's concepts."[40] These appear to be straightforward identity claims. Properties and relations are two kinds of abstract objects and they are identical with divine concepts. But how are we to understand divine concepts here?

We were told that "divine intellective activity [is] a causally efficacious or productive sort of divine conceiving."[41] Thus, there is a causal relation between the divine intellective activity and the existence of abstract objects. In addition, "properties are not ontologically independent, but rather depend on certain divine activities."[42] So there is a dependence relation between abstract objects and divine activities. And it seems clear from Menzel and Morris's discussion that they see this dependence relation as causal. Welty suggests that the most plausible way to think about this picture is by analogy with the thinker/thought relation in human beings. Thus, suggests Welty, the best way to understand this concerning God is that "he thinks the thoughts he does because he *purposely intends* to think those thoughts; that is, he wills to think them."[43] Even as human thoughts are created by the internal and intentional human activity of thinking, so abstract objects are created by God's active thinking, which is internal to God. Applied to robust logical non-voluntarism, Menzel and Morris' view would suggest that whatever kind of abstract objects constitute logical consequence, they

---

39. Alfred Freddoso, "Review of *Does God Have a Nature?*" 80.
40. Morris and Menzel, 166.
41. Ibid.
42. Ibid.
43. Welty, "Theistic Conceptual Realism," 193.

LOGICAL NON-VOLUNTARISM

are identical with divine concepts that result from God's intentional active thought.

However, as we've already discussed, this leads to a regress. For if abstract objects are God's concepts, then one can naturally ask, "Does God create his concepts according to his concept of what he is to create?" Or, as Welty asks, "in general, if abstract objects are divine ideas and God creates abstract objects, then what divine idea is exemplified in (i.e., serves as the exemplar for) the act of creating the abstract object?"[44] It seems no answer can be given without the same sort of question arising.

But an absolute creationist may try to get out of answering this dilemma with a third response, claiming that God creates abstract objects but that this act has no exemplar or model. In other words, the absolute creationist tries to cut off the regress by claiming that abstract objects are created *sui generis*. This may seem like a cheat, but I believe it fits well with an adherence to the traditional doctrine of *creatio ex nihilo*. However, anotherproblem arises here for the absolute creationist in that this response would be a major reconfiguration of his view. Remember the absolute creationist claimed that abstract objects are the result of the intentional thoughts of God. But if God created X without a model that he intentionally worked from, then this suggests that X, though a creation of God, is not an *intentional* creation of God. In essence, this response harks back to neo-Platonic views of emanation: that there are objects whose existence is causally dependent upon God but God did not intentionally bring about; they are merely emanated from God with no reference to (or perhaps even in spite of) God's will. This is, of course, an abandonment of the traditional doctrine of divine creation where everything created by God is the result of his divine intentions to do so. But more importantly, in this context, it would be more than a mere modification to absolute creationism. As Welty puts it, this response is equivalent to: "God doesn't *create* abstract objects at all."[45] As Welty words it, this response turns the view into an absolute emanationist picture, not an absolute *create*-ionist one.

4.2.5 Summary Assessment of Platonic Logical Non-Voluntarism

Let me now summarize our discussion of robust or Platonic logical non-voluntarism. We saw that Plato's *Timeaus* picture of the Divine Craftsman

44. Ibid., 200.
45. Ibid.

was very suggestive for logical non-voluntarism. In the same way that the Divine Craftsman could not affect the Platonic Forms, so this view claims that God cannot and does not affect logical entailment and all of the arguments that obey it. This comparison suggested that logical arguments are constituted by abstract objects. So this construal of logical non-voluntarism claims that the reason the validity of logical arguments is independent of God's power and being is because all such arguments are constituted by abstract objects (whatever those objects might be). Given that such objects are resistant to divine omnipotence (commands or will, or creating or sustaining power), the logical arguments constituted by them are also so resistant. But we've seen various problems that make this view unacceptable for many traditional Western theists. In general, every Platonist theory, including absolute creationism, violates, in some way, either the aseity intuition or the sovereignty intuition of traditional theism by (1) making God dependent upon abstract objects (thus violating the aseity intuition), or (2) making abstract objects uncreated (thus violating the creation condition), or (3) making abstract objects continued existence independent of God (thus violating the dependence and uniqueness conditions). Since these intuitions, with their included conditions, are core beliefs of traditional Western theism, theists in this tradition should reject robust logical non-voluntarism.

However, at this point, one wonders does logical non-voluntarism really need to appeal to such metaphysically rich notions as abstract objects? Maybe the *Timaeus* picture has simply misled us. For logical non-voluntarism seems to primarily be a theory about dependency, not ontology.[46] Couldn't logical entailment be construed as independent of God apart from appealing to abstract objects, and thus still affirm the thesis of logical non-voluntarism? This seems to me to be a *prima facie* promising possibility. Moreover, it's an alternative that actually more than one theistic philosopher has opted for. Let's investigate whether such a conception of logical non-voluntarism can do any better than its Platonistic cousin.

4.3 LOGICAL NON-VOLUNTARISM AND NOMINALISM

I describe a Platonist theory, generally, as one that appeals to abstract objects to explain some phenomenon. For many analytic philosophers, especially,

---

46. Much thanks goes to Scott Brown, again, for helping me to see this point more clearly.

LOGICAL NON-VOLUNTARISM

abstract objects are usually appealed to in order to explain some domain of discourse. Nominalist theories are described in various ways, but always in contrast with Platonist theories such as robust logical non-voluntarism. Thus, for my purposes here I define a nominalist theory, generally, as any theory that claims that some discourse in view can be fully explained *without* appealing to abstract entities. So, even when a particular discourse might reference things that are traditionally understood to be abstract objects (like possible worlds or propositions), a nominalist theory would intentionally interpret these words as *not* referencing abstract objects.

In the same way, given the problems we've seen with robust logical non-voluntarism, it seems to me that a logical non-voluntarist might also claim that logical discourse can be explained without reference to abstract entities of any kind. If this view of logical non-voluntarism can be made good, it would follow that logical consequence is *not* dependent upon, or constituted by, abstract objects but be dependent upon non-abstract objects of some kind. Moreover, as a form of non-voluntarism, whatever these objects may be, they must still exist independent of God's control and being. Call this picture of logic *lean* or *nominalist* logical non-voluntarism.

The obvious upshot of this form of logical non-voluntarism is that since it does not appeal to abstract objects, then it seems to avoid all of the problems that come from violating the aseity or sovereignty intuitions that burdened robust logical non-voluntarism. However, some immediate questions arise: Does lean logical non-voluntarism successfully explain logical discourse as well as respecting commonly held intuitions concerning logic? Likewise, does nominal logical non-voluntarism explain how the non-abstract entities that make up logic (whatever these may be) are independent of God's being or his ability to change or modify? In sum, are there any successful theistic logical nominalist theories out there?

Despite all the problems we've laid out in §4.2 above, Platonist theories of all kinds are still very popular among theistic philosophers. In fact, I know of only two such philosophers who could be categorized as logical nominalists. In the remainder of this chapter we will primarily investigate one of these theistic philosopher's attempts to construe logical discourse as a nominalist theory. As I believe we'll see, there are serious problems as to whether any theory of nominalism can adequately explain logical discourse as well as respect common logical intuitions. Moreover, I think lean logical non-voluntarism does not successfully protect the independence of logic as logical non-voluntarism desires and this seems to be a problem for any sort of logical nominalism one might put forward. Let's now investigate these attempts to ground logical non-voluntarism in nominalistic fashion.

4.3.1 Craig and Nominalism

As we've seen above, William Lane Craig takes the existence of abstract objects, of any kind, to be problematic because it violates core intuitions of traditional Western theism. Given these problems, his writings have investigated and suggested various views that attempt to evade any sort of Platonic theory with Western theism.[47] We've already looked at some of these attempts in §4.2 above. Craig's overwhelming conclusion is clear: there is no way to circumvent the problems that abstract objects create for traditional theistic belief. Therefore, he claims that traditional Western theists must opt for nominalism. This is a sweeping claim. Craig gives this recommendation in full generality: Platonism is *never* acceptable for the traditional theist in *any* domain. Thus, even though Craig never discusses the specific implications for logic, his recommendation implies a full endorsement of logical nominalism as well.

However, it must be noted, up to the time the research for this book was done, Craig has done little to offer any sort of positive nominalist proposal of any kind.[48] Up to now his discussions have taken the following general outline:

(1*) Traditional theists must take either a Platonist or nominalist construal of any discourse.

(2*) Due to various problems, such theists should reject a Platonist construal of any such discourse.

(3*) So, traditional theists must have a nominalist construal of any discourse.

But I believe that this conclusion is *too* sweeping in that discussions concerning Platonism and nominalism should be taken on a subject-by-subject basis. For example, suppose we discovered a nominalist theory of reference and predication that could explain well our talk of properties. If this was

---

47. For these various attempts and their problems see Copan and Craig, *Creation Out of Nothing*, and Craig, "Nominalism and Divine Aseity," 43–64 and his "Propositional Truth—Who Needs It?," 355–64. Also, see Gould, "The Problem of God and Abstract Objects," 255–74 for a good general overview of the available options.

48. At the time of this publication Craig's *God Over All* is still forthcoming.

LOGICAL NON-VOLUNTARISM

indeed our conclusion, I don't see what this state of affairs would have to do, at least directly, with whether nominalism or Platonism should be adopted to explain, say, mathematical discourse, or modal discourse, or even logical discourse. Even if nominalism could explain our property talk, that does not necessarily imply that nominalism can explain our math, modal, or logic talk.

Since Craig's criticisms against abstract objects are fully general, applying to even a Platonist construal of logical non-voluntarism, it follows that Craig's recommendation of nominalism implies an endorsement of lean logical non-voluntarism (like most theistic philosophers he denies universal possibilism and thus logical voluntarism as well). Nevertheless, regardless of the problems we saw with robust logical non-voluntarism, it seems to me that we are owed at least something of a theory of logical nominalism before we endorse a nominalist construal of logical non-voluntarism. Fortunately, another theistic philosopher has done some work toward that goal.

4.3.2 Swinburne and Logical Nominalism

Theistic philosopher Richard Swinburne has developed a view of logic that fits squarely with logical nominalism. His understanding of logic arises from his treatment of logical necessity, or what some philosophers call "broadly logical necessity."[49] It is clear from his discussion of this issue that "broadly logical necessity" includes what I'm calling logical entailment or logical consequence. According to Swinburne, logical necessity is "not a very deep feature of the world."[50] He claims that at least one major reason that it has been supposed so is that logical necessity has often been thought to characterize abstract entities like propositions, possible worlds, and the like—a picture that we are already familiar with. As I pointed out with the ultimacy problem above (see §4.2.2 of this chapter), one reason Swinburne seems motivated to reject this Platonist picture, at least for logic, is because of the implication this view has for God.[51] However, it's interesting to note

---

49. Since Kripke, "Naming and Necessity," 253–55 and Plantinga, *The Nature of Necessity*, chapter 1.

50. Swinburne, *The Christian God*, 96.

51. Benjamin Murphy suggests similar in his "Are God's Hands Tied By Logic?" 4.

that Swinburne seems to be mainly motivated by two other issues in adopting his nominalist picture of logical necessity.[52]

First, Swinburne seems uncomfortable with the implications that logical Platonism would have for our world. He clearly sees that if logical Platonism is true, then this means there is a world of abstract entities that governs, in some sense, the nature and behavior of ordinary mundane things in our world. For logical necessities and relations of the abstract world have consequences for how things must be in our physical world. For example, if modus ponens is a valid logical argument constituted by abstract entities in some Platonic realm, then it seems that in our world (when it's true) that if it rains the sidewalk will be wet, then when it rains, necessarily, it is the case that the sidewalk is wet. Swinburne rightly states that, "Logical necessities, claims the Platonist, make it inevitable that the world is one sort of place rather than another—by a hard inexorable necessity than which there is none harder."[53] Though Swinburne does not give an explicit argument against this point, it's clear from the tone of his discussion that he is bothered in some way by this "other-worldly" control or effect on our world.

The second reason that motivates Swinburne to reject logical Platonism is more explicit though. Swinburne clearly has a philosophical commitment to theoretical parsimony. He claims: "There is no need to postulate a timeless realm [of abstract entities] since everything that the Platonist adduces as grounds for adopting his way of talking can be redescribed without the need for it. I shall argue that the nominalist is basically correct."[54] This claim is worded generally. But Swinburne has logical Platonism particularly in sight so he goes on to argue specifically for a form of logical nominalism. Swinburne defines logical nominalism as the view that logic is mainly concerned with facts about how humans use language. Swinburne explicitly claims:

> [T]he only logical relations and necessary truths that we have any reason to believe to exist are put forwards on the basis of facts of language that can be described without this apparatus [i.e., abstract objects]—in terms of how speakers of a language treat

---

52. Swinburne, *The Christian God*, chapter 5 and his "In Defence of Logical Nominalism," 311–30.

53. Swinburne, *The Christian God*, 105–6.

54. Ibid., 106.

its sentences, together with facts about the referential context in which those sentences are used.[55]

Swinburne builds up his view of logical nominalism with what he takes to be the basic notions of negation, self-contradiction, and minimal entailment. He claims that these notions belong only to token sentences. Swinburne's overall picture is not really all that novel and so is similar to other types of logical nominalism; therefore I don't see the need to go into too much detail here on how his view operates.[56] But, basically, Swinburne claims that valid logical arguments "are simply generalizations about language."[57] He summarizes:

> Logic . . . concerns only relations of public sentences to each other. It codifies the rules for which sentences commit their utterer to which other sentences, it binds together a packet of sentences to which a speaker is committed by a given sentence. Logic is thus concerned with human behavior—a matter of psychology; not of how we reason casually, but of which minimal entailments we would publicly recognize if pushed.[58]

For example, on Swinburne's view, the valid logical argument of modus ponens is just one of the ways that we've agreed to be committed in our discourse. So, if someone makes a claim of "If p then q" to be true and also claims "p" as true, then we believe this person is committed to "q" as being true as well. Logical necessity is thus redefined as, not being

---

55. Ibid. By appealing to "facts about the referential context" Swinburne admits that this is not a pure, but a modified, nominalism since it's a theory that appeals to more than just token words or token sentences. However, as I defined at the beginning of §4.3, I take a nominalist theory to be one that does *not* appeal to abstract objects. Therefore, despite Swinburne's appeal to "referential context," his view of logic still counts as a purely nominalist theory by my definition.

56. In fact, Swinburne's account seems to be a classic example of psychologism—logic is the study of human inferential practice—which is almost universally rejected in logic today due to the historic criticisms of Frege and Husserl. See Hill, *Word and Object in Husserl, Frege, and Russell*, 7–11. However, a minority of philosophers, including myself, finds the charge of psychologism to be fairly vague and overblown. Philosopher Dale Jacquette has been a seemingly lone voice in the wilderness in this respect. See his "The Dialectics of Psychologism," v–vii, "Psychologism the Philosophical Shibboleth," 312–31 and his "Psychologism Revisited in Logic, Metaphysics, and Epistemology," 261–78 for detailed discussions of the real, and not so real, threats of psychologism. Little of my criticisms here against Swinburne overlap with these issues though.

57. Swinburne, *The Christian God*, 108.

58. Ibid., 114.

a come-what-may relation between abstract entities, but as the rules of a linguistic game such that if someone does not "play" by the rules of the game we would conclude that this person is either confused, ignorant, or cognitively deficient in some way of the linguistic rules.

In similar fashion, Swinburne holds that the logical nominalist can still *use* the language of logical Platonism—such as "propositions," "possible worlds," etc.—as long as such words are understood as shorthand, or stand-in fictions, with no Platonist commitments. In this sense, Swinburne admits that logical Platonist talk is useful, but ultimately dispensable

On Swinburne's view, it should be clear here that if logic is concerned with just how people use language, then logical rules are just as conventional as grammatical rules. In other words, since grammatical rules differ from language to language, logical rules just happen to be one of the ways that people have decided to understand the modal relations between their words and sentences. Thus, on Swinburne's view, the relation of logical entailment is just a description of convention established by human usage. Individual valid logical arguments are just characterizations of linguistic conventional patterns.[59]

4.3.2.1 *Problems for Swinburne's Account*

Let's now return to our overall dialectic. Following the broad outline of Craig's argument, we saw above that theistic philosophers and logicians can either construe logic along Platonist or nominalist lines. Given the

---

59. In some ways, Swinburne's view is incredibly naive. Inferentialists—philosophers who emphasize the role of inferential practice for philosophy of logic—understand that the sort of view that Swinburne is advocating here is far too sparse. Note the following quote from inferentialist Robert Brandom: "Even if, to begin with, attention is restricted to inferential properties, it is clear that not just any notion of correctness of inference will do as a rendering of the sort of content we take our claims and beliefs to have. A semantically adequate notion of correct inference must generate an acceptable notion of conceptual content. But such a notion must fund the idea of *objective* truth conditions and so of *objectively* correct inferences. Such properties of judgment and inference outrun actual attitudes of taking or treating judgments and inferences as correct. They are determined by how things actually are, independently of how they are taken to be. Our cognitive attitudes must ultimately answer to these attitude-transcendent facts" (Brandom, *Making it Explicit*, 137). At minimum, Brandom recognizes that focusing purely upon inferential practice *alone* is not enough for establishing objective truth conditions and thus objectively correct inferences (i.e., inferences that match valid logical argument forms). Though I don't develop this criticism exactly in this way here, a later criticism of Leftow, which I do discuss, seems to get at some of the same issues.

LOGICAL NON-VOLUNTARISM

problems that arise with abstract objects in relation to God, we concluded that a traditional Western theist should reject logical Platonism. However, I pointed out that a theist should not so quickly adopt Craig's proposal for nominalism—of any sort—without a theory. Swinburne has offered a nominalist theory of logic. Is this a successful account of logic? And if so, does it work as a metaphysical account of logical non-voluntarism?

Unfortunately, I think Swinburne's theory is a very poor account of logic. Brian Leftow, for one, has taken up criticisms specifically against Swinburne's logical nominalism, only two of which I will focus on here.[60] Though I only gave a rough summary of Swinburne's view, Leftow notes that Swinburne never actually gives an explicit description of his notion of "minimal entailment." So Leftow provides one. For any language L, minimal entailment is:

> (ME) L-sentence r_1 minimally entails L-sentence r_2 iff most L-speakers would take L's rules to commit someone to asserting r_1 to r_2.[61]

But Leftow highlights that there is a problem with this description, namely that the word "most" creates problems for Swinburne's account.

> [T]here does not appear to be a precise minimum per cent of the speaking population at which it becomes the case that "most" speakers are primed to assent that the rules commit someone asserting r_1 to r_2. Rather, there are cases when it is clear that enough are primed to constitute 'most' (99.9 per cent), cases where it is clear that not enough are (4 per cent), and cases in a middle zone where it is just unclear whether there are enough to be "most" in this context (56 percent?). So some account of the semantics of vagueness must fill out our understanding of Swinburne's theory.[62]

Leftow's main point here is that on Swinburne's view of logic, we cannot always clearly know when r_1 minimally entails r_2. The inherent vagueness in relying upon what most people would affirm leaves the validity of many logical arguments up in the air. (Not to mention that this means we have to do statistical analysis in order to determine the validity of an argument!)

---

60. Leftow takes on Swinburne's overall view of modality, something that I'm not interested in doing here.

61. Leftow, "Swinburne on Divine Necessity," 143. In a footnote, Leftow speaks of a personal correspondence with Swinburne, thus I think we can conclude that Swinburne finds (ME) to be an acceptable characterization of his notion of minimal entailment.

62. Ibid.

This is a far cry from our usual understanding of logical necessity. However, in the spirit of philosophical charitableness, Leftow attempts to supply Swinburne's account with the materials it needs.

Swinburne's notion of minimal entailment assumes, or includes, a notion of rules that commit a speaker of a language to other sentences in the language. Thus, Leftow claims that this notion of minimal entailment encapsulates the following notion of determinate commitment:

> (DC) If the rules commit someone to P, it is determinate that they commit him/her to P.[63]

I think (DC) is fairly self-evident, so I won't provide Leftow's full argumentation for it. But, in short, Leftow believes it is implausible that there can be rule commitment without determinate commitment. Note then, that on Swinburne's account of logic it follows from (DC) that where the rules are indeterminate, there are no minimal entailments. Once he makes the vagueness in this notion clear, Leftow goes on to investigate whether Swinburne's account of logic can be saved by any of the major theories of vagueness. It turns out, as Leftow argues, that Swinburne's account of logic is either incompatible with any of these theories, or the vagueness theory in question is just implausible.

For example, supplying Swinburne's logical view with a supervaluationist or "gap" theory of vagueness, the middle zone in question that most speakers are primed to assent to some particular argument's validity would be neither true nor false (i.e., there is no fact of the matter). But given (DC), this is incompatible with Swinburne's view of logic. So a supervaluationist account of vagueness will not help Swinburne. Another example, an epistemicist account of vagueness would claim, despite appearances, that there is some precise cut-off percentage that definitely determines what arguments speakers would or would not assent to the validity of. However, epistemicism is massively implausible. Leftow looks at a couple of other theories of vagueness with similar negative results.

Leftow concludes from his investigation that there is no major theory of vagueness that is either plausible or compatible with Swinburne's notion of minimal entailment. Since the notion of minimal entailment is central to Swinburne's nominalist account of logic, it follows that his account fails. Leftow thinks this result is unsurprising since we have strong intuitions

---

63. Ibid., 144.

LOGICAL NON-VOLUNTARISM

that logical necessity is about more than just what most people will assent to. As Leftow states:

> [E]ntailment does not actually turn on what "most" speakers are primed to say. Standard modal accounts of entailment define it in non-vague terms. They have found wide acceptance because there are widespread intuitions that entailment is *not* a vague concept. On a standard strict-implication account, P entails Q just if it cannot be the case that P is true while Q is false. This is no vague matter. . . .
>
> Nor does entailment seem a matter of convention. It may be a matter of convention what "P" and "Q" say. But given sufficient conventions to settle what they say, it is not a matter of convention whether it cannot be the case that P is true while Q is false.[64]

But Leftow pushes further problems upon Swinburne's account by drawing attention to Swinburne's understanding of the law of non-contradiction (LNC). Swinburne states:

> Philosophers postulate propositions as what is meant by some sentence, and then endow these with (sharp) properties. A sentence means either this proposition or that one. They decide that they are either true or false. So contradictions must be false . . . the "impossibility" of [a contradiction being true] is a consequence of the understanding of "contradiction" in this framework. In ordinary language, "it is raining and it isn't raining" can be true. That's why it doesn't express a proposition of the form "p & ~p" . . . the necessity arises from the framework that we have . . . created; the rules of classical logic as opposed to human language.[65]

Based on the above, Leftow agrees that we do sometimes use ordinary-language constructions like "it is raining and it isn't raining" to say something true—in this example to express that the weather is a borderline case, perhaps misting.[66] Such examples, claims Swinburne, show that when we insist that contradictory sentences cannot say anything true in our logic, we are just adopting a convention to treat such sentences differently. But, as Leftow points out, this explanation sits ill with Swinburne's overall account

---

64. Ibid., 145–46.

65. Swinburne (private correspondence), cited in ibid., 146, note 13.

66. Or, a somewhat common phenomenon when I lived in Florida, on some occasions I could look out the windows on one side of my house and see that it was raining (and sometimes it was quite the downpour) while looking out the windows on the opposite side of the house it was bright and sunny!

THE LOGIPHRO DILEMMA

of logical laws being "generalizations about language"[67] or "of logical relations between sentences recognizable in many particular cases."[68] For, if we do in fact violate the LNC in ordinary speech, then including it as a valid argument form in our logic textbooks would mean that logic is not really a generalization of what most people would affirm, as Swinburne so claims. Moreover, Leftow argues against Swinburne that sentence constructions like "it is raining and it isn't raining" are not affirmations of contradictory sentences.

> If someone says "it's raining and it's not" and I say "You've contradicted yourself," the reply will surely be: "Not really. You're missing the point." Ordinary speakers do not think that this is both a contradiction and true, even speakers innocent of formal logic. They take it as a striking way to say something true indirectly; the conventions are not that contradictory sentences are sometimes true, but that false sentences can sometimes be used as a way to suggest true ones. There is a perfectly good ordinary-language way to say what someone who tokens "it is raining and it is not raining" wants to suggest which does not violate [LNC]—viz. "it's misting."[69]

Given the plausibility of this explanation, such utterances are not affirmations of contradictory sentences, which in turn takes away much of the steam that Swinburne used to claim that the LNC, like all valid logical arguments, is simply an adopted logical convention.

Leftow seems to focus upon this issue because he claims, and I agree, that "we have strong intuitions that [LNC's] truth does not depend on us."[70] Therefore, unless Swinburne can give us a good argument for the conventionality of LNC, it seems we should go with our strong intuitions concerning logic first. The closest Swinburne comes to giving such an argument is that he claims contradictions lack "ultimate sense": if the consequences of sentences include an explicit contradiction,

> although it is prima facie conceivable that these sentences be true, it is not ultimately conceivable; they only make initial sense. They do not make *ultimate sense*. [They are] not conceivable by

---

67. Swinburne, *The Christian God*, 108.
68. Ibid., 109.
69. Leftow, "Swinburne on Divine Necessity," 147. He uses the equivalent "principle of non-contradiction," i.e., PNC, instead of my use of LNC.
70. Ibid., 148.

someone who begins to fill out . . . what a world would be like in which [they were] true.[71]

But this notion of inconceivability is problematic for Swinburne. If inconceivability is just being unable to imagine or picture a world that would make a contradiction true, then Swinburne's account is in trouble. For example, as Leftow points out, we can't imagine or picture the null-set's existence or non-existence. But regardless of our cognitive or imaginative abilities, the null-set surely either exists or it does not. Thus, inconceivability does not seem sufficient for logical impossibility, or for lacking sense. Leftow concludes that if being inconceivable is just entailing a contradiction, it can't explain Swinburne's claim that contradictions lack ultimate sense. On the other hand, if being inconceivable is something other than entailing a contradiction, there is another problem for LNC's supposed conventionality. Swinburne affirmed that contradictions could not be true because we cannot conceive of them being true. But this is presumably something beyond our control. Since conventions are within our control (i.e., we establish them), it follows that the LNC cannot be a matter of convention.

In summary, I believe we can conclude that Swinburne's nominalist explanation of logical necessity is not a successful account of logic.[72] Along with Brian Leftow, we've investigated at least two big problems for this account. Swinburne's logical nominalism fails to successfully explain logical discourse and it violates common intuitions concerning logic. And as I think is clear, if an account of logic fails as a successful or plausible explanation, then it surely won't help as a non-voluntarist explanation of the relationship between God and logic.

But this is only one version of logical nominalism. It does not follow that there are no other successful versions of logical nominalism that the logical non-voluntarist may appeal to. Are there any other better nominalist logical theories?

---

71. Swinburne, *The Christian God*, 111, 113.

72. To be fully fair, I note here that I gave a version of this section of the chapter at the Evangelical Philosophical Society annual meeting in November of 2013. Richard Swinburne was present at that paper. He was very gracious and admitted that the account of logic he gave in his 1994 *The Christian God* was insufficient and was seeking to bolster it. However, I have not read any recently published updated account.

4.3.3 Problems for Logical Nominalism (Generally)

I believe any account of logical nominalism has little hope of being any more successful. I won't be so bold as to offer an argument that claims to defeat every form of logical nominalism. Rather, I'll look at two other classic approaches that attempt to establish a thoroughly nominalist account of logic.[73] I'll then show how a similar criticism applies to both forms, as well as Swinburne's own nominalist account. I believe this will be good evidence for inductively concluding that any form of logical nominalism will most likely suffer from the same problem and thus logical nominalism is not available to the logical non-voluntarist as a plausible way of construing the relationship between God and logic.

4.3.3.1 Empirical Logical Nominalism.

One nominalist account of logic that seems initially quite plausible is the idea that we establish valid logical arguments by experience. For example, we might claim that we have good reason to believe that if it rains, the sidewalk will be wet and since it is raining, this indeed logically implies that the sidewalk is wet because we have seen many cases of this form—where "if p then q" and "p is the case"—and every time it turned out that "q is the case." This sort of approach seems straightforwardly intuitive. Unfortunately though, it faces one overwhelming obstacle: the very process of confirming a logical generalization by examination of its instances presupposes at least some logic. For instance, in the above example it seems that one must use modus ponens in order to confirm modus ponens, as well as the law of universal introduction. Therefore, empirical logical nominalism seems to beg the question in establishing logic: experientially, you need logic to establish logic.

More modern forms of empirical-type logical nominalism have not fared any better. In W. V. Quine's work logic is empirically confirmed as part of its place in the seamless whole of our best scientific theory[74]:

> A self-contained theory which we can check with experience includes, in point of fact, not only its various theoretical hypotheses

---

73. This section is highly indebted to Maddy, *Second Philosophy*, 202–6.

74. It could be that Quine abandoned this view later. See Maddy, "Three Forms of Naturalism," 437–59 for an examination of Quine's development of his views.

LOGICAL NON-VOLUNTARISM

of so-called natural science but also such portions of logic and mathematics as it makes use of.[75]

Given that logic is part of this overall theory, Quine believes that if we are presented with some recalcitrant datum, we could choose to revise even the valid laws of logic:

> Revision even of the logical law of excluded middle has been proposed as a means of simplifying quantum mechanics; and what difference is there in principle between such a shift and the shift whereby Kepler superseded Ptolemy, or Einstein Newton, or Darwin Aristotle.[76]

For Quine, the supposed necessity of logic just arises from its centrally located place in our "webs" of belief (i.e., the complex and interrelated epistemic relations between all of our beliefs). Centrally located beliefs are thought to be insulated from sharp empirical input at the sensory periphery of the web, where such beliefs are regularly revised due to new empirical input. But, as Quine says, logic can be revised if enough recalcitrant data (i.e., enough contrary empirical experiences) pushes us to do so. But, similar to the prior approach, it's hard to see how revision, in light of recalcitrant data, does not presuppose some logic—at minimum the law of non-contradiction (LNC). For how does one know that there is conflicting data unless one assumes the LNC?

Though this is primarily an epistemological point, I think it's clear that highlighting this problem shows that an empirical approach provides no help in establishing that logical arguments are constituted by non-abstract entities as logical nominalism claims. Therefore, since the empirical testing of the validity of logical arguments cannot be done without presupposing at least some of those arguments as already existing, an empirical approach to logic provides no help in establishing logical nominalism either.

4.3.3.2 Conventional Logical Nominalism.

Another nominalist account of logic, one that was very popular at one time, is what we might call conventional logical nominalism. This view is fairly close to Swinburne's account. Conventional logical nominalism claims "that we are free to adopt any logic we want to without coming into conflict

---

75. Quine, *The Ways of Paradox*, 121.
76. Quine, *From a Logical Point of View*, 43.

with any pre-existing facts, that we choose the logic we have for its various pragmatic virtues, that we both create and come to know the logical truths through this act of decision."[77] Quine is often credited with the fatal argument against conventional logical nominalism. As we saw illustrated earlier (see §4.2.3 of this chapter) the number of valid logical arguments is infinite. Since we are finite beings, we obviously cannot list them all. Therefore, a logical conventionalist must give a finite list of general arguments from which we can derive all of the rest. But, as Quine points out:

> Each of these conventions in general, announcing the truth of every one of an infinity of statements conforming to a certain description; derivation of the truth of any specific statement from the general convention thus requires a logical inference.... In a word, the difficulty is that if logic is to proceed *mediately* from conventions, logic is needed for inferring logic from the conventions.[78]

According to Quine, it seems that we must presuppose at least some valid logical arguments in order to be able to list all of the other valid logical arguments, as conventionalism so requires. In other words, logical conventionalism seems to assume some logical arguments while simultaneously claiming that all such arguments are simply matters of conventions. (Given the criticism against Quine's empirical view of logic, it is ironic that Quine points out a similar problem for conventional logical nominalism.)

4.3.3.3 Overall Problem for Logical Nominalism.

It's interesting to note that Swinburne's nominalist account also suffers from this very same problem. One of Swinburne's former students, philosopher Benjamin Murphy, argues that any possible language must operate within the bounds of certain necessary truths, including the necessary truths of valid logical arguments.[79] He thus concludes that it is no accident, generalization, or convention that we have arrived at affirming the validity of the logical arguments that we do. For the validity of argument forms does not seem to be based upon contingent truths about human decisions but based upon necessary logical truths. In essence, Murphy is arguing that at least some logic must be presupposed in order for people to affirm the valid-

---

77. Maddy, *Second Philosophy*, 204.
78. Quine, *The Ways of Paradox*, 103, 104.
79. See Murphy, "Are God's Hands Tied by Logic?" 6–9.

ity of other argument forms. Brian Leftow makes a similar point against Swinburne:

> Convention comes in at the level of what sentences say what. But once it is determinate what they say, whether we can conceive what they say is a fact about our powers of conception. We do not determine what these are. Our natures, not our language, impose their limits: it is up to us what sentences say what, but it is not up to us what is conceivable to us, and so it is not up to us what conceivable situations we can use sentences to express. If narrow logical modalities are relative to anything, then, they are relative to our natures, not our conventions.[80]

I'll not take the time to trace out Leftow's argument, but he goes on to claim that our natures are dependent on, what he calls, an "absolute modality." In short, Leftow claims that our natures are dependent upon deeper necessities beyond conventions or generalizations, which include the valid arguments of logic. If this is correct, then our "choice" of logic is constrained by logic. So, again, we see the same criticism brought against Swinburne as other forms of logical nominalism: logic must be presupposed in affirming logic.

Given that all of the forms of logical nominalism we have looked at here suffer from the same problem, it is reasonable to conclude that most any form of logical nominalism will have the same sort of problem. Therefore, I inductively conclude that logical nominalism is a problematic account of logic. It does not serve as a successful account of logical discourse. And moreover, given our main topic, if it's not a successful account of logic, then it also cannot serve the logical non-voluntarist in their explanation of the relationship between God and logic. A lean account of logical non-voluntarism will not work.

4.3.4 Summary Assessment of Nominalist Logical Non-Voluntarism

But one might object that all of this argumentation concerning logical nominalism is completely beside the point for logical non-voluntarism. For, as I've already pointed out, logical non-voluntarism is a theory primarily about dependence and independence relations, not a theory primarily about ontology. However, as I've tried to argue, what one theorizes about ontology will more than likely have implications about dependency or independency.

80. Leftow, "Swinburne on Divine Necessity," 148.

Nevertheless, I'll take the above criticism seriously in the following way. For the sake of argument, let's imagine that all of the above criticisms against nominalist accounts of logic were overcome. In other words, let's assume that there exists some nominalist account of logic that successfully explains logical discourse *and* also adequately explains our widely held intuitions concerning logic. If this were the case, would the logical non-voluntarist then have a successful basis for claiming that the validity of the logical consequence relation is fully independent of God's will or commands? And would this also show that logic is truly independent (ontologically or otherwise) where God's being does not cause, explain, or ground the logical consequence relation?

I think not. For if valid logical arguments are just generalizations about language, mere conventions established by pure fiat, or empirical verifications, then surely all of these contingent entities are within God's power to affect. Language is presumably always changing and evolving due to human usage and change. And conventions, by definition, are things simply established by human beings while empirical verifications are the result of investigating the world of contingent experience. It should be obvious that linguistic entities and conventions are something that human beings can and do change. But if logic is constituted by linguistic or conventional entities, per the claims of some logical nominalist theory, then one can hardly claim that linguistic and conventional entities are independent of God as logical non-voluntarism wants to so claim. If humans can change such things, surely God can as well. And if a successful logical nominalism was built upon empirically verified contingent realities, then surely these contingent things are entities that an omnipotent divine being can affect as well. Therefore, I see no help for the logical non-voluntarist by appealing to logical nominalism. Even if there was a nominalist theory that successfully explained logical discourse and respected common logical intuitions, such a theory would not have the resources to keep the non-voluntarist's primary thesis intact, namely that logic is independent of God's will or commands, or independent from his creating or sustaining power.

4.4 CONCLUSION

In this chapter we investigated logical non-voluntarism: the view that the validity of logical arguments is a feature independent of and antecedent to God's willing or commands and independent of God's creating and

LOGICAL NON-VOLUNTARISM

sustaining power in the sense of causing, grounding or explaining logical consequence. We first clarified and then investigated a Platonist construal of logical non-voluntarism. We saw that it suffered from several problems violating components of core intuitions of traditional Abrahamic theism thus making the view an unacceptable explanation of the relationship between God and logic. As an alternative we investigated nominalist construals of logical non-voluntarism. Though the nominalist approach initially gets us around the problems brought on by a robust logical non-voluntarism, we've seen that logical nominalism fails as a viable explanation of logical discourse and does not respect commonly held intuitions concerning logic. Moreover, even if this were not the case, I've argued that logical nominalism is insufficient to uphold the non-voluntarist position.

Since these two alternatives exhaust the options for conceiving logical non-voluntarism, I conclude that logical non-voluntarism is not a viable option for explaining the relationship between God and logic.

So what now?

5

A VIABLE THIRD ALTERNATIVE

It appears that our investigation of how to think about the relationship between God and logic has given us rather disappointing results. Following the map set out by the Logiphro dilemma, we asked: Are valid logical arguments valid because God's commands or wills to make them so (i.e., logical voluntarism) or, like the rest of us, does God acknowledge valid logical arguments as valid because their validity is something independent and antecedent to his commands or will (i.e., logical non-voluntarism)?

Our investigation in chapter 3, of the first option of logical voluntarism, encountered various objections; but we saw that the vacuity objection ultimately made this position untenable for traditional Western theists. For such theists hold that God has intelligibly communicated (i.e., specially revealed himself) to certain individuals in history, which in many instances has been faithfully recorded and disseminated via Scripture. But the vacuity objection shows that logical voluntarism exacts too high a price from theists who hold such a position for one could not justifiably believe that a logical voluntarist God's special revelation means what we would normally take such utterances or words to mean. Thus, logical voluntarism destroys the point of special revelation and so theists who hold to the importance of special revelation must reject it.

Unfortunately our next investigation in chapter 4, of the second available option of logical non-voluntarism, also ran into its share of problems. As we saw, logical non-voluntarism can be construed as either a Platonist or nominalist theory. For Platonist logical non-voluntarism we saw that it

A VIABLE THIRD ALTERNATIVE

violated indispensable intuitions and conditions of the aseity-sovereignty doctrine, a core part of traditional Western theism. However, we also saw that a nominalist construal of logical non-voluntarism is also problematic, and not for theological reasons, but given issues strictly related to logic. For the evidence suggests that logical nominalism is not an adequate account of logic, among other problems. And moreover, even if logical nominalism was an adequate account of logic, it could not uphold the main thesis of logical non-voluntarism. Thus, logical nominalism cannot help the logical non-voluntarist position. Since both Platonist and nominalist logical non-voluntarism are problematic, logical non-voluntarism should be rejected as the way to think about the relationship between God and logic.

In summary then, neither logical voluntarism nor logical non-voluntarism seem to be tenable ways of conceiving the relationship between God and logic. And perhaps this should be an unsurprising result for, as we discussed in chapter 2, one objection to approaching the question concerning the relationship between God and logic with a Euthyphro dialectical structure is that it would more than likely fail. This pessimistic prediction was based upon the almost universally perceived success of the original Euthyphro dilemma in supposedly overcoming any philosophical attempt that seeks to ground or explain morality in God's will or commands. We have attempted a similar sort of explanation between logic and God's commands or will; and it appears we have failed as well. So perhaps we have indeed entered a lame horse into a philosophical horse race.

However, remember that we gave some reason back in chapter 2 to question whether the original Euthyphro dilemma is as successfully damning as usually believed. I noted there that there is a growing body of philosophical literature that challenges this age-old critique. In this chapter I propose we look at some of this literature to see how the Euthyphro dilemma has been challenged. I think we will see that some of the perceived success of the Euthyphro dilemma comes from it being nested within a larger critique against any sort of theologically based ethics in general. So, in §5.1.1, I want us to see how the Euthyphro dilemma fits within this larger critique. In §5.1.2 we'll briefly re-investigate the original Euthyphro dilemma and then introduce a long-held, but rarely spelled out or fully addressed, theistic counter that lays claim to a viable third alternative to moral voluntarism or moral non-voluntarism. In §5.1.3 we'll try to clarify what this alternative is. Starting in §5.2, I will attempt to re-fashion this third alternative to the original Euthyphro dilemma into a working logical theory that might operate as a legitimate third alternative to the Logiphro dilemma. In §5.2.1 we'll revisit absolute creationism to see a hint at what sort of model we'll need. In §5.2.2 and §5.2.3 we'll look at the recent work of philosopher Greg Welty as he builds upon some notions from Aquinas in order to construct a model of the relationship of necessary truths to God. And then in §5.3 I'll attempt to build upon Welty's work and provide a model of God's relationship to logical consequence, one that to my knowledge has never been given before. In conclusion, I will present what I believe is a satisfying philosophical position that explains the relationship between God and logic, but one that overcomes all the problems associated with both logical voluntarism and (robust) logical non-voluntarism.

5.1 RETURNING TO THE EUTHYPHRO DILEMMA

When we investigated the updated (to our context) Euthyphro dilemma back in chapter 2 we saw that it basically challenged a specific kind of ethical theory—one that attempts to explain or ground morality in acts of divine will or divine commands. But, as briefly mentioned in that chapter, there are other ways to conceive of ethics in relation to God. Thus, I find it interesting that the Euthyphro dilemma is usually referenced as justification for rejecting *any* theologically based moral theory. Therefore, before returning to the Euthyphro, I think it might be helpful to back up and see how a general rejection of any theologically based ethic might go. Then I'll suggest how I believe the Euthyphro critique fits within this outlook such that the Euthyphro dilemma can then be simply sighted as the primary reason for rejecting any theologically based ethical theory.

5.1.1 Theologically Based Ethics[1]

The notion that morality is grounded in or depends primarily upon God was once widespread and very popular in Western thought. And to reject this claim was once considered completely devastating to ethical theory and practice. The following comment from John Locke (1632–1704) is fairly emblematic of this historical perspective: "[T]hose are not to be tolerated who deny the being of God. Promises, covenants, and oaths, which

---

1. This section is highly indebted to Garcia and King, eds., *Is Goodness without God Good Enough?* 1–8.

A VIABLE THIRD ALTERNATIVE

are the bonds of human society, can have no hold upon an atheist. The taking away of God, though but even in thought, dissolves all."[2] At minimum here, Locke seems to think that unless God exists, or unless human beings believe that God exists, then ethical notions (particularly promises and other types of obligations) don't really exist either. For without God, Locke claims, these ethical notions simply "dissolve." And if such notions do not exist, presumably moral notions like promises and obligations lose their normative force. I think this is why Locke claims that the "bonds of human society" would not exist either since he presumably thinks that without a general belief in God, we would be causally left with anarchy. Thus Locke contends that God, or again at least belief in God, is necessary for the efficacy of ethics in practically maintaining human civilization. According to Locke, in order to have morality it must be theologically grounded.[3]

In similar fashion, this supposed close connection between God and morality arises in other philosophical contexts. For instance, some theistic philosophers have taken the connection between God and morality to be so close or so intuitive that it is sometimes given as a premise in what are called moral arguments for God's existence. Such arguments usually take something like the following general form:

(1) If God does not exist, then some apparent and important feature F of ethics is illusory.

(2) The apparent and important feature F of ethics is not illusory.

(3) Thus, God exists.

Note how claim (1) is similar to what Locke claimed above. However, in our own day, there's a very clear consensus among many philosophers that claim (1) should be considered just outright false. So the idea that God is necessary for *any* sort of ethical feature seems completely false to most.[4] In fact, some believe that a God-based morality has actually *impeded* moral and philosophical progress, as Derek Parfit claims, "Belief in God, or in many gods, prevented the free development of moral reasoning."[5] Thus, the

---

2. Locke, *A Letter Concerning Toleration*, 52.

3. I'll not discuss the supposed validity of this argument here. I merely offer it for illustrative purposes.

4. It should be noted that some contemporary theistic philosophers reject this claim as well.

5. Parfit, *Reasons and Persons*, 454. As with Locke above, I'm not interested in discussing the validity of this view.

idea that ethics is, or must be, theologically based, or that the connection between God and morality is close or even helpful, is considered a very outmoded idea indeed by many philosophers in our day. The complete history of how God-based morality fell out of philosophical favor is a more complex picture I'm sure. But I believe philosophers Robert Garcia and Nathan King give a plausible summary of how this result most likely came about:

> During the Enlightenment, belief in God waned while moral reasoning flourished. Moreover, the idea that God plays an essential role in ethics was subjected to serious critique. It is fair to say that in the wake of the Enlightenment, belief in God was widely taken to be unsupportable by reason. Theism was defrocked, in no small part, by numerous published critiques of the traditional arguments for the existence of God; the impact of such objections is still with us. As a result, many thinkers have concluded that God is either unreal or unknowable—and in either case, unavailable to play a role in an ethical theory.[6]

We see here that Garcia and King mainly lay the blame for theologically based ethics' demise upon the overturn of traditional arguments for God's existence, especially those that rose in favor during the Enlightenment (approximately 1650–1800). This explanation is plausible, for if there is no good reason or argument to believe in God, and if we still want to hold to the objective reality of ethics (i.e., claim (2) above), then it clearly follows that ethics cannot be grounded in God. Since it's probably the case that most contemporary philosophers are atheists or agnostics, this explanation of the unpopularity of conceiving ethics as based upon God makes much sense.

However, it seems to me, that the *primary* reason or argument often appealed to against any sort of theologically based ethic is not an atheistic or agnostic presupposition. Though the spirit of the Enlightenment and the rise of atheism and agnosticism surely popularized attacks against God-based morality, I find that the main reason that such conceptions of morality are pooh-poohed today, particularly in philosophical literature, is that God-based morality is usually associated with the Euthyphro dilemma from ancient philosophy. But again, we've seen that the Euthyphro dilemma operates mainly as a criticism of theories that attempt to explain morality explicitly in terms of God's *commands* or *will*. If so, how does the Euthyphro dilemma operate as a justification for rejecting *any* theological conception

---

6. Garcia and King, *Is Goodness Without God Good Enough?* 2.

A VIABLE THIRD ALTERNATIVE

of morality? I think there is a sort of implicit reasoning that goes something like the following: *even if* God exists, the Euthyphro dilemma shows that God plays no integral or interesting role in ethics. For the moral voluntarist picture is wracked with problems (e.g., the no reasons objection, the abhorrent commands object, etc.) and the moral non-voluntarist position shows that since God is merely a reporter of those moral truths we might discover on our own, then, at best, all God can really contribute to moral thought is the role of being a moral advisor, or perhaps a life coach. Thank you very much, so the reasoning goes, but we humans are just fine on our own without bringing religion into the mix. If I'm right, this explains why someone like Harvard psychologist Steven Pinker can simply claim concerning God-based morality, in one clean sweep, "Plato made short work of it 2,400 years ago."[7] It is in this way, I believe, that the Euthyphro dilemma often operates as a general justification for rejecting any sort of theologically based ethic. And I think it should go without saying that this sort of reasoning would seem to transfer fairly easy over to our investigation. For even if God exists, then trying to argue for some theory that explains logic in relation to God will seem fairly useless as well if our examination of the Logiphro dilemma is correct.

However, as stated earlier, there are various criticisms in a growing body of philosophical literature that have questioned whether the Euthyphro dilemma is such a slam-dunk against any theologically based moral theory. So I now want to return to the Euthyphro dilemma and examine what some of these philosophers have said in response to it.

5.1.2 The Euthyphro Dilemma Revisited

We've already given some time to investigating the Euthyprho dilemma back in chapter 2. However, to help reorient us, theistic philosopher Keith Yandell gives a concise presentation of the Euthyprho dilemma in the following, which should sound very familiar to us by now:

> One argument for the autonomy of ethics from religion starts from the old dilemma taken from the Platonic dialogue *Euthyphro*. Succinctly it goes: either the good is good because the gods choose it or the gods choose it because it is good. We can easily revise this so that it applies to monotheism: either God arbitrarily decides what

---

7. Pinker, "The Moral Instinct." http://www.nytimes.com/2008/01/13/magazine/13 Psychology-t.html?pagewanted=all& r=3&. Accessed on June 7, 2016.

is good or bad, right or wrong, or what is good or bad, right or wrong, is determined by something independent of God's choice. In the former case, nothing is intrinsically good or bad, right or wrong. In the latter, God's sovereignty is compromised. Either alternative is incompatible with traditional monotheism. So ethics is autonomous from religion. This has been taught in countless introductory courses in philosophy and ethics.

The argument is a dilemma: there are just two possibilities. Neither is compatible with ethics being based on monotheism. So ethics cannot be, and so is not, based on monotheism.[8]

Yandell explains that the Euthyphro dilemma purports that there are only two options for conceiving of a theory that grounds ethics in God's will or commands, and both are problematic. One, ethics becomes completely arbitrary upon God's capricious choice (i.e., moral voluntarism); or two, ethics actually turns out to be superfluous to God's will and commands (i.e., moral non-voluntarism). This should be old hat to us by now. But let me restate the criticism in another way: the Euthyphro dilemma shows that either moral voluntarism makes ethics *too dependent* upon God; or, moral non-voluntarism makes ethics *too independent* from God.[9] Neither option is acceptable, especially to traditional Western theists. Since, according to the Euthyphro dilemma, these are the only two options available, then it seems that any sort of divine command ethical theory—or as we saw in the last section, *any* sort of theologically based ethic—is out the door.

But there has been a growing body of philosophical literature by those who wish to defend a God-based morality from this infamous argument. It's at this point that I believe our investigation becomes instructive. For many theistic thinkers (not only now but throughout history) have charged that the Euthyphro dilemma is a *false* dilemma. Yandell explains: "A dilemma argument is successful only if the alternatives presented exhaust all possibilities. Offering only two possibilities, this dilemma does not."[10] Thus, to claim that a dilemma is false is to point out that there are one or more legitimate possibilities *other than* what the dilemma in question offers. In other words, a false dilemma is false in the sense that it claims the presented two options are the *only* available options, when in fact there may be other viable alternatives. Moreover, a false dilemma can be false in a further way

---

8. Yandell, "Moral Essentialism," 101. Note how Yandell also seems to assume that the Euthyphro is a critique of any theologically based ethic.

9. I borrow this characterization from Baggett and Walls, *Good God*.

10. Yandell, "Moral Essentialism," 101.

A VIABLE THIRD ALTERNATIVE

if it turns out that at least one of these further possibilities is a successful option.

So Yandell claims that moral voluntarism and moral non-voluntarism are not the only two available options to the Euthyphro dilemma. And this is exactly what the growing body of philosophical literature I keep referring to is often claiming. And, moreover, this is not a new criticism but one with much historical precedence. David Baggett and Jerry Walls explain:

> [There is a] third alternative, though [it] is hardly a philosophical novelty. It has a venerable history in the tradition of Christian thought [as well as traditional Western theism generally] that has taken a number of notable forms, including the following: Augustine's "divine ideas tradition"; Leibniz's effort to root mathematical truth in God's noetic activity; Aquinas's insistence that anything, that in any way is, is from God; Berkeley's radical idealism; Descartes' view of constant creation; and even Jonathan Edwards's misguided attempt at temporal parts theory—all of these were efforts motivated by the theological conviction that God is at the root of all that is.[11]

So if there is indeed a third viable alternative as the above philosophers claim (for this quote does not say exactly what that alternative is), this would mean that the Euthyphro dilemma is a false dilemma and thus does not serve as an attack on a theologically based conception of ethics.

Let me reiterate again though that our primary interest here is not to resolve the Euthyphro dilemma for theistic ethical theorizing. Rather we are looking for some insight on how to overcome our own version of the dilemma. For if there is a viable third alternative to the original Euthyphro dilemma, perhaps an analogous third alternative can be offered against the Logiphro dilemma as well. Given this hopeful thought, it behooves us to investigate and get clear on what this third alternative to the Euthyphro dilemma exactly is.

Before doing so though I believe some attention should be drawn to what I see as a major shortcoming in this literature concerning this historical third alternative. As Baggett and Walls claim, this third alternative is not novel and has taken sundry forms in the writings of many different major thinkers of the Western theistic tradition. However, many of the philosophers in the *current* literature who claim to defend or uphold some version of this third alternative rarely give much explanation or detail to this

---

11. Baggett and Walls, *Good God*, 87. The longer bracketed thought is my own.

supposedly successful option. Contemporary defenders seem to do little more than list historical adherents as authorities, as Baggett and Walls have done above here (though they go on later in their 2011 work to spell out their own view), *or* they purposely give incomplete explanations. Philosophical theologian Gijsbert Van Den Brink makes a typical comment in this regard:

> Fortunately, there is a rather easy way out of this [Euthyprho-like] dilemma, which is hinted at (but not straightforwardly worked out) by some of the authors discussed in the preceding subsections, and which is in fact so well-known and well-founded in the classical tradition that it will suffice here to sketch out only its main lines.[12]

As Van Den Brink notes, this third alternative is "not straightforwardly worked out," but only "hinted at," by many authors. And, frustratingly, Van Den Brink himself does little more than "sketch out" this alternative as well.

Therefore, going against this trend, I want to try and clearly lay out this third alternative to the Euthyphro dilemma—again, in order that, hopefully, we can construct our own version for the Logiphro dilemma. To that end, I've found the thoughts of theistic philosopher Alvin Plantinga to be most helpful in this regard. I think an investigation of Plantinga on this subject will go far in aiding us to clearly explain the third alternative to the Euthyphro dilemma and thus how it might be extended to our own problem.

5.1.3 Answering the Euthyphro Dilemma[13]

Does God Have a Nature? is the result of Alvin Plantinga's Aquinas Lecture given at Marquette University in 1980. As the title suggests, Plantinga seeks to establish whether God has a nature, and if so to offer an explanation of just what that nature consists in. Though this subject may seem fairly far

---

12. Van Den Brink, *Almighty God*, 201–12. Likewise, Copan and Craig, *Creation Out of Nothing*, 189: "Historically, the mainstream position in response to the challenge of Platonism has been conceptualism." Yet, they also do little to spell out exactly how this third view of conceptualism goes.

13. Though §5.1.3 is primarily taken from Plantinga's work, the outline and flow of this section is highly indebted to Baggett and Walls, *Good God*, 87–92. Their discussion in this section is excellent and worth reading for anyone interested in the significance of Plantinga's thought for the issues discussed here.

A VIABLE THIRD ALTERNATIVE

afield from the moral issues of the Euthyphro dilemma, Plantinga engages in a host of questions about the relationship of God to necessary truths, including the supposedly necessary truths of morality. I personally find the whole of this little book incredibly interesting. But it is at the end of this book that Plantinga gives the following alluring suggestions:

> Can we ever say a pair of necessary propositions A and B that A makes B true or that A is the explanation of B? Could we say, perhaps, that [Necessarily 7 + 5 = 12] is *grounded in* [It is part of God's nature to believe that 7 + 5 = 12]? If so, what are the relevant senses of "explains," "makes true" and "grounded in"? These are good questions, and good topics for further study. If we can answer them affirmatively, then perhaps we can point to an important dependence of abstract objects upon God, even though necessary truths about these objects are not within his control.[14]

Here Plantinga is particularly talking about God and abstract objects. But let's sidestep this metaphysical furniture for what I take to be the more interesting and important point here, which is, as Baggett and Walls suggest,[15] the last sentence where Plantinga makes a distinction between *dependence* and *control*. What Plantinga hints at here is, as Baggett and Walls emphasize, an important distinction for resolving the Euthyphro dilemma. For with it the theist might explain that, say, moral truths are dependent on God (thus denying moral non-voluntarism) yet maintain that such truths are not within God's control (thus denying moral voluntarism). If this suggestion could be made good, then this would supply the theist with a legitimate alternative to the Euthyphro dilemma. Again though, we only have a hint here from Plantinga's concluding comment.

Fortunately Plantinga returned to this issue two years later in his presidential address to the American Philosophical Association entitled "How to Be an Anti-Realist," where he offered a way to affirm a non-control dependence relation between God and necessary truths. What Plantinga calls "anti-realist" here, following Kant, is any view that posits that things in the world owe their fundamental structure and perhaps existence to some activity of minds. Plantinga spends much of this address arguing against versions of this anti-realism represented by arguments from former American Philosophical Association presidents Hilary Putnam and Richard Rorty. For all the problems he points out for anti-realism, Plantinga still

---

14. Plantinga, *Does God Have a Nature?* 146.
15. Baggett and Walls, *Good God*, 90.

admits that there is strong intuitive support for such a view, or something closely akin to it:

> How could there be truths totally independent of minds or persons? Truths are the sort of things persons know; and the idea that there are or could be truths quite beyond the best methods of apprehension seems peculiar and *outré* and somehow outrageous. What would account for such truths? How would they get there? Where would they come from? How could the things that are in fact true or false—propositions, let's say—exist in serene and majestic independence of persons and their apprehension? How could there be propositions no one has ever so much as grasped or thought of? It can seem just crazy to suppose that propositions could exist quite independent of minds or persons or judging beings. That there should just *be* these truths, independent of persons and their noetic activities can, in certain moods and from certain perspectives, seem wildly counterintuitive. How could there be truths, of for that matter, falsehoods, if there weren't any person to think or believe or judge them?[16]

Of course Platonism, like the version of robust logical non-voluntarism discussed in chapter 4, goes strongly against this anti-realist intuition since versions of it affirm that there are certain truths that exist independently of anybody knowing them. Plantinga quips that such views are "realism run amok."[17] Despite Plantinga's critical perspective here, it's clear that he is not rejecting the objectivity associated with Platonism, but only its mind-independence. Plantinga attempts to resolve these competing notions in the following:

> So what we really have here is a sort of antinomy. On the one hand there is a deep impulse towards anti-realism; there can't really be truths independent of noetic activity. On the other hand there is the disquieting fact that anti-realism, at least of the sorts we have been considering, seems incoherent and otherwise objectionable. We have here a paradox seeking resolution, a thesis and antithesis seeking synthesis. And what is by my lights the correct synthesis, was suggested long before Hegel. This synthesis was suggested by

---

16. Plantinga, "How to Be an Anti-Realist," 67–68. I should be clear here that I am in no way sympathetic to Plantinga's anti-realist sympathies. However, his anti-realist intuitions motivate him to a conclusion that I *am* sympathetic with, as I'll show, which I don't think relies upon his anti-realism.

17. Ibid., 68. Of course, there is a whole tradition of philosophers who see nothing quite so "crazy" about such forms of realism.

A VIABLE THIRD ALTERNATIVE

Augustine, endorsed by most of the theistic tradition [Note again the appeal to traditional authorities], and given succinct statement by Thomas Aquinas:

Even if there were no human intellects, there could be truths because of their relation to the divine intellect. But if, *per impossible*, there were no intellects at all, but things continued to exist, then there would be such reality as truth." (*De Veritate* Q.1, A.6 Respondeo). The thesis, then, is that truth cannot be independent of noetic activity on the part of persons. The antithesis is that it must be independent of *our* noetic activity. And the synthesis is that truth is independent of our intellectual activity but not of God's.[18]

Let's try to slowly piece together what Plantinga is claiming here. On the side of anti-realism, Plantinga wants to affirm the intuition that truth is mind-dependent—truths cannot exist without some mind knowing them. On the side of Platonism, Plantinga wants to affirm the intuition that there are many true propositions that are independent of our mental input or control (this is the objectionable incoherence of anti-realism he refers to). His suggested resolution to these competing intuitions, following Aquinas, is that truth is independent of *human* intellectual activity, but it must be dependent on some *other* intellectual activity. Plantinga thinks that the best candidate mind for upholding *all* true propositions is God's mind.

As Baggett and Walls suggest, Plantinga's suggestion here hearkens back to the distinction he made in the concluding thoughts of *Does God Have a Nature?* For he is attempting to show here how propositions (i.e., "truths") depend on God without their truth being subject to his control. But what exactly is the nature of this relation between God and propositions? Plantinga clarifies his position: "It is thus not the case that a proposition is true because God believes it. On the other hand it is the case, I think, that a proposition *exists* because God thinks or conceives it."[19] Plantinga is *not* suggesting that propositions are true or made true just because God *believes* them, which invites a voluntarist interpretation; rather, God believes a proposition because it is true. Yet, the proposition exists because God *thinks* it, which denies non-voluntarism—that truths exist independently of some mind. Plantinga concludes with the following:

---

18. Ibid. The bracketed comment is my own.
19. Ibid., 70.

> [T]he fundamental anti-realist intuition—that truth is not independent of mind—is indeed correct. This intuition is best accommodated by the theistic claim that necessarily, propositions have two properties essentially: *being conceived by God* and *being true if and only if believed by God*. So how can we sensibly be anti-realists? Easily enough: by being theists.[20]

I'm not particularly interested entering into the details of Plantinga's overall argument here. But I am interested in the fact that we have now identified some resources for filling out the sought-for third alternative for overcoming the Euthyphro dilemma. For on this proposal God could be said to believe propositions that represent moral truths *because* they are true. Thus, his believing does not make them true and so moral voluntarism is denied. But these same propositions exist because God thinks them. Thus, the existence of moral truths is dependent upon God and so moral non-voluntarism is denied. Baggett and Walls attempt to fill out Plantinga's picture as it applies, more specifically, to ethics:

> [C]onsider the proposition that it is bad to torture sentient creatures for the fun of it. Such a proposition is plausibly taken as necessarily true. On Plantinga's creative anti-realist view, God believes such a proposition because it is true, rather than its being true because God believes it. Consistent with Plantinga's rejection of universal possibilism [i.e., voluntarism], not even God could alter the truth value of the proposition. . . . His version . . . is not, however, a pure divine independence theory [i.e., Platonism or non-voluntarism] . . . for the proposition expressing such a truth exists due to God's thinking it, which he always had and always will. So the proposition expressing such a necessary truth depends on God, even though God does not and cannot alter its contents. Of course God has not the slightest intention to alter it, for there's perfect resonance between his nature and will. From this perspective, Plantinga affirms a substantive dependence relation of necessary truths on the creative activity of God, carefully distinguishing such dependence from the issue of control.[21]

Again, this approach is not novel, but resonant with, even if not as explicit as, other theistic philosophers' response to the Euthyphro dilemma. For example, Paul Copan claims, "the ultimate resolution to this Euthyphro dilemma is that *God's good character* or *nature* sufficiently grounds objective

---

20. Ibid., 68.
21. Baggett and Walls, *Good God*, 90–91.

A VIABLE THIRD ALTERNATIVE

morality."[22] Note that Copan appeals to God's nature as opposed to Plantinga's notion of God thinking or conceiving, while Baggett and Walls claim that the propositions expressing such truths exist "due to God's thinking [them], which he always has and always will." Moreover, "God has not the slightest intention to alter [them], for there's perfect resonance between his nature and will."[23] So Baggett and Walls idea coheres with Copan's claim that God's thoughts (at least concerning necessary propositions) are the result of his nature, which according to the classical picture is immutable and eternal. Similarly, William Lane Craig states: "On the theistic view, objective moral values are rooted in God. He is the locus and source of moral value. God's own holy and loving nature supplies the absolute standard against which all actions are measured." And so, adds Craig, God's "commands flow necessarily from his moral nature."[24]

Let me try to pull all of this together and clearly recapitulate this third alternative to the Euthyphro dilemma. Applying Plantinga's (and others') ideas, we have the following. Our third alternative claims that the Euthyphro dilemma is a false dilemma. Moral voluntarism and moral non-voluntarism are not the only two available options for conceiving of a God based ethic. Moral truths or principles are neither constituted by God's commands (moral voluntarism), nor are they completely independent of God (moral non-voluntarism). Rather, moral truths and principles are constituted by God's mental activity of conceiving or thinking of them according to his immutable and eternal nature (third alternative). God believes the moral truths because they are true, independently of his believing they are true. He doesn't make them true by his believing them (thus

22. Copan, "God, Naturalism, and the Foundations of Morality," 158. As worded, appealing to God's "good" nature makes it look as if Copan is begging the question. If the adjective "good" is left out, I believe Copan's reasoning is the following: the moral character of moral truths is grounded or parasitic upon the moral nature of God.

23. I think Baggett and Wells state this poorly here. Given what else they claim about God, I believe they should've said: "God *could not* have any intention to change any moral truth."

24. Kurtz and Craig, "The Kurtz/Craig Debate," 30. This response is so common among theistic philosophers I'm shocked that it's rarely addressed in most ethics textbooks in discussions concerning the Euthyphro dilemma. Other theistic philosophers who have given various but similar responses to the Euthyphro dilemma include Adams, *The Virtue of Faith*, 97–122; Frankena, "Is Morality Logically Dependent on Religion?" 295–317; Helm, ed. *Divine Commands and Morality*; and Quinn, *Divine Commands and Moral Requirements*. Much more could be said here; but again, I'm not necessarily interested in solving the Euthyphro dilemma, but rather in mining it for answers to my own dilemma.

denying moral voluntarism). However, the moral truths only exist because he thinks or conceives of them (thus denying moral non-voluntarism). So God's mental activity is responsible for the existence of moral truths, but God is not in voluntaristic control of their moral content.

Therefore, by claiming that morality is grounded in God's thinking or conceiving, and ultimately his nature, the theist appears to get around the objections of both horns of the Euthyphro dilemma. Contra moral voluntarism, God doesn't command what is good based upon a purely arbitrary will; rather, God commands what is good based upon his thoughts, which is subject to his eternal and immutable nature. Since God's nature is good, and immutably and eternally so, his moral commands are good as well—God could not command otherwise. Thus, unlike moral voluntarism, this third alternative does not make ethical principles *too dependent* upon God. It claims moral truths are dependent on God in the right way: upon God's immutable nature, not upon a purely arbitrary will. Contra moral non-voluntarism, this third alternative gets around the sovereignty worries. Since morality is grounded in God's immutable nature, ethical principles are not completely independent of God. Moral truths are not something outside of God that he must consult. Rather, God's ethical "consultations," so to speak, are with his own self. His own nature determines the moral character of what is good. Unlike moral non-voluntarism, this third alternative does not make ethical principles *too independent* from God. Thus, for the traditional Western theist, this third option ensures moral truths are independent in the right way: from God's arbitrary will, but dependent in the right way on his nature and thus not completely independent of God.

I take the above to be the classic theistic response to the Euthyphro dilemma, and one that the recent growing body of philosophical literature is trying to recapture. I don't claim to have given an exhaustive presentation of how such a theory would work in every detail. Nor have I dealt with any possible objections to this view.[25] Rather, my main aim here has been to show that the Euthyphro dilemma can be answered with a promising third alternative, which suggests that there might be a similar promising third alternative to the Logiphro dilemma. And, if that's so, this further suggests that there might be a way of explaining the relationship between God and logic. It's to this task we now turn.

---

25. For two such objections, see Antony, "Atheism as Perfect Piety" and Sinnott-Armstrong, "Why Traditional Theism Cannot Provide an Adequate Foundation for Morality." Let me comment though that I think these objections are answerable.

A VIABLE THIRD ALTERNATIVE

5.2 OVERCOMING THE LOGIPHRO DILEMMA

As we've seen, the structure and end result of the Logiphro dilemma is very similar to the Euthyphro dilemma. The Logiphro dilemma purports that there are only two options for conceiving of the relationship between God and logic. One, valid logical arguments become completely arbitrary upon God's capricious choice (i.e., logical voluntarism); or two, valid logical arguments are outside of, and thus superfluous, to God's will and sovereignty (i.e., (robust) logical non-voluntarism). Roughly speaking, it seems that logical voluntarism makes logic *too dependent* upon God (i.e., the vacuity objection exacts too high a price for traditional Western theism) while (robust) logical non-voluntarism makes logic *too independent* from God (i.e., it violates core intuitions concerning the nature of God), or in its nominalistic version logical non-voluntarism is just an inadequate account of logic or doesn't help in supporting the logical non-voluntarist's main thesis. Since, according to the Logiphro dilemma, these are the only two options available, then it seems we have exhausted the options for conceiving of any sort of interesting relationship between God and logic. And thus, as with the original Euthyphro dilemma, it seems that any sort of theologically based view of logic is unavailable.

However, as with the classic theistic response to the Euthyphro dilemma, I want to propose that the Logiphro is a false dilemma as well—that there is at least one viable alternative to logical voluntarism and (robust) logical non-voluntarism. And, as I've alluded to throughout this chapter, I believe that this alternative will be roughly analogous to the alternative provided against the Euthyphro dilemma. However, some work will have to be done in translating the third alternative from applying to necessary moral truths to logically valid arguments. What might this alternative look like applied to the Logiphro dilemma?

I had complained earlier that the *current* philosophical literature that makes claim to the classic theistic response to the Euthyphro dilemma is often vague and incomplete in its explanation of this response. My complaint applies doubly so when looking at the literature concerning the relation between God and other necessary entities (like valid logical arguments). For, again, such philosophers often say that there is a "classic" response that upholds a particular view of the relation between God and necessary entities, a view that is usually accompanied by a notable list of adherents such as Augustine, Aquinas, Leibniz, among others. But again, usually little detail is give to this response. I believe our investigation of Plantinga

THE LOGIPHRO DILEMMA

above went some way towards helping us to see how a general outline of a third alternative to the Logiphro dilemma might go: necessary entities are dependent upon God, but outside of his control. But can we find any additional help that might more particularly explain the relationship between God and logic? I believe the recent work of Oxford-trained philosopher Greg Welty is some of the best, current work on the subject. Though Welty is primarily concerned with the relationship between God and *all* necessary entities, his work has obvious implications for God and logic as well. Therefore, I suggest we investigate his view for help.

We will have a good introduction to Welty's theory if we see what he is mainly reacting against—a view we've already been introduced to back in chapter 4: Christopher Menzel and Thomas Morris's absolute creationism.[26] Remember, absolute creationism claims that *all* entities, abstract as well as concrete objects, are created by God. Welty has investigated absolute creationism and has found various problems with it, some of which we've already discussed in (See §4.2.4 of chapter 4). To review, we saw that absolute creationism concerning abstract objects results in a regress problem. For example, on the absolute creationist view of robust logical non-voluntarism, God is not free to make the abstract objects that constitute logical consequence in just any old way he wants. Such objects have intrinsic natures or structures that necessitate what sort of entities they are to be if created. If God decides to create one of these abstract objects, call it X, then his creation of X *must* come about in a certain result. But then this seems to imply that God must follow the pattern of some other thing, call it Y. And so the same problem seems to arise for object Y that absolute creationism was invoked in order to solve for object X. Therefore, we have a regress. We also saw, as Welty pointed out, that any absolute creationist attempt to overcome this problem only invited further problems that were endemic to their project. Since in chapter 4 we were only concerned with whether absolute creationism could save a Platonistic construal of logical non-voluntarism, we didn't pursue any further analysis of it. But Welty goes on to explain in more detail what he thinks went wrong with absolute creationism. It's clear that Welty's goal is to provide a superior view, what he calls *theistic conceptual realism*, which overcomes the problems of abso-

---

26. As footnoted back in chapter 4, this view is sometimes called "Theistic Activism," and is in fact dubbed so by Morris and Menzel, "Absolute Creation," 353–62. However, the name of that article is "Absolute Creation" and so their view is often interchangeably called both in the literature discussing it. Since I started with the name "absolute creationism," I'll stick with that instead of "theistic activism."

A VIABLE THIRD ALTERNATIVE

lute creationism. Therefore, in order to see how Welty arrives at his view, I believe we should investigate in more detail how he responds to absolute creationism.

5.2.1 Absolute Creationism Revisited

In chapter 4 we introduced the following quote from Menzel and Morris, which was cited as a nice crisp synopsis of their absolute creationist view. Here is that quote again:

> [A]ll properties and relations are God's concepts, the products, or perhaps better, the contents of the divine intellective activity, a causally efficacious or productive sort of divine conceiving. Unlike human concepts, then, which are graspings of properties that exist ontologically distinct from and independent of those graspings, divine concepts are those very properties themselves; and unlike what is assumed in standard Platonism, those properties are not ontologically independent, but rather depend on certain divine activities.[27]

Earlier I presented this view as it seems to be presented by its authors, viz., absolute creationism asserts that there is a causal, creative relation between divine intellectual activity and abstract objects. But Welty makes a very interesting observation about the above paragraph. He reflects that there is a significant ambiguity that runs throughout the set of claims here, which, contends Welty, amount to two very different theses. The first Welty calls the *causal dependence thesis*, where abstract objects causally depend upon a divine intellective activity, which seemed to me back in chapter 4 to be the obvious interpretation of their view. This causal dependence thesis can be clearly recognized by highlighting claims in the above, such as: "All properties and relations are . . . the products . . . of divine intellective activity"; the "divine intellective activity [is] a causally efficacious or productive sort of divine conceiving"; and "Those properties . . . depend on certain divine activities." But Welty observes that there is a second thesis here that he calls the *identity thesis*, where, as he puts it, "abstract objects are identical to divine intellective activity (or, at the very least, constituted by one aspect of such activity, namely, its 'content')."[28] Welty claims that the main problem

---

27. Morris, *Anselmian Explorations*, 166. Note the similarity in language here with the things said by Plantinga, and Baggett and Walls, back in §5.1 of this chapter.

28. Welty, "Theistic Conceptual Realism," 211.

with Menzel and Morris's absolute creationism stems from reading their view as a causal dependence thesis, which include the problems we've already looked at. Moreover, Welty notes that the identity thesis reading of absolute creationism does "little theoretical work" for Menzel and Morris since they mainly treat their view with a "profusion of causal language in their articulation of their theory."[29] In other words, Menzel and Morris clearly present absolute creationism as a causal dependence theory, as I also presented it back in chapter 4. So, despite the ambiguous language that presents a possible identity thesis reading, it seems clear that Menzel and Morris go for the causal dependence interpretation of their view. But Welty suggests there is another interesting and perhaps promising theory lurking in the identity thesis reading of absolute creationism.

Again, our interest here is whether Menzel and Morris's view (similar to Plantinga's view) has the rudiments of a successful theory for construing the relationship between God and logic. Welty thinks absolute creationism is a *partially* correct. But he claims: "I submit that the best way to construe the relation between abstract objects and divine intellective activity is in terms of an [identity thesis], and that all proponents of such a view should purge their treatments of any causal language. Otherwise they will be saddled with unnecessary problems."[30] Thus, Welty proposes to give a view of the relationship between God and abstract objects that capitalizes upon the identity thesis reading of absolute creationism, and which supposedly gets around the problems identified with causal dependence reading of this view. However, as we'll see, this is not a return to a view that is similar to what we've designated as robust logical non-voluntarism. As I'll endeavor to show, Welty's view squarely fits with a third alternative approach to the Logiphro dilemma that we are aiming for. But, in order to give a clearly successful third alternative here, we must first see the particulars and resources of Welty's own theistic conceptual realism. Then we'll be in a better position to see how we might apply it to our own Logiphro problem.

5.2.2 The Resources of Theistic Conceptual Realism

In contrast to the theistic activism of absolute creationism, Welty explains why he dubs his view what he does:

29. Ibid.
30. Ibid.

A VIABLE THIRD ALTERNATIVE

> I prefer to call my model "theistic conceptual realism" (hereafter, TCR) rather that "theistic activism" in order to purge all reference to divine *activity*, specifically, the activity of *creating* abstract objects. TCR claims that (at least some of) the divine thoughts can be regarded as functionally equivalent to abstract objects, due to the unique and determinative relation they sustain to any created realm.[31]

There are a couple of things to note here as far as they pertain to our goal. One, as we've already investigated, Welty's TCR model will attempt to pattern itself upon something like the identity thesis reading of Menzel and Morris's view. Thus, he will argue that abstract objects are identical to divine thoughts.[32] Two, this model patterns itself on something akin to Platonism (i.e., "realism"). For the central claim of the TCR model is that at least some of the divine thoughts *function* as equivalents to traditional, Platonistic, abstract objects. Welty continues:

> As a version of *realism*, TCR asserts that abstract objects (such as propositions and possible worlds) are *real* objects. They are not (as in creative antirealism) mere products of human intellective activity, but have the extramental existence relative to finite minds. However, as a version of *conceptual* realism, TCR asserts that such objects are ultimately mental in character. This is because what is being considered is a *theistic* version of conceptual realism, where the abstract objects in question are uncreated ideas in the divine mind; i.e., God's thoughts.[33]

Largely building his TCR model upon the thought of Thomas Aquinas, Welty claims that TCR need affirm only three resources: divine aseity, essential omniscience, and God as intelligent creator. Welty claims with these "we will have the resources for developing an account of (at least some of the divine ideas which enable them [to] satisfy the functional concept of 'proposition' and 'possible world,' but in a way that avoids the pitfalls of" theistic activism (i.e., the causal thesis reading of Absolute Creationism)."[34] Let's look at his explication of each of these three resources.

---

31. Ibid., 213.

32. Given that Welty is attracted to an "identity" reading of Menzel and Morris's view, it seems clear that Welty himself wants to make identity claims between abstract objects and God's thoughts, as we'll shortly see.

33. Welty, "Theistic Conceptual Realism," 213–14.

34. Ibid., 214.

First, Welty appeals to God's *a se* existence. We've already discussed this classical theistic doctrine and its importance for rejecting a Platonist construal of logical non-voluntarism. But to recall, what we termed the aseity intuition of traditional Western theism was the following: God, uniquely, does not depend upon anything distinct from himself for his existence. Thus, there is not at any time, any cause for God's existence. Additionally, Welty claims that this intuition includes God's *character* in that not only God's existence, but every aspect of his nature as well, does not depend upon anything distinct from God. Though this additional aspect was not emphasized in our discussion back in chapter 4, I think it should be obvious that it was assumed within the traditional Western picture of classical theism.

Second, Welty appeals to the idea that God is *essentially* omniscient. Obviously omniscience is included in classical theism as well—God exhaustively knows all things. But Welty emphasizes the idea that God is essentially omniscient because, as traditional Western theists hold, God is *necessarily* the kind of person he is, that he *necessarily* has (at least some of) the properties he has. For example, Swinburne notes that theists claim, among other things,

> that God is an animate being of a certain kind which can only have thoughts of certain kinds and perform actions of certain kinds. He could not have thoughts other than true thoughts or perform actions other than ones which effect their desired result. . . . [It is] logically impossible that he commit suicide, or abandon his omnipotence.[35]

Therefore, the second major component of Welty's TCR model is that God is essentially, and thus necessarily, omniscient, which, again, is part of the classical understanding of God that traditional Western theists have long held.

Welty elaborates that there is a vital connection between the first two components that we must be clear about. He says, "Crucial to TCR is the claim that God's omniscience ought to be understood in light of his aseity."[36] Why say this and what work is aseity doing with omniscience here? Welty claims, "The best way to [understand this claim] is to construe such omniscience as [God's] self-knowledge. That is, God perfectly knows himself, and in knowing himself, he knows all creatures, both possible and actual

---

35. Swinburne, *The Coherence of Theism*, 285–86.
36. Welty, "Theistic Conceptual Realism," 215.

A VIABLE THIRD ALTERNATIVE

[i.e., those that are actual]."[37] Welty's articulation of God's omniscience is not new. Thomas Aquinas claimed: "Now if anything is perfectly known, it follows of necessity that its power is perfectly known. But the power of anything can be perfectly known only by knowing to what its power extends."[38] Aquinas claims here that perfect knowledge of X includes knowledge of all actual states of affairs that X has brought about *and* all possible states of affairs that X is capable of bringing about. On this conception, since God perfectly knows, for example, President Obama, he not only knows every state of affairs that President Obama has ever brought about, God also knows every possible state of affairs that President Obama ever could bring about. As this applies to God's perfect knowledge of himself, this constitutes knowledge of *all* possible states of affairs.

Welty notes here that Aquinas construes divine omniscience in a way that coheres with divine aseity. He articulates the above more acutely, that according to Aquinas "God's knowledge of *possible* things is his knowledge of his own *power*, while his knowledge of *actual* things is his knowledge of his own *will*." This, claims Welty, "follows the Thomistic distinction between the *scientia intelligentiae* and the *scientia visionis*, the knowledge of understanding and the knowledge of vision, the knowledge of possibility and the knowledge of actuality."[39] Aquinas expounds this in the following:

> Whatever therefore can be made, or thought, or said by a creature, as also whatever He Himself can do, all are known to God, although they are not actual. And in so far it can be said that He has knowledge even of things that are not. Now a certain difference is to be noted in the consideration of those things that are not actual. For though some of them may not be in act now, still they were, or they will be; and God is said to know all these with the knowledge of vision [i.e., *scientia visionis*] . . . . But there are other things in God's power, or the creature's, which nevertheless are not, nor will be, nor were; and as regards these He is said to have knowledge, not of vision, but of simple intelligence [i.e., *scientia intelligentiae*].[40]

---

37. Ibid.
38. Thomas Aquinas, *Summa Theologica*, Part I, Q.14, A.5, Respondeo.
39. Welty, "Theistic Conceptual Realism," 216. The reference to God's "own will" I take to be his actual will.
40. Aquinas, *Summa Theologica*, Part I, Q.14, A.9, Respondeo.

Welty comments here that Aquinas takes his starting point for the above distinction from Augustine's remarks that God's knowledge of creatures are prior to the existence of the creatures themselves. Aquinas goes on to develop from this idea a model of God's knowledge in terms of something like a blueprint which an architect has for whatever he intends to build. Note the similarity to the Divine Craftsman metaphor originally found in Plato's *Timaeus*:

> The knowledge of God is the cause of things. For the knowledge of God is to all creatures what the knowledge of the artificer is to things made by his art. Now the knowledge of the artificer is the cause of things made by his art from the fact that the artificer works by his intellect . . . . Nevertheless, we must observe that a natural form, being a form that remains in that to which it gives existence, denotes a principle of action according only as it has an inclination to an effect . . . , hence His knowledge must be the cause of things, in so far as His will is joined to it.[41]

To put this another way, according to Aquinas the divinely omniscient architect, God, has knowledge of all possible blueprints, which is his knowledge of his own power (what God can and cannot do), and thus knowledge of all possible things.[42] In addition, God's knowledge also includes which blueprints he has decided to enact, which is his knowledge of his own actual will, and thus knowledge of all actual things. According to Welty, "These two aspects of self-knowledge are jointly sufficient to define divine omniscience."[43]

So, because of divine aseity, God's knowledge of himself—of his power and of his will—is not to be understood as knowledge obtained from creatures, but is completely independent of and prior to creatures. This is in complete contrast to our own human knowledge of natural objects. For our knowledge of such things depends on what exists—our genuine knowledge of X is primarily the result of X independently existing. But God's knowledge of such objects is the very basis of natural objects in an analogous way to the architect's plans being the basis of what gets built. Again Aquinas:

> Natural things are midway between the knowledge of God and our knowledge: for we receive knowledge from natural things, of

---

41. Ibid., Part I, Q.14, A.8, Respondeo.

42. Note here that Aquinas is ruling out universal possibilism, just as we also did concerning logical voluntarism.

43. Welty, "Theistic Conceptual Realism," 216.

A VIABLE THIRD ALTERNATIVE

> which God is the cause by His knowledge. Hence, as the natural objects of knowledge are prior to our knowledge, and are its measure, so, the knowledge of God is prior to natural things, as is the measure of them; as, for instance, a house is midway between the knowledge of the builder who made it, and the knowledge of the one who gathers his knowledge from the house already built.[44]

Welty summarizes the above in the following way, including an appeal to his third resource.

> [I]f God is a person, then he has beliefs, powers, and intentions. And if God is not only the creator of the universe, but is an *intelligent* creator, then his creative acts consist of divine power actualizing divine intentions. . . . Most theists in the [Western theistic tradition] have wanted to eschew a neo-Platonic notion of creation as divine "emanation" (wherein the creation is ultimately an unintended but inevitable byproduct of the divine nature) in favor of a model wherein God is seen as an artificer or architect who purposefully chooses to create according to a distinct "blueprint" in his mind.
>
> Thus intelligent creation presupposes *the existence of divine ideas*, insofar as it presupposes a correspondence between God's idea of the world he wishes to create and the world that gets created.[45]

Thus, Welty emphasizes that the existence of any created world entails the existence of the divine ideas, according to which the world was purposefully (and thus intelligently) created; but the existence of the divine ideas does not entail the existence of a world created according to them. For God could have refrained from creating any world and still he would have the ideas of the worlds that he could have created.

Now that we have the resources of divine aseity, essential omniscience (construed as divine self-knowledge), and God as intelligent creator, what does Welty do with these notions?

5.2.3 Theistic Conceptual Realism

Welty takes the considerations we've investigated in the preceding section to build his model of theistic conceptual realism (TCR). Again, Welty is

---

44. Aquinas, *Summa Theologica*, Part I, Q.14, A.8, Reply 3.
45. Welty, "Theistic Conceptual Realism," 217–18.

attempting to build a picture of abstract objects as *identical* with divine ideas, such that these ideas *function* as abstract objects have traditionally thought to function in most Platonist theories. According to Welty, since the divine aseity of God's knowledge of all possibilities (of everything he can bring about and has brought about) is completely independent of creatures, "then a whole range of God's thoughts can be seen to function as abstract objects in relation to the created realm."[46] Welty thus goes on to specifically argue for a model of abstract objects as divine thoughts or divine ideas. He claims that this model accounts for two types of abstract objects: possible worlds, and propositions.[47]

As claimed above, God is an omniscient being. And as we've seen, one consequence of this notion is that God perfectly knows the capacities of his own power, and therefore all possibilities. And since modal notions are usually taken to be interdefinable, then from knowledge of possibility is derived knowledge of impossibility, necessity, and contingency.[48] So the impossible is what is not possible. The necessary is what is not possibly not, and the contingent is what is possible and not necessary. Therefore, Welty claims that

> [P]ossible worlds are simply God's knowledge of his own power, of what he is able to instantiate. The notion of "God's knowledge" is not just a useful fiction, and so neither are possible worlds. God truly has this knowledge—it is as real as his own thoughts—and he creates in accordance with it.[49]

Welty goes on to comment that this conception naturally leads to a theistic version of an actualist conception of possible worlds, akin to the modal pictures embraced by philosophers such as Alvin Plantinga, Robert M. Adams, and Robert Stalnaker (but rejected by David Lewis). I think an actualist

---

46. Ibid., 218.

47. Earlier in Welty's work he argues for the existence of both possible worlds and propositions. In brief summary, Welty argues that both types of abstract objects are indispensable to our theorizing. In other words, he claims that both types of abstract objects are needed in order for our theoretical explanations to be able to do the work they are intended to do. He then goes on to give his TCR model of how to think about these two types of abstract objects. In this project, I approach this subject quite differently. I start with Welty's model of how to think about possible worlds and abstract objects. I then go on to use these entities as an integral part of my answer to the Logiphro dilemma.

48. One example of how such terms are interdefinable is Swinburne, *The Christian God*, 96.

49. Welty, "Theistic Conceptual Realism," 219.

A VIABLE THIRD ALTERNATIVE

picture of possible worlds is probably most easily comprehended in contrast to David Lewis' concretist picture of possible worlds. In short, Lewis claimed that possible worlds are spatiotemporal wholes existing separately from the world elsewhere in logical space and each actual in itself—as actual as our own world is. But the contrasting actualist picture claims that *all* possible worlds are abstract objects existing in *the* world (i.e., the physical universe that we live in) and only one of these possible worlds obtains (i.e., the actual world). It must be emphasized here that on the actualist conception of possible worlds even the "actual world" is identified with an abstract object: it is just one *way* the world could be. Unlike other possible worlds, the actual world happens to accurately represent *the* world. Welty notes that on a theistic conception of actualist possible worlds, existence claims about nonfactual possible worlds are reducible to existence claims about things in the actual world, for God's knowledge of his own power is a mental item in the actual world.

However, Welty points out that this is not a "reductive" analysis of modality. Rather, modal facts about God ground modal facts about the world. Welty notes:

> In this connection it is crucial to remember that, because of the divine aseity, it is simply a "brute fact" that God is the kind of God he is, with the powers that he has. There is no cause of God's nature and existence, and thus no cause or ultimate explanation of why God's knowledge of his nature has the content that it does. This is significant, because it follows that *what* God is able to do (the possible), and *knowledge* of what he is able to do, is not dependent in any way upon the existence of anything distinct from God (such as, for instance, human sentences).[50]

No doubt that in order for human beings to *describe* these and other facts about God, they must use human sentences. But, following Aquinas, our order of knowing does not determine, and is completely independent of, the order of God's being and knowing. In sum, "God's knowledge of necessary truths about himself—for instance, the range of possible universes he could create—is a function of who God is in and of himself, not a function of our contingent ability to describe such knowledge."[51]

---

50. Ibid., 219–20.
51. Ibid., 220.

Welty then turns his attention to clarifying what propositions are in TCR.[52] Propositions are usually defined as the content being asserted in a declarative sentence, where this content can be clarified with a that-clause. For example, in the declarative sentence "Columbus is the capital of Ohio" the proposition being asserted is *that Columbus is the capital of Ohio*. If this example seems redundant, note that by this same account the English speaker who says "The cat is black" and the Spanish speaker who says "El gato es negro" are both expressing the same proposition, namely *that the cat is black*. And, as philosopher of metaphysics Michael Loux says, "Platonists never tire of pointing out, for example, that there is a nondenumerable infinity of propositions specifying, in turn, that each irrational less than the number one is less than the number two."[53] Therefore, an account of propositions is usually thought to entail that there is an infinite plenitude of propositions. On the TCR model, Welty believes this condition is met. So any proposition, such as *that Columbus is the capital of Ohio*, *that Granny Smith apples are red*, and *that there is an interstellar speck of carbon so small and so distant from human beings that no human has any knowledge of it* are all represented by declarative sentences that "describe possibilities that God has the power to bring about, and God knows this about himself, and therefore has the corresponding thought."[54] Since God is omniscient, then, at the very least, for any possible way something could be, God knows whether or not he could bring it about. Welty thus concludes that God has an infinite number of thoughts (i.e., propositions).[55]

---

52. Again, Welty has already argued for the existence of propositions as abstract objects and he now takes himself to be giving a theistic model of how to think about these entities. Additionally, he has argued that possible worlds cannot be reduced to propositions. I'll address this issue in §5.3.1 below.

53. Loux, "Toward an Aristotelian Theory of Abstract Objects," 499.

54. Welty, "Theistic Conceptual Realism," 220.

55. This is actually a highly contentious claim that has been debated by theistic scholars for centuries. Most contemporary Western theists hold that God's knowledge is infinite, in some sense. But is divine knowledge *exhaustively* infinite, which has been thought to entail that there exists an infinity of (say) propositions, all known by God; or is God's knowledge *potentially* infinite, which would entail that any (say) proposition that might come into being is capable of being known by God? It seems clear that Welty is opting for the former notion of exhaustively infinite divine knowledge. It's not clear to me that I need to take a stand on this issue either way. It seems to me that all I really need is to say is that there are *enough* propositions (i.e., divine thoughts) available to capture logical validities. If this entails an *actual* infinity of divine thoughts, so be it.

A VIABLE THIRD ALTERNATIVE

But what about necessary propositions represented by such sentences as "If 1 is less than 2, then 1 is less than 3"? Welty explains how his TCR model accounts for these:

> Here God knows that he can *not* "bring these about," since their truth does not depend upon his will or any act of intentional creation. Rather, it depends upon his essence, for it is a primitive modal fact about God's power that *any* world created according to divine power will be correctly described by these and other thoughts (whereas, it is a primitive modal fact about God's power that any world created according to divine power will be *in*correctly described by other propositions, such as "3 is less than 2"). Since God, if omniscient, knows all of this about himself, the thoughts which comprise such knowledge can function as the full range of propositions there are.[56]

But don't necessary propositions (and contingent ones for that matter) have something to do with possible worlds? Given that Welty has both categories of abstract objects on the table in TCR, he needs to address the connection between possible worlds and propositions.

In doing so, he makes three distinctions between (1) the existence of a proposition, (2) its truth-value, and (3) the modal status of its truth-value. According to Welty, "the divine thoughts constitute the *existence* of all propositions (regardless of modal status), whereas the divine essence (specifically, the divine power) is the truth-maker for necessary truths (including, of course, necessary truths pertaining to possibilities)."[57] In short, the divine thoughts supply the requisite truth-bearers (i.e., propositions), whereas the divine power supplies the relevant truth-makers (i.e., possible worlds). So, according to Welty, for any proposition p that represents some necessary truth, p exists because it is a divine thought and will be the bearer of its requisite truth-value. But what makes p true, according to Welty, are the possible worlds, which are God's knowledge of what he is able to bring about.

But what, according to Welty, is the truth-maker for *contingent* propositions? Here Welty is much more tentative. He claims, "Perhaps that is,

---

56. Welty, "Theistic Conceptual Realism," 221. Note that Welty is ruling out universal possibilism, as we did with logical voluntarism back in chapter 3.

57. Ibid. Following Plantinga's actualist interpretation of possible worlds, Welty's model adopts modal logic S5, which counts the following two implications as valid (where N is a necessity operator and P is a possibility operator): (Np→NNp) and (Pp→NPp). For further explanation see Haack, *Philosophy of Logics*, 177.

ultimately, solely a function of the divine will. Or perhaps it is instead partly constituted by the contribution of human wills. What I say here is not affected by this question."[58] Welty understands that how one answers this question has implications for, among other things, one's view of human freedom, the problem of evil, and various other related sticky issues. Since Welty is mainly concerned with explaining necessary truths and necessarily existing entities, I think he can be excused for sidestepping the potential landmines here. Similarly, since our prime target is about logic, which doesn't seem to be integrally related to the notion of contingent propositions, I think I can put such considerations to one side as well.[59]

In summary, the TCR model of abstract objects claims traditional Western theists have the resources within the classical conception of God to hold that there are mental entities within the mind of God that equivalently function as certain abstract objects (namely propositions and possible worlds) as they are traditionally thought to function. According to Welty, these divine thoughts are not created by God, but nonetheless exist because of God.

5.3 CONSTRUCTING A THIRD ALTERNATIVE TO THE LOGIPHRO DILEMMA

Welty claims that his TCR model can account for all necessary truths. Maybe so. For my purposes I am only concerned with whether TCR has the resources to construct a theory that accounts for logical consequence (and thus respects the intuitions congruent with it) but avoids the problems we saw for logical voluntarism and robust logical non-voluntarism. I think Welty's TCR model does indeed provide the resources needed for constructing a viable third alternative to the Logiphro dilemma. However, I believe I need to say a little more about these resources before laying out my suggested answer.

---

58. Ibid.

59. Just for the record, I'm quite satisfied with a compatibilist reading of human freedom. So I don't see a problem with claiming that the truth-value of all contingent propositions is dependent on God's will alone (i.e., human wills make no significant contribution to the truth-value of contingent propositions). However, contemporary theists are not united on how to think about issues related to human freedom, including the problem of evil. So, like Welty, I'd rather not get into those issues here. Nevertheless, I think that my ultimate answer to the Logiphro dilemma (similar to Welty's view) might have implications for these issues.

A VIABLE THIRD ALTERNATIVE

As I've already said, Welty follows Plantinga's actualist conception of possible worlds. Since I am largely following Welty's picture, I'll be appealing to Plantinga's conception of possible worlds as well.[60] That being the case, let's investigate this particular conception of possible worlds as well as investigating the notion of propositions a bit more, especially exploring how propositions relate to possible worlds.

5.3.1 More Details on Possible Worlds and Propositions

Plantinga defines the notion *a state of affairs* as "a way things could have been."[61] Strictly speaking, a state of affairs is not the sort of thing that can be either true or false, i.e., a state of affairs cannot instantiate what Welty calls the property of "alethicity." A state of affairs is the sort of thing that either obtains or does not obtain. So, for example, *Michael Jordan's being more than six feet tall* is a state of affairs, as is *Mitch Romney being President of the United States of America*. Though both are states of affairs, the former obtains, or is *actual*, while the latter is only a *possible* state of affairs since it does not obtain. Plantinga then defines a possible world as a *maximal* or *complete* state of affairs.[62] Thus, any possible world is simply a maximal state of affairs that has not obtained and the actual world is a maximal state of affairs that has obtained.[63]

Plantinga also addresses the relationship between possible worlds and propositions. He claims that a proposition like

(1) *that Socrates is mortal*

is intimately related to a state of affairs like

(2) *Socrates' being mortal.*

---

60. Plantinga, *The Nature of Necessity*, 44–46.
61. Ibid., 44.
62. According to Plantinga, "a state of affairs S *includes* a state of affairs S' if it is not possible (in the broadly logical sense) that S obtain and S' fail to obtain—if, that is, the conjunctive state of affairs S *but not S'* (a state of affairs that obtains if and only if S obtains and S' does not) is impossible.... [So] a state of affairs S is *complete* or *maximal* if for every state of affairs S', S includes S' or S precludes S'." Ibid., 44–45.
63. Furthermore, Plantinga argues that there is at least one, and at most one, actual world among all of the possible worlds. The proof: "for suppose two worlds W and W* both obtained. Since W and W* are distinct worlds, there will be some state of affairs S such that W includes S and W* precludes S. But then if both W and W* are actual, S both obtains and does not obtain; and this, as they say, is repugnant to the intellect." Ibid., 45.

Some have argued that the relation is so intimate that propositions should just be identified with states of affairs in possible worlds.[64] But, following Welty, I think there are good reasons to avoid this identification. For one, propositions can be true or false, while states of affairs and possible worlds cannot (at best they obtain or do not obtain). Thus, propositions have a property that states of affairs and possible worlds do not (capable of being true or false, i.e., alethicity) and so states of affairs or possible worlds cannot be propositions. Second, states of affairs and possible worlds are neither believed nor disbelieved (i.e., they don't serve as the content of such thoughts) but propositions can be believed or disbelieved. Therefore, I think we're justified in concluding that states of affairs and possible worlds should not be identified with propositions.[65]

But what is the relationship between propositions and possible worlds? It should be clear that the above proposition (1) has a corresponding relationship to the state of affair (2). Thus, Plantinga comments, "it is impossible, in that broadly logical sense, that (1) be true and (2) fail to obtain" and "equally impossible that (2) obtain and (1) be false."[66] Plantinga additionally claims that, "for any possible world W and proposition p, W entails p or the denial of p."[67]

In addition, Plantinga, along with Welty's earlier explanation, understands propositions to be truth-bearers. Whereas the possible worlds operate as the truth-makers for propositions, understood in the following way. The "book on a world W" is the complete set of propositions true at W. So,

---

64. For examples of this view see Chisholm, "Events and Propositions," 15–24, and his "States of Affairs Again," 179–89, and Lycan, "The Trouble with Possible Worlds" 274–316.

65. One possible exception here: note that some possible worlds may be so simple (e.g., containing only one object) that they could be believed or disbelieved. However, many possible worlds will be far too complex to be believed or disbelieved by we mere mortals.

66. Plantinga, *The Nature of Necessity*, 45–46.

67. Ibid, 46. In addition, Plantinga notes that for any possible world W, Plantinga defines *the book on W* as the maximal set S of propositions such that p is a member of S if W entails p. The proofs for maximality and uniqueness of any book: "if B is a book, then for any proposition p, either p is a member of B or else not-p is. And clearly for each possible world W there will be one book. There is at least one, since for any world W and proposition p, W entails either p or its denial; so the set of propositions entailed by W is maximal. There is also at most one; for suppose a world W had two (or more) distinct books B and B'. If B differs from B', there must be some proposition p such that B contains p but B' contains the denial of p. But then W would entail both p and its denial, in which case W would not be a possible state of affairs after all." Ibid.

A VIABLE THIRD ALTERNATIVE

to say that p is true at a world W is to say that if W had been actual, then p would have been true. And to say that p is necessarily true is to say that p is true at every W.

With Plantinga's metaphysical picture in place, I now want to additionally argue that there are some propositions that have logical, as well as non-logical, content.[68] Since some sentence tokens have distinguishable logical and non-logical terminology, and since I take sentence tokens to represent corresponding propositional content, it follows that these corresponding propositions are structured by logical and non-logical content as well. In chapter 1 I argued for how we are epistemically justified in making such a distinction. The only additional point I'm making here is that this distinction is found within the very content of some propositions themselves, i.e., those propositions that are represented with this very distinction. With these more clarified notions in place, I think we can begin to build a more nuanced picture of possible worlds and propositions.

5.3.2 A Theistic Interpretation of Possible Worlds and Propositions

Back in chapter 1, I argued that (LC) best represents the extra-systematic notion of the logical consequence relation:

> (LC) Φ is a logical consequence of Γ, if at every possible world in which the uniform substitution of the non-logical content in Γ and Φ renders every member of Γ true, then it also renders Φ true.

I argued there that this characterization of logical consequence captures many of the major intuitions shared by many concerning logic. In addition, because we did not want to assume any particular ontological commitments at the outset of our investigation, we opted for a neutral metaphysical stance. However, I now claim that Φ and Γ should be thought of as divine mental entities that function as the traditional abstract objects called propositions. I additionally now claim that the modal language in (LC) should be thought of as divine mental entities that function as the traditional abstract objects called possible worlds. Again, I am not actually claiming that the entities represented in (LC) *are* the traditional, Platonic, abstract object of propositions and possible worlds. Rather, similar to Welty's TCR model, I am claiming that certain of God's thoughts *function* as these traditional abstract objects and so the entities represented in (LC) are identical with

---

68. See chapter 1 for what I take this distinction to amount to.

certain divine thoughts. Thus, my conception of logical consequence (LC) claims that God's thoughts function (to be spelled out below) in ways that propositions and possible worlds have traditionally thought to function within Platonic theories that appeal to such entities.

Since I am identifying God's thoughts as being functionally equivalent to propositions and possible worlds, I need to be clear on how exactly these different sorts of divine thoughts operate before addressing how they explain logical consequence.

Following Aquinas and Welty's TCR model, I hold that the classical understanding of God's *a se* existence includes every aspect of his nature, including his omniscience. Thus, I hold that the entirety of God's knowledge (of what is actual and what is possible) is not dependent upon anything outside of God. As this conception suggests, the following are jointly sufficient to define God's omniscience: (a) God's knowledge of his will and (b) God's knowledge of his power. But where do divine thoughts enter in here? And how exactly do such thoughts relate to propositions and possible worlds?

Taking my lead from Welty (and Aquinas), I believe God's knowledge of his own will should be understood in the following way: God knows all the actual states of affairs he has brought about (i.e., all those that obtain) *and* he knows all of their corresponding propositions, which are thus true. This facet of divine knowledge is constituted by God's own thoughts, which can be distinguished into two categories, each category with a different functional role: divine thoughts that function as actual states of affairs (or the actual world) or divine thoughts that function as propositions corresponding to those states of affairs. God's knowledge of his own will includes individual divine thoughts that function as a state of affairs. In addition, God's knowledge of his own will also has the divine thought that represents the maximal state of actual affairs, in the sense that this additional thought functions as the actualist abstract object known as the actual world. Likewise, I understand God's knowledge of his own will to include all the divine thoughts that truth-functionally evaluate all of the individual actual states of affairs, in the sense that each of these thoughts functions as a proposition, and each proposition is true given that it corresponds to the actual state of affairs, i.e., what God had brought about. In summary, God's knowledge of his own will is constituted by all the divine thoughts that function either as the actual states of affairs (or the maximal actual states of affairs) he has brought about *or* function as the propositions that truthfully correspond to

A VIABLE THIRD ALTERNATIVE

these (or the book of the world). Again, to reiterate, because God has an *a se* existence, and his omniscience is included in this existence, then God's knowledge of his own will is the antecedent *to*, not the result *of* (like it is for us), the actual world. God's knowledge of the actual world—knowledge of his own will—is thus one facet of God's omniscience.

But God's *a se* omniscience is constituted not only by his knowledge of his will, it is also constituted by his knowledge of his power—what he is able to bring about. Again taking my lead from Welty (and Aquinas), I think God's knowledge of his power should be understood in the following way: God knows all possible (non-obtaining) states of affairs (i.e., he knows all possible states of affairs that he could bring about) *and* he knows all of their correspondingly true propositions. This facet of divine knowledge is constituted by God's own thoughts, which can also be distinguished into two similar categories, each category with a different functional role: divine thoughts that function as possible states of affairs (or possible worlds) or divine thoughts that function as propositions that are correspondingly true to those respective worlds. In detail, God's knowledge of his power includes individual divine thoughts that function as possible states of affairs. Likewise, God's knowledge of his power includes the divine thoughts that represent the different maximal states of possible affairs, in the sense that these additional divine thoughts function as the abstract objects known as possible worlds. In addition, I understand God's knowledge of his power to include all the divine thoughts that truth-functionally evaluate all of the individual possible states of affairs, in the sense that each of these thoughts functions as a proposition, and each proposition has a truth-value that corresponds to its accompanying possible state of affairs. In summary, God's knowledge of his power is made up all the divine thoughts that function either as possible states of affairs (or the maximal possible states of affairs) *or* they function as the propositions that correspond to these possible states of affairs. And thus God's knowledge of his own power is knowledge of his divine thoughts that function as all possible worlds and his divine thoughts that function as all the propositions corresponding to these possible worlds. Like Welty, I take both facets of divine omniscience—God's knowledge of his own will (and thus actuality) and his own power (and thus possibility)—to be jointly sufficient to define divine omniscience.

However, there's one additional wrinkle I think I must address concerning God's knowledge of his power. Earlier we saw that Welty suggested that God's omniscience includes all the possible ways something could be, which, as worded, I affirm as well. But Welty claimed that this affirmation implies that God has an infinite number of divine thoughts. In other words, as I've explicated above, God would have to have an infinite number of divine thoughts that function as possible states of affairs as well as those infinite number of divine thoughts that function as propositions corresponding to those states of affairs. Welty thinks that "intuitively, there are an infinite number of propositions."[69] He's partially motivated to this claim by examples like the following: "For each real number r, for example, there is the proposition that r is distinct from the Taj Mahal."[70] It's obvious how such examples could be multiplied. But Welty also reasons in the following way:

> If God is omniscient, then at the very least, for any possible way things could be, God knows whether or not he could bring it about. This is sufficient for God to have thoughts that match the infinity of propositions that there must be. While there are surely propositions not thought of by any human being, due to lack of imagination or energy on their part, or perhaps due to the complexity of the proposition in question, this is not the case with God. And so the plenitude condition is easily satisfied.[71]

What Welty is calling the plenitude condition is the claim that any successful theory of propositions must guarantee that there are as many propositions as we think there are. If this condition on my own theory requires that I need an infinite number of propositions, I accept it. Given the details of my theory, this would mean that God's knowledge of his power includes an infinite number of divine thoughts that function as possible states of affairs and an infinite number of corresponding divine thoughts that function as propositions.

5.3.3 Applying the Model to Logical Consequence

With all of the pieces now in place, I think we are now in a position to explicate a theistic explanation of logical consequence—one that avoids the problems of both logical voluntarism and (robust) logical non-voluntarism.

---

69. Welty, "Theistic Conceptual Realism," 109.
70. Plantinga, "God, Arguments for the Existence of,"
71. Welty, "Theistic Conceptual Realism," 126.

A VIABLE THIRD ALTERNATIVE

Remember that (LC) is our representation of the logical consequence relation:

> (LC) Φ is a logical consequence of Γ, if at every possible world in which the uniform substitution of the non-logical content in Γ and Φ renders every member of Γ true, then it also renders Φ true.

We explain (LC) in the following way. Φ represents a proposition and Γ represents zero or more propositions. At least some of the propositions represented by Γ (and of course the proposition represented by Φ) must contain both logical and non-logical content.[72] This clarified, a valid logical argument (i.e., Γ ⊢ Φ) is one in which at every possible world where the uniform substitution of the non-logical content of both Γ and Φ renders all members of Γ (if any) true, then Φ is true as well. Of course, in our theistic model there are no abstract objects referenced in (LC). Rather, our reference to "possible worlds" and "propositions" is understood as identifying certain sorts of divine thoughts. Namely, those thoughts that function equivalently to the traditional Platonic entities so named.

So logical consequence (LC), and thus the validity of any instance of a valid logical argument, (partially) holds in virtue of certain divine thoughts that are functionally equivalent to propositions. But to fully explain (LC), these sorts of divine thoughts must receive their respective truth-values. And they do so in virtue of other sorts of divine thoughts that are functionally equivalent to possible worlds. And these latter sorts of divine thoughts are the kinds of things that they are in virtue of God perfectly knowing the capacity of his own power, and thus all possibilities. So logical consequence, the primary focus of logic, ultimately holds in virtue of God's knowledge of his own power—of what he is able to instantiate.

I think it might be helpful to give a few examples of how validity is explicated by (LC) by seeing how our theistic model would explain them.

Take modus ponens, a valid logical argument, recognized by just about any formal system of logic. How would we explain the validity of this argument interpreted by our proposed theistic model? Modus ponens is usually represented as {p, ($p \rightarrow q$)} ⊢ q. Remembering that "possible worlds" and "propositions" are phrases that actually represent two sorts of divine thoughts, (LC) would explain this argument's validity by saying that p, ($p \rightarrow q$), and q represent propositions, which contain logical, as well as

---

72. This condition on Γ ⊢ Φ is to rule out any non-logical implications, i.e., conceptual implications, material implications, etc.

non-logical, content. At every possible world where the uniform substitution of the non-logical terminology of p, $(p\to q)$, and q renders p and $(p\to q)$ true, then it is also the case that q is true at all of those possible worlds as well. Put negatively, our theistic model would claim that it is not within God's power to bring about any state of affairs at which the propositions p and $(p\to q)$ are true, but where the proposition q is also false. Invalidity should be fairly easy to see here as well. Taking affirming the consequent, i.e., $\{q, (p\to q)\} \vdash p$, as a clear example of invalidity, according to (LC) this argument's invalidity would mean that at every possible world where the uniform substitution of the non-logical content of the propositions q and $(p\to q)$ are true, there is at least one of these possible worlds where the proposition p turns out false. Our model would interpret this to mean that it is within God's power to bring about a state of affairs at which q and $(p\to q)$ are true, but p is false.

Additionally, our model would interpret a logical truth (i.e., $\vdash \Phi$) in the following way. Again pointing out that "possible worlds" and "propositions" are actually two sorts of divine thoughts, according to (LC), the logical truth represented by the proposition Φ is true at every possible world regardless of what is substituted in for the non-logical content of Φ.[73] Our model explains this as it not being within God's power to ever instantiate a state of affairs that would make Φ false. In similar fashion, our model would interpret a logical contradiction Δ in the following way.[74] According to (LC), the proposition represented by Δ is not true at *any* possible world regardless of what is substituted in for the non-logical content of Δ. By this model it is not within God's power to ever instantiate a state of affairs that would make Δ true.

Remember that, ultimately, logical consequence holds in virtue of God's knowledge of his own power. But how are we to interpret the extent of God's power? Following Welty's TCR model, I take the above interpretations of logical validity to be brute facts about God. Welty claimed:

> [I]t is crucial to remember that, because of the divine aseity, it is simply a "brute fact" that God is the kind of God he is, with the powers that he has. There is no cause of God's nature and

---

73. Note that Φ must be a proposition with both logical and non-logical content in order that others sorts of necessarily true propositions do not counts as "logical" truths.

74. Note that Δ must be a proposition with both logical and non-logical content in order that others sorts of necessarily false propositions do not counts as "logical" falsehoods.

existence, and thus no cause or ultimate explanation of why God's knowledge of his nature has the content that it does. This is significant, because it follows that *what* God is able to do (the possible), and *knowledge* of what he is able to do, is not dependent in any way upon the existence of anything distinct from God (such as, for instance, human sentences).[75]

Therefore, the fact that when Γ logically implies Φ means simply that God cannot bring about a state of affairs where the uniform substitution of the non-logical content of the propositions (if any) represented by Γ are true and Φ false, and this is just a brute fact about God's power and nature. As Brian Leftow was quoted in the last chapter: "it is part of the ordinary theist's concept of God that no regress of true explanations can go past God's existence, i.e., that when one has traced some phenomenon back to the fact that God exists, one can go no further."[76]

5.3.4 Answering the Logiphro Dilemma

Now that we have the metaphysical components in place (i.e., divine thoughts), and now that I think we see how this model explains logical consequence as represented by (LC), does the above theistic, metaphysical model of logical consequence avoid the problems associated with logical voluntarism and robust logical non-voluntarism? Do we indeed have a viable third alternative to the Logiphro dilemma?

In short, I believe we do. For example, the above account denies logical voluntarism for it claims there are certain limitations to God's power. (LC) is, in essence, a representation of at least part of God's *a se* omniscient knowledge of his power. On this model (LC) claims that it is beyond God's power to bring about certain states of affairs or combinations of certain states of affairs—namely those states of affairs that would violate logical validity. Though logical consequence is ultimately dependent on God, and thus the validity of any valid logical argument is dependent on God, the model presents God as not in control of logical consequence—logic is not *too dependent* on him. Thus, this model denies what we labeled logical voluntarism and so this model thus does not suffer the vacuity objection laid out back in chapter 3.

---

75. Welty, "Theistic Conceptual Realism," 219–20.
76. Leftow, "Is God an Abstract Object?" 584.

But is this model just a form of logical non-voluntarism? Is it guilty of the sins of (robust) logical non-voluntarism since it seemingly appeals to abstract, Platonist entities? As we saw, robust logical non-voluntarism ran up against the aseity and sovereignty intuitions of traditional Western theism in various ways. In general, the appeal to Platonic, abstract objects either (1) makes God dependent, in some way, on such objects (violating divine aseity); or (2) such objects turn out to be uncreated (violating *creatio ex nihilo*); or (3) such objects are beyond need of God's continued sustainment (violating divine sovereignty). However, the above theistic model is not at fault concerning any of these issues. Concerning (1), the "objects" that (LC) represent are God's own thoughts, part of his very essence. So God does not depend on some object outside of himself. For example, the necessary existence usually attributed to God would be interpreted on this model as God being unable to bring about a state of affairs where God does not exist. Thus, God does not depend on some abstract objects outside of himself, such as propositions or possible worlds, in order to necessarily exist. His necessary existence is just a fact about God's own essence. Concerning (2), since the divine thoughts that are represented by (LC) are part of God's nature—it's a brute fact that God thinks the thoughts he does—they are not creatures and thus not created. Concerning (3), neither are the divine thoughts represented in (LC) objects that are independent of God's sustaining power. Since they are part of God himself, they are not objects independent of God. In sum, since on this model logical consequence is rooted in God himself—logic is not *too independent* of God. Therefore, it is not guilty of the problems associated with robust logical non-voluntarism and thus denies that view.

The only thing missing is giving this model a name. Though fairly clunky, in honor of Welty's model, I'll call this model *theistic conceptual logical realism*.

Therefore, our question, "What is the relationship between logic and God?" or more precisely, "What is the relationship between what constitutes logical consequence, as characterized by (LC), and the God of classical theism?" is answered with the model provided by theistic conceptual logical realism. I conclude that it is a viable third alternative to the Logiphro dilemma. It avoids the problems of logical voluntarism as well as those of robust logical non-voluntarism. Therefore, I think the best way to think about the relationship between God and logic, is the model provided by theistic conceptual logical realism.

BIBLIOGRAPHY

Adams, Marilyn McCord. *William Ockham*. 2 vols. South Bend, IN: University of Notre Dame Press, 1987.
Adams, Robert Merrihew. *The Virtue of Faith*. Oxford: Oxford University Press, 1987.
Antony, Louise. "Atheism as Perfect Piety." In *Is Goodness without God Good Enough?*, edited by Robert K. Garcia and Nathan L. King, 67–84. Lanham, MD: Rowman and Littlefield, 2009.
Aquinas, Thomas. *Summa Theologica*. 3 vols. Translated by Fathers of the English Dominican Province. New York: Benziger Brothers, 1947.
Armstrong, A. H. *An Introduction to Ancient Philosophy*. Boston: Beacon, 1947.
Baggett, David, and Jerry L. Walls. *Good God: The Theistic Foundations of Morality*. Oxford: Oxford University Press, 2011.
Beall, J. C., and Greg Restall. *Logical Pluralism*. Oxford: Oxford University Press, 2006.
Beany, Michael. *The Frege Reader*. Malden, MA: Blackwell, 1997.
Bencivenga, E. "What Is Logic About?" In *The Nature of Logic*, edited by Achille C. Varzi, 5–19. Stanford: CSLI, 1999.
Bergmann, Michael, and Jeffrey E. Brower. "A Theistic Argument against Platonism (and in Support of Truthmakers and Divine Simplicity)." In *Oxford Studies in Metaphysics*, vol. 2, edited by Dean Zimmerman, 357–86. Oxford: Clarendon, 2006.
Boersma, Hans. *Heavenly Participation: The Weaving of a Sacramental Tapestry*. Grand Rapids: Eerdmans, 2011.
Boyer, Stephen D., and Christopher A. Hall. *The Mystery of God: Theology for Knowing the Unknowable*. Grand Rapids: Baker Academic, 2012.
Brandom, Robert B. *Making it Explicit: Reasoning, Representing, and Discursive Commitment*. Cambridge: Harvard University Press, 1994.
Burgess, John. "Proofs About Proofs: A Defense of Classical Logic, I." In *Proof, Logic and Formalization*, edited by Michael Detlefsen, 8–23. London, Routledge, 1992.
Chisholm, Roderick. "Events and Propositions." *Noûs* 4 (1970) 15–24.
———. "States of Affairs Again." *Noûs* 5 (1971) 179–89.
Clouser, Roy. "Religious Language: A New Look at an Old Problem." In *Rationality in the Calvinist Tradition*, edited by Hendrick Hart, Johan Van Der Hoeven, and Nicholas Wolterstorff, 385–407. Lanham, MD: University Press of America, 1983.
Conee, Earl. "The Possibility of Power Beyond Possibility." *Philosophical Perspectives* 5 (1991) 447–73.
Cooper, John M., ed. *Plato: Complete Works*. Indianapolis, IN: Hackett, 1997.

BIBLIOGRAPHY

Copan, Paul. "God, Naturalism, and the Foundations of Morality." In *The Future of Atheism: Alister McGrath and Daniel Dennett in Dialogue*, edited by Robert B. Stewart, 141–61. Minneapolis: Fortress, 2008.

Copan, Paul, and William Lane Craig. *Creation Out of Nothing: A Biblical, Philosophical, and Scientific Exploration*. Grand Rapids: Baker Academic, 2004.

Copleston, Frederick. *A History of Philosophy: Volume III: Late Medieval and Renaissance Philosophy*. New York: Image, 1993.

Craig, William Lane. "Anti-Platonism." In *Beyond the Control of God? Six Views on the Problem of God and Abstract Objects*, edited by Paul M. Gould, 113–26. New York: Bloomsbury, 2016.

———. *God Over All: Divine Aseity and the Challenge of Platonism* Oxford: Oxford University Press, 2016.

———. "Nominalism and Divine Aseity." In *Oxford Studies in Philosophy of Religion*, vol. 4, edited by John Kvanvig, 43–64. Oxford: Oxford University Press, 2012.

———. "Propositional Truth—Who Needs It?" *Philosophia Christi* 15 (2013) 355–64.

Curley, E. M. "Descartes on the Creation of the Eternal Truths." *The Philosophical Review* 93 (1984) 569–97.

Darwall, Stephen. *The Second-Person Standpoint*. Cambridge: Harvard University Press, 2006.

Davidson, Herbert. *Proofs for Eternity, Creation and the Existence of God in Medieval Islamic and Jewish Philosophy*. Oxford: Oxford University Press, 1987.

Descartes, René. *The Philosophical Writings of Descartes, vol. 3*, edited by John Cottingham, Robert Stoothoff, Dugald Murdoch, and Anthony Kenny. Cambridge: Cambridge University Press, 1991.

Dummett, Michael. *Frege: Philosophy of Language*, 2nd ed. Cambridge: Harvard University Press, 1981.

Endres, J. A. "Die Dialektiker und ihre Gegner im 11. Jahrhundert." *Philosophisches Jahrbuch* 19 (1906) 20–33.

———. *Petrus Damiani und die weltliche Wissenschaft*. Beiträge zur Geschichte der Philosophies des Mittelalters 8.3. Münster: Aschendorff, 1910.

Estlund, David M. *Democratic Authority: A Philosophical Framework*. Princeton, NJ: Princeton University Press, 2008.

Feinberg, John S. *No One Like Him*. Wheaton, IL: Crossway, 2001.

Fine, Kit. "Essence and Modality." *Philosophical Perspectives* 8 (1994) 1–16.

Frankena, William F. "Is Morality Logically Dependent on Religion?" In *Religion and Morality: A Collection of Essays*, edited by Gene Outka and John P. Reeder, Jr., 195–317. Garden City, NY: Anchor, 1973.

Frankfurt, Harry G. "Descartes on the Creation of the Eternal Truths." *The Philosophical Review* 86 (1977) 36–57.

———. "The Logic of Omnipotence." *The Philosophical Review* 73 (1964) 262–63.

Freddoso, Alfred. Review of *Does God Have a Nature?* by Alvin Plantinga. *Christian Scholars Review* 12 (1983) 78–83.

Frege, Gottlob. "Thought" (1918–19). In *The Frege Reader*, edited by Michael Beaney, 325–45. Malden, MA: Blackwell, 1997.

Garcia, Robert K., and Nathan L. King, eds. *Is Goodness without God Good Enough?* Lanham, MD: Rowman and Littlefield, 2009.

Geach, P. T. "Omnipotence." *Philosophy* 48 (1973) 7–20.

———. "Plato's *Euthyphro*: An Analysis and Commentary." *Monist* 50 (1966) 369–82.

BIBLIOGRAPHY

Gomez-Torrent, Mario. "The Problem of Logical Constants." *The Bulletin of Symbolic Logic* 8 (2002) 1–37.

Gould, Paul, ed. *Beyond the Control of God? Six Views on the Problem of God and Abstract Objects.* London: Bloomsbury, 2014.

———. "The Problem of God and Abstract Objects." *Philosophia Christi* 13 (2011) 255–74.

Haack, Susan. *Philosophy of Logics.* Cambridge: Cambridge University Press, 1978.

Hare, John E. *Plato's Euthyphro.* 2nd ed. Bryn Mawr, PA: Bryn Mawr Commentaries, 1985.

Harman, Gilbert. *Change in View: Principles of Reasoning.* Cambridge: MIT Press, 1973.

———. *Thought.* Princeton, NJ: Princeton University Press, 1986.

Helm, Paul, ed. *Divine Commands and Morality.* Oxford: Oxford University Press, 1981.

Hill, Claire Ortiz. *Word and Object in Husserl, Frege, and Russell.* Athens, OH: Ohio University Press, 2001.

Holopainen, Toivo J. "Peter Damian." In *Stanford Encyclopedia of Philosophy* (Spring 2009 Edition), edited by Edward N. Zalta. Online: http://plato.stanford.edu/entries/peter-damian/.

Horton, Michael. *The Christian Faith: A Systematic Theology for Pilgrims on the Way.* Grand Rapids: Zondervan, 2011.

Jacquette, Dale. "The Dialectics of Psychologism." *Philosophy and Rhetoric* 30 (1997) v–viii.

———. "Psychologism the Philosophical Shibboleth." *Philosophy and Rhetoric* 30 (1997) 312–31.

———. "Psychologism Revisited in Logic, Metaphysics, and Epistemology." *Metaphilosophy* 32 (2001) 261–78.

Janowski, Zbigniew. *Cartesian Theodicy: Descartes' Quest for Certitude.* Dordrecht, Netherlands: Kluwer Academic, 2000.

Karger, Elizabeth. "Ockham's Misunderstood Theory of Intuitive and Abstractive Cognition." In *The Cambridge Companion to Ockham*, edited by Paul Vincent Spade, 204–26. New York: Cambridge University Press, 1999.

Kenny, Anthony. *The God of the Philosophers.* Oxford: Clarendon, 1979.

King, Peter. "Ockham's Ethical Theory." In *The Cambridge Companion to Ockham*, edited by Paul Vincent Spade, 227–44. New York: Cambridge University Press, 1999.

Knuuttila, S. *Modalities in Medieval Philosophy.* London: Routledge, 1993.

Kretzmann, N. "Syncategorema, Exponibilia, Sophismata." In *The Cambridge History of Later Medieval Philosophy*, edited by N. Kretzmann, A. Kenny and J. Pinborg, 211–45. Cambridge: Cambridge University Press, 1982.

Kripke, Saul. "Naming and Necessity." In *Semantics of Natural Language*, edited by Donald Davidson and Gilbert Harman, 763–69. Dordrecht: Reidel, 1972.

Kurtz, Paul, and William Lane Craig. "The Kurtz/Craig Debate: Is Goodness without God Good Enough?" In *Is Goodness without God Good Enough?*, edited by Robert K. Garcia and Nathan L. King, 25–46. Lanham, MD: Rowman and Littlefield, 2009.

Leftow, Brian. "Is God an Abstract Object?" *Noûs* 24 (1990) 581–98.

———. *God and Necessity.* Oxford: Oxford University Press, 2012.

———. "Necessity." In *The Cambridge Companion to Christian Philosophical Theology*, edited by Charles Taliaferro and Chad Meister, 15–30. Cambridge: Cambridge University Press, 2009.

———. "Swinburne on Divine Necessity." *Religious Studies* 46 (2010) 141–62.

Lewis, David. *On the Plurality of Possible Worlds.* Oxford: Blackwell, 1986.

BIBLIOGRAPHY

Locke, John. *A Letter Concerning Toleration,* 2nd ed. 1689. Reprint. Indianapolis: Bobbs-Merrill, 1955.

Lossky, Vladimir. *The Mystical Theology of the Eastern Church.* Greenwood, SC: Attic, 1957.

Loux, Michael J. *Metaphysics: A Contemporary Introduction.* 2nd ed. London: Routledge, 2002.

———, ed. *The Possible and the Actual: Readings in the Metaphysics of Modality.* Ithaca, NY: Cornell University Press, 1979.

———. "Toward an Aristotelian Theory of Abstract Objects." In *Midwest Studies in Philosophy,* vol. 11: *Studies in Essentialism,* edited by P. French, T. Uehling, and H. Wettstein, 495–512. Minneapolis: University of Minnesota Press, 1986.

Lovejoy, Arthur O. *The Great Chain of Being.* Cambridge: Harvard University Press, 1957.

Lycan, William. "The Trouble with Possible Worlds." In *The Possible and the Actual: Readings in the Metaphysics of Modality,* edited by Michael J. Loux, 274–316. Ithaca, NY: Cornell University Press, 1979.

MacFarlane, John. "Logical Constants." In *The Stanford Encyclopedia of Philosophy* (Fall 2009 Edition), edited by Edward N. Zalta. Online: http://plato.stanford.edu/archives/fall2009/entries/logical-constants/.

Mackie, J. L. "Evil and Omnipotence." *Mind* 64 (1955) 200–212.

Maddy, Penelope. *Second Philosophy: A Naturalistic Method.* Oxford: Oxford University Press, 2007.

———. "Three Forms of Naturalism." In *The Oxford Handbook of Philosophy of Mathematics and Logic,* edited by Stewart Shapiro, 437–59. Oxford: Oxford University Press, 2005.

Mann, William E. "Modality, Morality, and God." *Noûs* 23 (1989) 83–99.

Mavrodes, George. "Some Puzzles Concerning Omnipotence." *The Philosophical Review* 72 (1963) 221–23.

McGrade, A. S. "Natural Law and Moral Omnipotence." In *The Cambridge Companion to Ockham,* edited by Paul Vincent Spade, 273–301. New York: Cambridge University Press, 1999.

Menzel, Christopher. "Theism, Platonism and the Metaphysics of Mathematics." *Faith and Philosophy* 4 (1987) 365–82.

Miller, Ed. L. *God and Reason.* New York: Macmillan, 1972.

Miller, Leonard G. "Descartes, Mathematics, and God." *The Philosophical Review* 66 (1957) 451–65.

Milliken, John. "Euthyphro, the Good, and the Right." *Philosophia Christi* 11 (2009) 145–55.

Moreland, J. P., and William Lane Craig. *Philosophical Foundations for a Christian Worldview.* Downers Grove, IL: IVP, 2003.

Morris, Thomas V. *Anselmian Explorations: Essays in Philosophical Theology.* Notre Dame, IN: Notre Dame University Press, 1987.

———, ed. *God and the Philosophers: The Reconciliation of Faith and Reason.* New York: Oxford University Press, 1994.

Morris, Thomas V., and Christopher Menzel. "Absolute Creation." *American Philosophical Quarterly* 23 (1986) 353–62.

Murphy, Benjamin. "Are God's Hands Tied By Logic?" *Ars Disputandi* 3 (2003) (No page numbers given, pagination represents pdf).

Parfit, Derek. *Reasons and Persons.* Oxford: Oxford University Press, 1986.

BIBLIOGRAPHY

Peterson, Michael, William Hasker, Bruce Reichenbach, and David Basinger. *Reason and Religious Belief.* 2nd ed. Oxford: Oxford University Press, 1998.

Pinker, Steven. "The Moral Instinct." *New York Times*, January 13, 2008. Online: http://www.nytimes.com/2008/01/13/magazine/13Psychology-t.html?pagewanted=all&_r=3&.

Philo. *The Works of Philo, Complete and Unabridged.* New updated version. Translated by C. D. Yonge. Peabody, MA: Hendrickson, 1993.

Plantinga, Alvin. *Does God Have a Nature?* Milwaukee, WI: Marquette University Press, 1980.

———. "God, Arguments for the Existence of." In *The Routledge Encyclopedia of Philosophy*, edited by Edward Craig, 85–93. London: Routledge, 1998.

———. "How to Be an Anti-Realist." *Proceedings and Addresses of the American Philosophical Association* 56 (1982) 47–70.

———. *The Nature of Necessity.* Oxford: Oxford University Press, 1974.

———. *Warranted Christian Belief.* Oxford: Oxford University Press, 2000.

Pojman, Louis P., ed. *The Theory of Knowledge: Classical and Contemporary Readings.* 3rd ed. Belmont, CA: Wadsworth, 2003.

Priest, Graham. *In Contradiction.* Expanded ed. Oxford: Clarendon, 2006.

Priest, Graham, J. C. Beall, and Bradley Armour-Garb, eds. *The Law of Non-Contradiction.* Oxford: Oxford University Press, 2007.

Quine, W. V. "Carnap and Logical Truth." 1954. Reprinted in *The Ways of Paradox*, rev. ed., 107–32. Cambridge: Harvard University Press, 1976.

———. *From a Logical Point of View.* 2nd ed. Cambridge: Harvard University Press, 1980.

———. *Philosophy of Logic.* 2nd ed. Cambridge: Harvard University Press, 1986.

———. "Truth by Convention." 1936. Reprinted in *The Ways of Paradox*, rev. ed., 77–106. Cambridge: Harvard University Press, 1976.

———. "Two Dogmas of Empiricism." 1951. Reprinted in *From a Logical Point of View*, 2nd ed., 20–46. Cambridge: Harvard University Press, 1980.

———. *The Ways of Paradox.* Rev. ed. Cambridge: Harvard University Press, 1976.

———. *Word and Object.* Cambridge: MIT Press, 1960.

Quinn, Philip L. *Divine Commands and Moral Requirements.* Oxford: Clarendon, 1978.

Rea, Michael C. "Introduction." In *Analytic Theology: New Essays in Philosophy of Theology*, edited by Oliver D. Crisp and Michael C. Rea, 1–30. Oxford: Oxford University Press, 2009.

Read, Stephen. *Thinking About Logic: An Introduction to the Philosophy of Logic.* Oxford: Oxford University Press, 1995.

Resnick, I. M. *Divine Power and Possibility in St. Peter Damian's De divina omnipotentia.* Leiden: Brill, 1992.

Resnik, Michael. "Logic, Normative or Descriptive? The Ethics of Belief or a Branch of Psychology." *Philosophy of Science* 52 (1985) 221–38.

Rigney, Joseph. "Restoring Virgins and Changing the Past: Peter Damian on God's Power and Possibility." Unpublished paper, 2012.

Rosen, Gideon. "Abstract Objects." In *Stanford Encyclopedia of Philosophy* (Fall 2014 Edition), edited by Edward N. Zalta. Online: http://plato.stanford.edu/entries/abstract-objects.

Schrader, David E. "Frankfurt and Descartes: God and Logical Truth." *Sophia* 25 (1986) 4–18.

BIBLIOGRAPHY

Sells, Michael A. *Mystical Languages of Unsaying*. Chicago: The University of Chicago Press, 1994.

Shafer-Landau, Russ. *Moral Realism: A Defence*. Oxford: Oxford University Press, 2003.

Shapiro, Stewart. *Foundations without Foundationalism: A Case for Second-Order Logic*. Oxford: Oxford University Press, 1991.

———. "Necessity, Meaning, and Rationality: The Notion of Logical Consequence." In *A Companion to Philosophical Logic*, edited by Dale Jacquette, 227–40. Malden, MA: Blackwell, 2002.

———, ed. *The Oxford Handbook of Philosophy of Mathematics and Logic*. Oxford: Oxford University Press, 2005.

———. "Simple Truth, Contradiction, and Consistency." In *The Law of Non-Contradiction*, edited by Graham Priest, J. C. Beall, and Bradley Armour-Garb, 336–54. Oxford: Oxford University Press, 2007.

———. *Thinking About Mathematics: The Philosophy of Mathematics*. Oxford: Oxford University Press, 2000.

Shapiro, Stewart, and Jack Arnold. "Where in the (World Wide) Web of Belief is the Law of Non-contradiction?" *Noûs* 41 (2007) 276–97.

Sharvy, Richard. "*Euthyphro* 9d–11b: Analysis and Definition in Plato and Others." *Noûs* 6 (1972) 119–37.

Sinnott-Armstrong, Walter. "Why Traditional Theism Cannot Provide an Adequate Foundation for Morality." In *Is Goodness without God Good Enough?* edited by Robert K. Garcia and Nathan L. King, 101–15. Lanham, MD: Rowman and Littlefield, 2009.

Sorabji, Richard. *Time, Creation, and the Continuum: Theories in Antiquity and the Early Middle Ages*. Ithaca, NY: Cornell University Press, 1983.

Spade, Paul Vincent, ed. *The Cambridge Companion to Ockham*. New York: Cambridge University Press, 1999.

Stencil, Eric. "Cartesian Modality: Possibility and Essence in Descartes and Arnauld." Ph.D. diss., University of Wisconsin, Madison, 2012.

Swinburne, Richard. *The Christian God*. Oxford: Oxford University Press, 1994.

———. *The Coherence of Theism*. Rev. ed. Oxford: Oxford University Press, 1993.

———. "In Defence of Logical Nominalism: Reply to Leftow." *Religious Studies* 46 (2010) 311–30.

———. *Faith and Reason*. 2nd ed. Oxford: Clarendon, 2005.

———. *Revelation: From Metaphor to Analogy*. 2nd ed. Oxford: Clarendon, 2007.

Van Den Brink, Gijsbert. *Almighty God: A Study of the Doctrine of Divine Omnipotence*. Kampen, Netherlands: Kok Pharos, 1993.

van Inwagen, Peter. "Quam Dilecta." In *God and the Philosophers: The Reconciliation of Faith and Reason*, edited by Robert V. Morris, 31–60. New York: Oxford University Press, 1994.

Varzi, Achille C. "Logic, Ontological Neutrality, and the Law of Non-Contradiction." In *Contradictions, Logic, History, Actuality*, edited by Elena Ficara, 53–80. Berlin: De Gruyter, 2014.

Wadell, Paul J. *Happiness and the Christian Moral Life*. 2nd ed. Lanham, MD: Rowman and Littlefield, 2012.

Weinberg, Julius R. *A Short History of Medieval Philosophy*. Princeton, NJ: Princeton University Press, 1964.

Weiner, Joan. *Frege Explained*. Chicago: Open Court, 2004.

BIBLIOGRAPHY

Welty, Greg. "Theistic Conceptual Realism: The Case for Interpreting Abstract Objects as Divine Ideas." D.Phil thesis, Oxford University, 2006.

Westphal, Merold. *Overcoming Onto-Theology*. New York: Fordham University Press, 2001.

Yandell, Keith E. "Moral Essentialism." In *God and Morality: Four Views*, edited by R. Keith Loftin, 97–116. Downers Grove, IL: IVP, 2012.

Yannaras, Christos. *Elements of Faith: An Introduction to Orthodox Theology*. Edinburgh, Scotland: T. & T. Clark, 1991.

Subject Index

abstract objects, xii, 5–7, 11–12, 23, 44, 56, 78, 86, 89–127, 137–41, 144–47, 152–66
  controlled by God, 137, 139
  created by God, 103, 105, 107–8 144
  dependence on God, 94, 98, 101–4, 108, 110, 137, 139
  equivalent to divine thoughts, 147
  identical to divine thoughts, 145, 147, 152
  ontological independence, 111, 117, 124–27, 139
  possible worlds, 5–7, 12, 44, 89, 92, 98–99, 101, 111, 113, 147, 152–55, 157–66
  problem of God and. *See* problem of God and abstract objects
  propositions, 5, 11, 23, 56, 78, 89, 99–101, 111, 113, 116, 119, 137–41, 147, 152, 154–66
absolute creationism, 103–10, 135, 138–55
  bootstrapping objection, 105
  causal dependence thesis, 145–46
  divine concepts, 103–5, 108–9, 140–55
  noetic activity, 103–5, 108–9, 135, 138–39, 145–46
  identity thesis, 145–46
  logical voluntarism objection, 105–8
analogical predication, 81–83
anti-realism/realism, xii, 107–8, 137–39, 144–52, 154–55, 162, 165–66
apophatic theology, 76–84

argument, 2, 4, 8–12, 36–38, 43–46, 55, 57, 60–69, 74, 79, 81, 83, 85, 87, 89–92, 96, 99–102, 104, 110, 114–18, 120, 122–26, 128, 143, 163–65
aseity-sovereignty doctrine, 19, 93–110, 129, 147–53, 164, 166
  aseity, 19, 129, 147–53, 164, 166
  creation condition, 94, 97, 100–104, 110
  dependence condition, 94, 98, 101–4, 108, 110
  uniqueness condition, 94, 98, 101–4, 107, 110
  aseity intuition, 94, 98, 101–4, 107, 110–11
  sovereignty intuition, 94, 97, 102–4, 107, 110

classical theism, xi–xii, 19, 22–26, 35, 45, 54, 84, 102–3, 148
creation, 35, 37, 45–46, 48, 57, 67, 74–75, 88, 93–97, 102–10, 112, 130, 135–36, 144–47, 151, 155

deductive (or logical) validity. *See* logical consequence relation.
dialetheias, 45, 56
divine command theory, 28–32, 36, 38, 42, 50, 89, 95, 110, 126, 130, 134
divine concepts, 103–5, 108–9, 140–55
  noetic activity, 103–5, 108–9, 135, 138–39, 145–46
divine thoughts, 147, 152, 155

Subject Index

divine concepts *(continued)*
   function as abstract objects, 145, 147, 152
divine omnipotence, 23, 46–55, 57, 65–69, 75, 95, 110, 126, 148, 164–65
divine omniscience, 19, 23, 147–54, 160–61, 164–65
   as knowledge of possibility, 148, 152
   as knowledge of power, 149–50, 152, 160–61
   as knowledge of will, 149–50, 160–61
   as self-knowledge, 148
   essential, 147–49, 152
   infinite, 154
divine thoughts, 147, 152, 155
divine transcendence, 63, 65–69, 78–80, 82–83, 88

epistemicism, 118
Euthyphro dialogue, xi, 28–29, 33–35, 42
Euthyphro dilemma, xi–xii, 27–42, 65, 85, 129–43
   alternatives to, 135–37, 140–42
   applicability of, 33–35
   divine command theory, 28–32, 36, 38, 42, 130, 134
   false dilemma, 38, 134–35, 141–42
   logical Euthyphro dilemma. *See* Logiphro dilemma.
   objections to, 31, 40–41, 129
   structure, 33–6, 65, 85, 129–37, 140–43
   updated Euthyphro dilemma, 28–30, 129
evidentialism, 18

fideism, 17–19

God, xi–xii, 19–26, 35, 47–57, 63, 65–75, 78–80, 82–84, 88–89, 93–95, 98, 100–105, 107, 110–12, 126, 129, 140–54, 160–61, 164–66
   abstract objects and. *See* problem of God and abstract objects.
   aseity, 19, 93–95, 98, 100–105, 107, 110–12, 129, 147–53, 164, 166. *See* aseity-sovereignty doctrine.
   classical theism, xi–xii, 19, 22–26, 35, 45, 54, 84, 102–3, 148
   communicable attributes, 23
   definition of, 19–25
   immutability, 19, 23, 48, 70, 72–73, 89, 141–42
   incommunicable attributes, 23
   intelligent creator, 35, 147, 151
   logically contradictory actions, 47–49, 65–74. *See also* pseudo-task.
   mental activity of, 140–41
   omniscience, 19, 23, 147–54, 160–61, 164–65
   omnipotence, 23, 46–55, 57, 65–69, 75, 95, 110, 126, 148, 164–65
   problem of evil, 23
   simplicity, 19
   sovereignty. *See* aseity-sovereignty doctrine.
   transcendence, 63, 65–69, 78–80, 82–83, 88
   truth (always tells), 70–73

language, 4–6, 10, 12, 17, 44–45, 53, 58–60, 66, 68–79, 82–84, 89–92, 114–20, 124–26, 145–46, 159
   formal, 4–6, 10, 12, 159
   natural, 10, 12, 17, 44–45, 53, 58–60, 66, 68–79, 82–84, 89–92, 114–20, 124–26, 145–46
law of non-contradiction (LNC), 38, 46, 48, 51, 56–57, 62, 66–67, 79, 119–21, 123
logic, 2–14, 36–38, 43–46, 55–57, 60–69, 74, 79, 81, 83, 85, 87, 89–92, 96, 99–102, 104, 106, 110–11, 114–18, 120, 122–28, 143, 159, 163–66. *See also* logical consequence relation.
   argument, 2, 4, 8–12, 36–38, 43–46, 55, 57, 60–69, 74, 79, 81, 83, 85, 87, 89–92, 96, 99–102, 104, 110, 114–18, 120, 122–26, 128, 143, 163–65
   axiomatic method, 3–4

Subject Index

choosing a logic, 106, 122–25
definition of, 2, 13–14
entailment. *See* also logical consequence relation.
epistemological justification of, 10–12
formal systems of, 4–6
logical constants, 9–10, 12. *See* also logical connectives.
logical/non-logical content, 7–9, 12–13, 159, 163–66
logical form, 8–9
logical terms, 9–10, 12
metaphysical basis of, 5–6
non-formal characterizations of, 6–7
non-voluntarism. *See* logical non-voluntarism.
ontological independence, 111, 117, 124–27
primary focus of, 2–3
revising beliefs of, 56, 122–25
truth-functional connectives, 9–10, 12–13, 159, 163–66
universal applicability, 8–9
validity/invalidity, 2. *See* also logical consequence relation.
voluntarism. *See* logical voluntarism.
logical connectives, 7–9, 12–13, 159, 163–66
logical consequence relation, 2, 4–7, 10, 12–14, 26, 92, 113, 115, 117–18, 159, 163, 165–66
broadly logical necessity, 113
completeness, 4, 10
definition of (LC), 7, 12–14, 26, 92, 159, 163, 165–66
epistemological justification of, 10–12
formal consequence (F), 7, 13
metaphysical basis of, 5–6
minimal entailment, 115, 117–18
modal consequence (M), 6
non-formal characterizations of, 6–13
non-voluntarism. *See* logical non-voluntarism.
possible worlds consequence (PW), 6, 13

rational consequence (R), 7, 13
semantic notion, 4
semantic consequence (S), 7, 13
soundness, 4, 10
syntactic notion, 4
universal applicability, 8–9, 92
voluntarism. *See* logical voluntarism.
logical Euthyphro dilemma. *See* Logiphro dilemma.
logical nominalism, 113–23
broadly logical necessity, 113
conventional logical nominalism, 123
empirical logical nominalism, 122–23
human language usage, 114–16
logic as linguistic convention, 116–21
minimal entailment, 115, 117–18
objections to, 121
theoretical parsimony, 114
vagueness, 117–18
logical/non-logical content, 7–9, 12–13, 159, 163–66
logical non-voluntarism, 7, 12, 37–40, 85–130, 138–40, 143–46, 148, 156, 162, 165–66
advantages of, 90–93
defined, 87–90
nominalist (lean) version of, 110–27
objections to, 39–40
ontological dependence/independence, 88–90, 99–100, 104, 108, 126, 145
too independent from God, 143
Platonic (robust) version of, 87–110
logical terms, 7–9, 12–13, 159, 163–66
logical voluntarism, xi–xii, 36–40, 42–84, 86–87, 90, 94, 96, 106, 109, 113, 128–30, 140, 143, 150, 155–56, 162, 165–66
abhorrent commands objection, 61–2
definition of, 45
incoherence objection, 63–65, 67–68
metaphysical basis of, 44
motivations for, 46–57
no reasons objection, 61

177

Subject Index

objections to, 38–39, 57–84
too dependent on God, 143
unintelligibility objection, 65–68
vacuity objection, 60–61, 68–76, 83–84
Logiphro dilemma, 35–42, 87, 134–35, 142–43, 146, 156–66
alternative to, 146, 156–66
false dilemma, 38, 87, 134–35, 142–43
non-voluntarist option. *See* logical non-voluntarism.
voluntarist option. *See* logical voluntarism.

mathematical truths, 51–52, 137, 155
moral non-voluntarism, 30–31, 44, 129, 134–35, 137, 140–42
too independent from God, 134, 137, 142
moral voluntarism, 30–32, 50, 58–9, 60–62, 85, 129, 134–35, 137, 141–42
abhorrent commands objection, 31, 59, 61–62
arbitrariness problem, 59
no reasons objection, 31, 58, 61
too dependent on God, 134, 137, 142
vacuity objection, 31, 58, 60–61

necessary connections, 51
necessary truths, 8, 35, 45, 55, 61, 67–8, 92, 114, 124, 130, 137–41, 143–44, 155–56
mind independence, 138–40

ontological arguments, 99–100
ontological dependence/independence, 88–90, 99–100, 104, 108, 126, 145

Philo, 103–8
Plato, xi, 23, 28–30, 33, 35, 42, 88–90, 97, 102–3, 109, 133, 150
Platonism, xii, 44, 86, 88–89, 93, 96–98, 100–5, 107, 109–14, 116–17, 127–29, 133, 136, 138–40, 144–45, 147–48, 151–52, 154, 159–60, 163, 166. *See also* antirealism/realism.
objectivity of, 138
mind independence, 138
platonic entities, 88–89, 93, 107, 147, 163, 166
possibilism (limited and universal), 37, 45–46, 53, 74–76, 87, 113, 140, 150, 155
possible worlds, 5–7, 12, 44, 89, 92, 98–99, 101, 111, 113, 147, 152–55, 157–66
actual world, 152–53
truth-makers, 155, 158
identical with divine thoughts, 159
relationship to propositions, 158–59
problem of evil, 23
problem of God and abstract objects, xii, 93–113, 117, 137, 144–46, 166
creatio ex nihilo problems, 100–110
objections to, 95–110
practical worries, 95–96
ultimacy problem, 96–100
propositions, 5, 11, 23, 56, 78, 89, 99–101, 111, 113, 116, 119, 137–41, 147, 152, 154–66
contingent, 155–56
existence of, 155
identical with divine thoughts, 159
modal status, 155
necessary, 155–56
relationship to possible worlds, 158–59
states of affairs, 157–58
truth-bearers, 56, 100, 155, 158
truth-makers, 155
pseudo-task, 65
psychologism, 11, 115

revelation (special), 14–16, 20–22, 25–26, 70–76, 82, 84, 90, 106, 128

Scripture, 15–16, 18, 20–26, 39, 70–71, 73–74, 76, 81–82, 84, 128
states of affairs, 157–58
supervaluationism, 118

178

Subject Index

theistic activism. *See* absolute creationism.
theistic conceptual realism, 144, 147–57
  See divine concepts.
theistic conceptual logical realism, 162–66
theologically based ethics, 130–33
  objections to, 131–32
  grounded in God, 140–42
theological method, 14–22, 76–84
  apophatic theology, 76–84
  challenges to natural theology, 16–20
  kataphatic theology, 76
  mystical theology, 76–84
  natural (philosophical) theology, 14–16
  revealed theology, 14–15
  synthesis of natural and revealed theology, 20–22
theoretical parsimony, 114
tradition of theism, 2, 15–17, 19–26, 32, 35, 38–39, 43–44, 46, 54–55, 57–58, 61, 68–76, 79–84, 86, 93–94, 97–98, 102, 107–8, 110, 112, 117, 127–29, 134–35, 142–43, 148, 151, 154, 156, 166
  Eastern, 24, 76–77, 80–81
  Western (or Abrahamic), 2, 15–17, 19–26, 32, 35, 38–39, 43–44, 46, 54–55, 57–58, 61, 68–76, 79–84, 86, 93–94, 97–98, 102, 107–8, 110, 112, 117, 127–29, 134–35, 142–43, 148, 151, 154, 156, 166
truth-bearers, 56, 100, 155, 158
truth-functional connectives, 7–9, 12–13, 159, 163–66
truth-makers, 100, 155, 158

vacuity objection, 31, 58–62, 67–76, 79–84, 90, 128, 143, 165
  "biting the bullet," 76, 79–84
  to logical voluntarism, 60–62, 67–76, 83–84
  to moral voluntarism, 31, 58–59, 60–61

Name Index

Adams, Marilyn McCord, 51
Adams, Robert Merrihew, 50, 141
Antony, Louise, 29, 40, 85, 142
Aquinas, Thomas, 81–82, 149–51, 160
Armstrong, A. H., 88
Arnold, Jack, 57

Baggett, David, 31, 41, 58, 59–60, 134–41
Basil of Nyssa, 24
Basinger, David, 22
Beall, J. C., 8, 92
Bencivenga, E., 9
Bergmann, Michael, 105
Blanks, David, 95
Boersma, Hans, 86
Boyer, Stephen D., 17
Brandom, Robert, 116
Brower, Jeffrey E., 105
Brown, Scott, 95, 110

Chisholm, Roderick, 158
Clifford, W. K., 18
Clouser, Roy, 45, 53
Conee, Earl, 37, 45, 69
Copan, Paul, 41, 93, 102, 112, 140–41
Copleston, Frederick, 50, 51
Craig, William Lane, 17, 21, 93, 100–103, 105, 112–13
Curley, E. M., 37, 45, 67

Damian, Peter, 46–49, 52, 53, 55, 67
Descartes, René, 52–54, 55, 65, 67, 77

Endres, J. A., 47, 48

Estlund, David, 33

Fine, Kit, 95
Frankena, William F., 141
Frankfurt, Harry G., 65, 67
Freddoso, Alfred, 107–8
Frege, Gottlob, 3, 13, 115

Garcia, Robert K., 130, 132
Geach, Peter T., 28, 75
Gomez-Torrente, Mario, 12
Gregory of Nyssa, 24
Gregory of Nazianzus, 17, 24
Gould, Paul, 93–5, 98, 104, 105, 112

Haack, Susan, 4, 155
Hall, Christopher A., 17
Hare, John E., 28
Harman, Gil, 2
Harnack, Adolph von, 19
Hasker, William, 22
Helm, Paul, 141
Hill, Claire Ortiz, 115
Holopainen, Toivo J., 47, 48, 49, 55
Horton, Michael, 17, 19, 20, 82, 96

Inwagen, Peter van, 18

Jacquette, Dale, 115
Janowski, Zbigniew, 53
Jerome, 47

Karger, Elizabeth, 50
Kenny, Anthony, 16
King, Nathan L., 130, 132

Name Index

King, Peter, 50
Knuutilla, S., 48
Kripke, Saul, 113

Leftow, Brian, 93, 97–98, 117–21, 125, 165
Lewis, David, 89
Locke, John, 130–31
Lossky, Vladimir, 76–77, 80
Loux, Michael J., 154
Lovejoy, Arthur O., 97
Lycan, William, 158

MacFarlane, John, 9, 12–13
Mackie, J. L., 65
Maddy, Penelope, 3, 122–24
Mann, William, 34–35
Mavrodes, George, 65
McGrade, A. S., 50
Menzel, Christopher, 93, 103–5, 108, 144–47
Miller, Ed., 14, 21–22
Miller, Leonard G., 67
Milliken, John, 41, 91
Moreland, J. P., 17, 21
Morris, Robert V., 18, 93, 103–5, 108, 144–47
Murphy, Benjamin, 113, 124

Parfit, Derek, 131
Parry, Robin, 32
Peterson, Michael, 22
Philo, 103–8
Pincock, Chris, 87, 97
Pinker, Steven, 133
Plantinga, Alvin, 23, 63, 93, 113, 136–40, 146, 155, 157–59, 162
Plato, xi, 23, 28–30, 33, 35, 42, 88–90, 97, 102–3, 109, 133, 150
Pojman, Louis P., 18
Priest, Graham, 37, 45, 56, 57, 66, 68, 71
Pseudo-Dionysius, 76–77

Putnam, Hilary, 137

Quine, W. V., 3, 7, 56–57, 65, 73, 122–24
Quinn, Philip L., 141

Rea, Michael, 80
Read, Stephen, 3, 4, 5
Reichenbach, Bruce, 22
Resnik, I. M., 48
Resnik, Michael, 11
Restall, Greg, 8, 92
Rigney, Joe, 48
Ritschl, Albrecht, 19
Rorty, Richard, 137
Rosen, Gideon, 89
Rudavsky, Tamar, 106

Schrader, David E., 53
Sells, Michael, 77–79, 81
Shafer-Landau, Russ, 34
Shapiro, Stewart, 5, 6, 10–11, 13, 29, 57, 58, 71, 79, 106
Sharvy, Richard, 28
Sinnott-Armstrong, Walter, 142
Stencil, Eric, 53
Swinburne, Richard, 15, 16, 86, 99, 113–21, 122, 124, 125, 148, 152

Tertullian, 19
Turretin, Francis, 19

Van Den Brink, Gijsbert, 66–67, 136

Walls, Jerry, 31, 41, 58, 59–60, 134–36
Weinberg, Julius R., 50
Weiner, Joan, 13
Welty, Greg, 107–9, 144–57, 160, 162, 164–65, 166
William of Ockham, 49–52, 53, 55, 67

Yandell, Keith, 133–35
Yannaras, Christos, 80–81

www.ingramcontent.com/pod-product-compliance
Lightning Source LLC
Chambersburg PA
CBHW051744230426
43670CB00012B/2154